Australasian Language Technology Association Workshop

(ALTA 2013)

Brisbane, Australia
4 – 6 December 2013

Editors:

S. Karimi
K. Verspoor

ISBN: 978-1-62993-557-7

Printed from e-media with permission by:

Curran Associates, Inc.
57 Morehouse Lane
Red Hook, NY 12571

Some format issues inherent in the e-media version may also appear in this print version.

Printed by Curran Associates, Inc. (2014)

Association for Computational Linguistics
209 N. Eighth Street
Stroudsburg, Pennsylvania 18360

Phone: 1-570-476-8006
Fax: 1-570-476-0860

acl@aclweb.org

Additional copies of this publication are available from:

Curran Associates, Inc.
57 Morehouse Lane
Red Hook, NY 12571 USA
Phone: 845-758-0400
Fax: 845-758-2634
Email: curran@proceedings.com
Web: www.proceedings.com

ALTA 2013 Workshop Committees

Workshop Co-Chairs

- Sarvnaz Karimi (CSIRO)
- Karin Verspoor (National ICT Australia)

Workshop Local Organiser

- Laurianne Sitbon (Queensland University of Technology)

Programme Committee

- Timothy Baldwin (University of Melbourne)
- Steven Bird (University of Melbourne)
- Wray Lindsay Buntine (NICTA)
- Lawrence Cavedon (NICTA and RMIT University)
- Nathalie Colineau (DSTO)
- Dominique Estival (University of Western Sydney)
- Graeme Hirst (University of Toronto)
- Nitin Indurkhya (UNSW)
- Su Nam Kim (Monash University)
- Francois Lareau (Macquarie University)
- Andrew MacKinlay (NICTA)
- David Martinez (NICTA)
- Meladel Mistica (The Australian National University)
- Diego Mollá (Macquarie University)
- Scott Nowson (Xerox Research Centre Europe)
- Cecile Paris (CSIRO)
- Luiz Augusto Pizzato (University of Sydney)
- Andrea Schalley (Griffith University)
- Rolf Schwitter (Macquarie University)
- Hanna Suominen (NICTA)
- Stephen Wan (CSIRO)
- Ingrid Zukerman (Monash University)

Preface

This volume contains the papers accepted for presentation at the Australasian Language Technology Association Workshop (ALTA) 2013, held at the Queensland University of Technology in Brisbane, Australia on 4–6 December 2013.

We would like to declare this the ALTA Year of the Woman, in recognition of the first-time all-female organisation of the conference, including our local organiser in Brisbane, Laurianne Sitbon. We initially thought to have a female-only line-up for the keynote speakers, but settled with a population representative 50%. Please note that no gender biases were intentionally introduced into paper reviewing or acceptance; however, the authors on the accepted papers are fully one third female.

The goals of the workshop are to:

- bring together the Language Technology (LT) community in the Australasian region and encourage interactions and collaboration;
- foster interaction between academic and industrial researchers, to encourage dissemination of research results;
- provide a forum for students and young researchers to present their research;
- facilitate the discussion of new and ongoing research and projects;
- increase visibility of LT research in Australasia and overseas and encourage interactions with the wider international LT community.

This year's ALTA Workshop presents 16 peer-reviewed papers, including nine full, four short papers, and three papers that will be presented as posters. We received a total of 24 submissions. Each paper, apart from two submissions that were deemed outside of the conference scope at submission time, was reviewed by three members of the program committee. The reviewing for the workshop was double blind, and done in accordance with the DIISRTE requirements for E1 conference publications. Furthermore, great care was taken to avoid all conflicts of interest; in particular, no paper was assessed by a reviewer from the same institution as any of the authors. In the case of submissions involving a co-chair, the double-blind review process was upheld, and acceptance decisions were made by the non-author co-chair.

The proceedings include abstracts of the invited talks by Mark Steedman and Bonnie Webber, both from the University of Edinburgh. We are delighted to take advantage of their visit to Australia to bring them to Brisbane and are honoured to welcome them to ALTA. This volume also contains an overview of the ALTA Shared Task, its use as a class project, and a description of the winning system. These contributions were not peer-reviewed.

We would like to thank, in no particular order: all of the authors who submitted papers to ALTA; the program committee for the time and effort they put into maintaining the high standards of our reviewing process; the local organiser Laurianne Sitbon for taking care of all the physical logistics and lining up some great social events; our invited speakers Mark Steedman and Bonnie Webber for agreeing to share their extensive experience and insights with us; the team from the NeCTAR Human Communication Science virtual laboratory (HCSvLab) and David Milne for agreeing to host two fascinating tutorials, and Paul Cook and Scott Nowson, the program co-chairs of ALTA 2012, for their valuable help and support. We would like to acknowledge the constant support and advice of the ALTA Executive Committee for providing input critical to the success of the workshop.

Finally, we gratefully recognise our sponsors: CSIRO, Google, and NICTA. Their generous support enabled us to fund student paper awards, as well as offer travel subsidies to three students to attend and present at ALTA. The University of Queensland also sponsored afternoon tea on Friday afternoon. We thank them as well.

Sarvnaz Karimi and Karin Verspoor
Programme Co-Chairs

ALTA 2013 Programme

ALTA will be held in P-block, the Queensland University of Technology Gardens Point campus.

Wednesday 4 December 2013 Pre-workshop tutorials (Room P-504)

10:00–14:30 (Lunch break 12-1) *Working with the HCS vLab*
Dominique Estival (University of Western Sydney) and Steve Cassidy (Macquarie University)

15:00–17:45 (Break 16:30-16:45) *Applying Wikipedia as a machine-readable knowledge base*
David Milne (CSIRO)

Thursday 5 December 2013

08:50–09:00	Opening remarks
09:00–10:00	Invited talk (Room P-512) Bonnie Webber *Concurrent Discourse Relations*
10:00–10:30	Coffee (Level 5)
Session 1 (Room P-512)	
10:30–11:00	Marco Lui and Paul Cook *Classifying English Documents by National Dialect*
11:00–11:30	Tim O'Keefe, Kellie Webster, James R. Curran and Irena Koprinska *Examining the Impact of Coreference Resolution on Quote Attribution*
11:30–12:00	Yvette Graham, Timothy Baldwin, Alistair Moffat and Justin Zobel *Crowd-Sourcing of Human Judgments of Machine Translation Fluency*
12:00–13:30	Lunch (Terrace, Level 6)
Session 2 (Room P-512)	
13:30–14:00	Shunichi Ishihara *The Effect of the Within-speaker Sample Size on the Performance of Likelihood Ratio Based Forensic Voice Comparison: Monte Carlo Simulations*
14:00–14:30	Hanna Suominen and Gabriela Ferraro *Noise in Speech-to-Text Voice: Analysis of Errors and Feasibility of Phonetic Similarity for Their Correction*
14:30–15:00	Robert Power, Bella Robinson and David Ratcliffe *Finding Fires with Twitter*
15:00–15:30	Coffee (Level 5)
Session 3 (Room P-512)	
15:30–16:00	Asif Ekbal, Sriparna Saha, Diego Molla and K Ravikumar *Multi-Objective Optimization for Clustering of Medical Publications*
16:00–16:20	Tatyana Shmanina, Ingrid Zukerman, Antonio Jimeno Yepes, Lawrence Cavedon and Karin Verspoor *Impact of Corpus Diversity and Complexity on NER Performance*
16:20–16:50	Rolf Schwitter *Working with Defaults in a Controlled Natural Language*
16:50–17:20	ALTA business meeting
19:00–	Conference dinner (Plough Inn, South Bank, Brisbane)

Friday 6 December 2013

09:00–10:00	Joint ADCS/ALTA Invited talk (Room P-421) Mark Steedman *Robust Computational Semantics*
10:00–10:30	Coffee (Level 5)
Session 4: ALTA/ADCS joint session (Room P-421)	
10:30–11:00	**ADCS paper** Takumi Sonoda and Takao Miura *Conditional Collocation in Japanese*
11:00–11:30	**ADCS paper** Hanna Suominen and Leif Hanlen *Visual Text Summarision for Surveillance and Situational Awareness in Hospitals*
11:30–12:00	Antti Puurula *Cumulative Progress in Language Models for Information Retrieval*
12:00–12:30	Oldooz Dianat, Cecile Paris and Stephen Wan *A Study: From Electronic Laboratory Notebooks to Generated Queries for Literature Recommendation*
12:30–13:30	Lunch (Terrace, Level 6)
Session 5: ALTA Shared Task (Room P-512)	
13:30–13:45	Diego Molla *ALTA 2013 Shared Task overview*
13:45–14:00	Marco Lui and Li Wang *Recovering Casing and Punctuation using Conditional Random Fields*
Session 6 and Poster Boasters (Room P-512)	
14:00–14:30	Shunichi Ishiharal *A Comparative Study of Likelihood Ratio Based Forensic Text Comparison in Procedures: Multivariate Kernel Density vs. Gaussian Mixture Model-Universal Background Model*
14:30–14:50	Farshid Zavareh, Ingrid Zukerman, Su Nam Kim and Thomas Kleinbauer *Error Detection in Automatic Speech Recognition*
14:50–15:05	Awards and final remarks
15:05–15:20	ALTA poster boasters
	Jared Willett, David Martinez, J. Angus Webb and Timothy Baldwin *Automatic Climate Classification of Environmental Science Literature*
	Jason Brown and Sam Mandal *Rhythm, Metrics, and the Link to Phonology*
	Shunichi Ishihara *Differences in Speaker Individualising Information between Case Particles and Fillers in Spoken Japanese*
15:20–17:00	Poster session with ADCS (Level 4)

Contents

Invited talks

Robust Computational Semantics

ALTA 2013/ADCS 2013 Joint Keynote

Mark Steedman
School of Informatics
The University of Edinburgh
Edinburgh, United Kingdom
steedman@inf.ed.ac.uk

Abstract

Practical tasks like question answering and machine translational ultimately require computing meaning representations that support inference. Standard linguistic accounts of meaning are impracticable for such purposes, both because they assume non-monotonic operations such as quantifier movement, and because they lack a representation for the meaning of content words that supports efficient computation of entailment. I'll discuss practical solutions to some of these problems within a near-context free grammar formalism for a working wide-coverage parser, in current work with Mike Lewis, and show how these solutions can be usefully applied in NLP tasks.

Concurrent Discourse Relations

ALTA 2013 Keynote Presentation

Bonnie Webber
School of Informatics
The University of Edinburgh
Edinburgh, United Kingdom
bonnie@inf.ed.ac.uk

Abstract

The Penn Discourse Treebank (PDTB) was released to the public in 2008 and remains the largest corpus of manually annotated discourse relations — both relations that are signaled explicitly (e.g., by a coordinating or subordinating conjunction, or by a discourse adverbial or other construction) and ones that otherwise appear implicit.

The Penn Discourse TreeBank also diverges from other discourse-annotated corpora in permitting more than one discourse relation to be annotated as holding concurrently. Annotators could indicate this by assigning multiple sense labels to an explicit connective. Or, in those cases where adjacent sentences had no explicit connective, annotators could indicate concurrent discourse relations by either annotating a single implicit connective that concurrently conveyed multiple senses or annotating multiple implicit connectives, each conveying one of the concurrent relation(s). Subsequent experiments carried out using Mechanical Turk showed that, when a discourse adverbial explicitly signalled a discourse relation, there was often a separate concurrent relation that could be associated with an implicit coordinating or subordinating conjunction.

There are different circumstances in which different sets of concurrent discourse relations are taken to hold. I will go through these, and conclude with what I take the implications of this to be for various language technologies, including statistical machine translation.

Full papers

Classifying English Documents by National Dialect

Marco Lui♡♣ **and Paul Cook**♡
♡ Department of Computing and Information Systems
The University of Melbourne
Victoria 3010, Australia
♣ NICTA Victoria Research Laboratory
{mhlui,paulcook}@unimelb.edu.au

Abstract

We investigate *national dialect identification*, the task of classifying English documents according to their country of origin. We use corpora of known national origin as a proxy for national dialect. In order to identify general (as opposed to corpus-specific) characteristics of national dialects of English, we make use of a variety of corpora of different sources, with inter-corpus variation in length, topic and register. The central intuition is that features that are predictive of national origin across different data sources are features that characterize a national dialect. We examine a number of classification approaches motivated by different areas of research, and evaluate the performance of each method across 3 national dialects: Australian, British, and Canadian English. Our results demonstrate that there are lexical and syntactic characteristics of each national dialect that are consistent across data sources.

1 Introduction

The English language exhibits substantial variation in its usage throughout the world with regional differences being noted at the lexical and syntactic levels (e.g., Trudgill and Hannah, 2008) between varieties of English such as that used in Britain and the United States. Although there are many varieties of English throughout the world — including, for example, New Zealand English, African American Vernacular English, and Indian English — there are a smaller number of so-called standard Englishes. British English and American English (or North American English) are often taken to be the two main varieties of standard English (Trudgill and Hannah, 2008; Quirk, 1995), with other varieties of standard English, such as Canadian English and Australian English, viewed as more-similar to one of these main varieties.

The theme of this work is *national dialect identification*, the classification of documents as one of a closed set of candidate standard Englishes (hereafter referred to as dialects), by exploiting lexical and syntactic variation between dialects. We make use of corpora of text of known national origin as a proxy for text of each dialect. Specifically, we consider Australian English, British English, and Canadian English, three so-called "inner circle" standard Englishes (Jenkins, 2009).[1]

This preliminary work aims to establish whether standard approaches to text classification are able to accurately predict the variety of standard English in which a document is written. The notion of standard English is differentiated from other factors such as style (e.g., formality) or topic Trudgill (1999), which are expected confounding factors. A model of dialect classification built on a single text type (e.g., standard national corpora) may be classifying documents on the basis of non-dialectal differences such as topic or genre. In order to control for the confounding factors, we utilize text from a variety of sources. By drawing training and test data from different sources, the successful transfer of models from one text source to another is evidence that the classifier is indeed capturing differences between different documents that are dialectal, rather than being due to any of the aforementioned confounding factors.

The main contributions of this paper are: (1) we introduce national dialect identification as a classification task, (2) we relate national dialect identification to existing research on text classification, (3) we assemble a dataset for national dialect identification using corpora from a variety of sources,

[1]We don't consider American English because of a rather surprising lack of available resources for this national dialect, discussed in Section 4.

(4) we empirically evaluate a number of text classification methods for national dialect identification, and (5) we find that we can train classifiers that are able to predict the national dialect of documents across data sources.

2 Related Work

National dialect identification is conceptually related to a range of established text classification tasks. In this section, we give some background on related areas, deferring the description of the specific methods we implement to Section 3.2.

2.1 Text Categorization

Text categorization has been described as the intersection of machine learning and information retrieval (Sebastiani, 2005), and is focused on tasks such as mapping newswire documents onto the topics they discuss (Debole and Sebastiani, 2005). A large variety of methods have been examined in the literature, due to the large overlap with the machine learning community (Sebastiani, 2002). One approach that has been shown to consistently perform well is the use of Support Vector Machines (SVM, Cortes and Vapnik, 1995). Joachims (1998) argued for their use in text categorization, observing that SVMs were well suited due to their ability to handle high-dimensional input spaces with few irrelevant features. Furthermore, he observed that most text categorization problems are linearly separable, a view that has been validated in a variety of studies (e.g., Yang and Liu, 1999; Drucker et al., 1999).

2.2 Language Identification

Language identification is the task of classifying a document according to the natural language it is written in. Recent work has applied language identification techniques to the identification of Dutch dialects, with encouraging results (Trieschnigg et al., 2012).

2.3 Native Language Identification (NLI)

Authorship profiling is an umbrella term for classification tasks that involve inferring some characteristic of a document's author, such as age, gender and native language (Estival et al., 2007). Native language identification (NLI, Koppel et al., 2005) is a well established authorship profiling task. The aim of NLI is to classify a document with respect to an author's native language, where this is not the language that the document is written in. One approach to NLI is to capture grammatical errors made by authors, through the use of contrastive analysis (Wong and Dras, 2009), parse structures (Wong and Dras, 2011) or adaptor grammars (Wong et al., 2012). Brooke and Hirst (2012) test a broad array of approaches to NLI, and specifically highlight issues with in-domain evaluation thereof.

2.4 Authorship Attribution

Authorship profiling focuses on identifying features which vary between groups of authors but are fairly consistent for a given group. In contrast, authorship attribution is the task of mapping a document onto a particular author from a set of candidate authors (Stamatatos, 2009), and is sometimes incorrectly conflated with authorship profiling. Mosteller and Wallace (1964) used a set of function words to attribute papers of disputed authorship. Other stylometric features used to identify authors include average sentence and word length (Yule, 1939). Modern features used for authorship attribution include distributions over function words (Zhao and Zobel, 2005), as well as features derived from parsing and part-of-speech tagging (Hirst and Feiguina, 2007). Author-aware topic models have also been proposed for authorship attribution (Seroussi et al., 2012).

2.5 Text-based Geolocation

Social media has recently exploded in popularity, with Twitter reporting that roughly 500 million tweets are sent each day (Twitter, 2013). There is a relationship between textual content and geolocation, with for example, texts containing words such as *streetcar*, *Maple Leafs*, and *DVP* likely being related to Toronto, Canada (Han et al., 2012).

Eisenstein et al. (2010) apply techniques from topic modeling to study variation in word usage on Twitter in the United States. Of particular relevance to our work, Wing and Baldridge (2011) and Roller et al. (2012) aggregate the tweets of users to predict their physical location in grid-based representations of the continental United States. These methods consider the KL-divergence between the distribution of words in a user's aggregated tweets and that of the tweets known to originate from each grid cell, with the most-similar cell being selected as the target user's most-likely location.

2.6 Computational Dialectal Studies

Although the specific issue of English national dialect classification has not been considered to date, a small number of computational studies have examined issues related to dialects. For example, Atwell et al. (2007) consider which variety of English, British or American, is most common on the Web. Peirsman et al. (2010) use techniques based on distributional similarity to identify lectal markers — words characteristic of one dialect versus another due to differences in sense or frequency — of dialects of Dutch. Zaidan and Callison-Burch (2012) studied dialect identification in Arabic dialects using automatic classifiers, and found that classifiers using dialectal data outperformed an informed baseline, achieving near-human classification accuracy.

Of particular relevance to our work, Cook and Hirst (2012) consider whether Web corpora from top-level domains (specifically `.ca` and `.uk`, in their work) represent corresponding national dialects (Canadian English and British English, respectively). They find that the relative distribution of spelling variants (e.g., the frequency of *color* relative to that of *colour*) is quite consistent across corpora of known national dialect. Furthermore, they show that these distributions are similar for corpora of known national dialect and Web corpora from a corresponding top-level domain.

3 Methodology

National dialect identification is a classification task, where each document must be mapped onto a single national dialect from a closed set of candidate dialects. We evaluate each method by training a classifier on a set of training documents and applying it to an independent set of test documents. For each experiment, we compute per-class precision, recall and F-score, using their standard definitions. We focus our evaluation on F-score, macroaveraged over all the per-class values, in order to maintain balance across precision and recall and across individual classes.

3.1 Cross-domain classification

A key challenge in evaluating national dialect identification as a text classification task is that documents in the training data may exhibit some non-dialectal variation that the classifiers may pick up on. For example, if British English were represented by a balanced corpus such as the British National Corpus (Burnard, 2000), but a corpus of say, newspaper texts, were used for American English (e.g., The New York Times Annotated Corpus, Sandhaus, 2008) then a classifier trained to distinguish between documents of these two corpora may pick up on differences in genre and topic as opposed to national dialect. Even if more-comparable corpora than those just mentioned above were chosen, because a corpus is a sample, certain topics or words will tend to be over- or under-represented. Indeed Kilgarriff (2001) points out such issues in the context of keyword comparisons of comparable corpora of British and American English, and Brooke and Hirst (2012) specifically highlight the same issue in native language identification.

In an effort to avoid this pitfall, we utilize text of known national origin from a variety of different sources. Specifically, we collect text representing each national dialect from up to 4 different sources (Section 4). In this paper, following the terminology of Pan and Yang (2010), we refer to each source as a *domain*, and acknowledge that this does not correspond to the topical sense of the term *domain* that is more common in NLP.

We cross-validate by holding out each source in turn, training a classifier on the union of the remaining sources and then applying it to the held-out source. By carrying out *cross-domain classification*, we mitigate the risk that confounding factors such as topic, genre or document length will misleadingly give high classification accuracy.

3.2 Classification Methods

We select methods from each field (Section 2) that are promising for national dialect identification.

3.2.1 BASELINE

We use a random classifier as our baseline, eschewing majority-class as it is not applicable in the cross-source context we consider; one of the primary differences anticipated between sources is that the relative distribution of classes will vary. The random classifier maps each document onto a dialect from our dialect set independently. It represents a trivial baseline that we expect all other classifiers to exceed.

3.2.2 TEXTCATEGORIZATION

We use the general text categorization approach proposed by Joachims (1998), applying a linear SVM to a standard bag-of-words representation.

3.2.3 NATIVELID

We use part-of-speech plus function word n-grams with a maximum entropy classifier (Wong and Dras, 2009). Wong and Dras aim to exploit grammatical errors, as contrastive analysis suggests that difficulties in acquiring a new language are due to differences between the new language and the native language of the learner, implying that the types of errors made are characteristic of the native language of the author. In national dialect identification, we do not expect grammatical errors to be as salient, because English is a national language of each of the countries considered. Nevertheless, part-of-speech plus function word n-grams are of interest because they roughly capture syntax — which is known to vary amongst national dialects (Trudgill and Hannah, 2008) — and are independent of the specific lexicalization.

3.2.4 AUTHORSHIPATTRIB

Authorship attribution is about modeling the linguistic idiosyncrasies of a particular author, in terms of some markers of the individual's style. Although in national dialect identification we do not assume that each document has a single unique author, we do assume that documents from the same country share stylistic properties resulting from the national dialect. We hypothesize that this results in systematic differences in the choice of function words (Zhao and Zobel, 2005). We capture this using a distribution over function words, which is a restricted bag-of-words model, where only words on an externally specified 'whitelist' are retained. We use the same stopword list as for native language identification as a proxy for function words. As per Zhao and Zobel (2005), we apply a naive Bayes classifier.

3.2.5 LANGID

We treat each dialect as a distinct language, and apply the language identification method of Lui and Baldwin (2011) in which documents are represented using a mixture of specially-selected byte sequences. The method specifically exploits differences in data sources to learn a set of byte sequences that is representative of languages (or in our case, dialects) across all the data sources. This feature selection is done by scoring each sequence using information gain (IG, Quinlan, 1993), with respect to each dialect as well as with each data source. This representation is then combined with a multinomial naive Bayes classifier.

3.2.6 GEOLOCATION

Our geolocation classifier is a nearest-prototype classifier using K-L divergence as the distance metric on a standard bag-of-words (Wing and Baldridge, 2011). The class prototypes are calculated from the concatenation of all members of the class. For both documents and classes, probability mass is assigned to unseen terms using a pseudo-Good-Turing smoothing, the parameters of which we estimate from the training data.

3.2.7 VARIANTPAIR

Motivated by Cook and Hirst's (2012) work on comparing dialects, our variant pair classifier uses the relative frequencies of spelling variants (e.g., *color/colour*, *yoghurt/yogurt*) to distinguish between dialects. For each of a set of $\sim$1.8k spelling variant pairs from VarCon,[2] we calculate the frequency difference in a document between the first and second variant (e.g., freq(*color*) − freq(*colour*)). A standard vector-space model of similarity is used: each dialect is modeled as the sum of the vectors of all documents for that dialect; Cosine is used to map a given document to the most similar dialect.

4 Text Sources

4.1 NATIONAL

Large corpora are available for British and Canadian English. The written portion of the British National Corpus (BNC, Burnard, 2000) consists of roughly 87 million words of a variety of genres and topics from British authors from the late twentieth century. The Strathy Corpus[3] consists of roughly 40 million words of a variety of text types by Canadian authors from a similar time period. We use these two corpora in this study.

Appropriate resources are not available for American or Australian English. The Corpus of Contemporary American English (COCA, Davies, 2009) currently consists of over 450 million words of American English, but can only be accessed through a web interface; the full text form is unavailable. The American National Corpus (ANC, Ide, 2009) is much smaller than the BNC and Strathy Corpus at approximately only 11 million words.[4] In the case of Australian English, the Aus-

[2] `http://wordlist.sourceforge.net`

[3] `http://www.queensu.ca/strathy/`

[4] This figure refers specifically to the written portion of the Open ANC, the freely-available version of this corpus.

Domain	Australia			Canada			United Kingdom		
	#	μ	σ	#	μ	σ	#	μ	σ
NATIONAL	0	–	–	10000	2415.8	2750.4	10000	2742.3	2692.9
WEB	10000	2111.7	3261.5	10000	2459.4	3839.5	10000	2098.1	3527.4
WEBGOV	10000	1237.2	2706.3	10000	3980.4	4522.4	10000	2558.1	3327.4
TWITTER	1857	12.1	6.3	3598	11.8	6.3	24047	12.0	6.5

Table 1: Characteristics of the ENDIALECT dataset. # is the document count, μ and σ are the mean and standard deviation of document length (in words).

tralian Corpus of English (Green and Peters, 1991) consists of just 1 million words.[5]

4.2 WEB

The Web has been widely used for building corpora (e.g., Baroni et al., 2009; Kilgarriff et al., 2010) with Cook and Hirst (2012) presenting preliminary results suggesting that English corpora from top-level domains might represent corresponding national dialects of English. Australia, Canada, and the United Kingdom all have corresponding top-level domains that contain a wide variety of text types — namely `.au`, `.ca`, and `.uk`, respectively — from which we can build corpora. However, the top-level domain for the United States, `.us`, is primarily used for more-specialized purposes, such as government, and so a similar Web corpus cannot easily be built for American English. Here we build English Web corpora from `.au`, `.ca`, and `.uk` which — based on the findings of Cook and Hirst (2012) — we assume to represent Australian, Canadian, and British English, respectively.

One common method for corpus construction is to issue a large number of queries to a search engine, download the resulting URLs, and post-process the documents to produce a corpus (e.g., Baroni and Bernardini, 2004; Sharoff, 2006; Kilgarriff et al., 2010). Cook and Hirst (2012) use such a method to build corpora from the `.ca` and `.uk` domains; we follow their approach here. Specifically, we select alphabetic types in the BNC with character length greater than 2 and frequency rank 1001–5000 in the BNC as *seed words*. We then use Baroni and Bernardini's (2004) BootCaT tools to form 18k random 3-tuples from these seeds. We use the BootCaT tools to issue search engine queries for these tuples in the `.au`, `.ca`, and `.uk` domains. Using the BootCaT tools we then download the resulting URLs, and eliminate duplicates. We further eliminate non-English documents using `langid.py` (Lui and Baldwin, 2012). Following Cook and Hirst we only retain up to three randomly-selected documents per domain (e.g., `www.cbc.ca`). The final corpora consist of roughly 77, 96, and 115 million tokens for the `.au`, `.ca`, and `.uk` domains, respectively.

4.3 WEBGOV (Government)

The government of each of the countries considered in this study produces an enormous number of documents which can be used to build corpora. Furthermore, because many government websites are in particular second-level domains (e.g., `.gov.uk`) it is possible to easily construct a Web corpus consisting of such documents.

To build governmental Web corpora we follow a very similar process to that in the previous subsection, this time issuing queries for each of `.gov.au`, `.gc.ca`, and `.gov.uk`.[6] The resulting Australian, British, and Canadian government corpora contain roughly 199, 161, and 148 million words, respectively.[7]

4.4 TWITTER

Twitter[8] is an enormously popular micro-blogging service which has previously been used in studies of regional linguistic variation (e.g., Eisenstein et al., 2010). Twitter allows users to post short (up to 140 characters) messages known as *tweets*, and a recent report from Twitter indicates that roughly 500 million tweets are sent each day (Twitter, 2013). Crucially for this project, roughly 1% of tweets include geolocation metadata and

[5] The Australian National Corpus (`http://www.ausnc.org.au/`) is much larger, but consists of relatively little written material from the same time period as our other corpora.

[6] In this case there is an obvious domain to use to build an American government corpus, i.e., `.gov`. However, because we did not have a general Web corpus, or an appropriate national corpus, for American English, we did not build a government corpus for this dialect.

[7] There is a small amount of overlap between WEB and WEBGOV, with 3.7% of the WEB documents coming from governmental second-level domains.

[8] `http://twitter.com/`

can be used to build corpora known to correspond to a particular geographical region.

Using the Twitter API we collected a sample of tweets from October 2011 – January 2012 with geotags indicating that they were sent from Australia, Canada, or the United Kingdom.[9] We then filtered this collection to include only English tweets (again using `langid.py`). The resulting collection includes roughly 140k, 240k, and 1.4M tweets from Australia, Canada, and the United Kingdom, respectively.

5 The ENDIALECT dataset

The ENDIALECT dataset (Table 1), consists of 109502 documents in 3 English dialects (Australian, British, and Canadian) across 4 text sources (NATIONAL, WEB, WEBGOV and TWITTER, described in Section 4). We conducted a pilot study, and found that across all the methods we test, the in-domain classification accuracy did not vary significantly beyond 5000 documents per dialect. Thus, for NATIONAL, WEB and WEBGOV, we retained 10000 documents per dialect. For WEB and WEBGOV, we randomly sampled 10000 documents (without replacement) from each dialect. For NATIONAL, the documents are substantially longer, and furthermore, documents from the (Canadian) Strathy Corpus are on average twice as long as those from the (British) BNC. In order to extract documents of comparable length to the WEB and WEBGOV, we divided each document in NATIONAL into equal-sized fragments (10 fragments per document for the BNC and 20 per document for the Strathy Corpus). We then sampled 10000 fragments from each, yielding pseudo-documents of comparable length to documents from WEB and WEBGOV.

Constructing documents from the Twitter data is more difficult because individual messages are very short; preliminary experiments indicated that trying to infer dialect from a single message is nearly impossible. For Twitter, we therefore concatenate all documents from a given user to form a single pseudo-document per user. The Twitter crawl available to us had insufficient data to extract 10000 users per country, so we opted to retain all the users that had 15 or more messages in our data, giving us a total number of user pseudo-documents comparable to the number of documents for our other data sources (albeit with a skew between dialects that is not present for the other text sources).

[9] Although an abundance of geolocated tweets are available for the United States, since we do not have corpora from the other sources for this national dialect we do not consider it here.

6 Results

The first set of experiments we perform is in a leave-one-out cross-domain learning setting over our 4 text sources (referred to interchangeably as "domains") and 7 classification methods. We train one classifier for each pair of classification method and target domain, for a total of 28 classifiers. The training data used for each classifier is leave-one-out over the set of domains. For example, for any given classification method, the classifier applied to WEB is trained on the union of data from NATIONAL, WEBGOV, and TWITTER.

Table 2 summarizes the macroaveraged F-score for each classifier in the cross-domain classification setting. We find that overall, the best methods for national dialect identification are TEXTCATEGORIZATION and NATIVELID. We also find that F-score varies greatly between target domains; in general, F-score is highest for NATIONAL, and lowest for TWITTER.

In this work, we primarily focus on cross-domain national dialect identification, for reasons discussed in Section 3.1. However, most of the methods we consider were not developed for cross-domain application, and thus in-domain results provide an interesting point of comparison. Hence, we present results from in-domain 10-fold cross-validation in Table 3 for comparison with the cross-domain outcome.

Our in-domain results are consistent with our cross-domain findings, in that methods that perform better in-domain tend to also perform better cross-domain, and target domains that are "easier" in-domain also tend to be "easier" cross-domain, "easier" meaning that all methods tend to attain better results. For most methods, the in-domain performance is better than the cross-domain performance, which is not surprising given that it is likely that there are particular terms that are predictive of a dialect in-domain that may not generalize across domains.

Overall, the results on in-domain and cross-domain classification suggest that TEXTCATEGORIZATION is consistently the best among the methods compared across multiple domains, and that some domains are inherently easier for national

Approach	Target Domain NATIONAL (2-way)	WEB (3-way)	WEBGOV (3-way)	TWITTER (3-way)
BASELINE	0.491	0.317	0.313	0.269
TEXTCATEGORIZATION	0.911	0.656	0.788	0.447
NATIVELID	0.812	0.606	0.480	0.314
AUTHORSHIPATTRIB	0.502	0.367	0.227	0.334
LANGID	0.772	0.538	0.597	0.043
GEOLOCATION	0.432	0.347	0.312	0.369
VARIANTPAIR	0.443	0.267	0.226	0.281

Table 2: Macroaverage F-score for cross-domain learning. For each domain/method combination, a classifier is trained on the union of the 3 non-target domains.

Approach	Target Domain NATIONAL (2-way)	WEB (3-way)	WEBGOV (3-way)	TWITTER (3-way)
BASELINE	0.499	0.336	0.328	0.329
TEXTCATEGORIZATION	0.975	0.762	0.870	0.773
NATIVELID	0.946	0.577	0.708	0.521
AUTHORSHIPATTRIB	0.591	0.368	0.489	0.451
LANGID	–	–	–	–
GEOLOCATION	0.861	0.532	0.544	0.316
VARIANTPAIR	0.532	0.359	0.333	0.337

Table 3: Macroaverage F-score for in-domain (supervised) classification for each domain/method combination. (We do not have in-domain LANGID results as the method of Lui and Baldwin (2011) specifically requires cross-domain training data.)

dialect identification than others. To better understand the difference between domains, we conducted a further experiment, where we trained a classifier using each method on data from only one of our domains. We then applied this classifier to every other domain. We conducted this experiment for the two best-performing methods in the cross-domain setting: TEXTCATEGORIZATION and NATIVELID. The results of this experiment are summarized in Table 4.

The performance of classifiers trained on all non-test domains is generally better than that of classifiers trained on a single domain. The only exception to this is with classifiers trained on WEB applied to WEBGOV, which could be due to the noted overlap between these domains. However, this relationship is not symmetrical: classifiers trained only on WEBGOV do not perform better on WEB than classifiers trained on WEBGOV +NATIONAL +TWITTER.

7 Discussion

The high performance of TEXTCATEGORIZATION provides strong evidence of the viability of the cross-domain approach to identifying national dialect. This can be partly attributed to the much larger feature set of this method — to which no feature selection is applied — as compared to the other methods. The total vocabulary across all the datasets amounts to over 3 million unique terms. From this, the SVM algorithm was able to learn parameter weights that were applicable across domains — this can be seen from how the cross-domain text categorization results (Table 2) comfortably exceed the baseline in all domains.

AUTHORSHIPATTRIB uses a set of ~ 400 function words, in contrast to the ~ 3 million terms in the text categorization approach. The AUTHORSHIPATTRIB results are very close to the baseline in the cross-domain setting, suggesting that stylistic variation as captured by these features is not characteristic of English dialects.

F-scores for NATIVELID comfortably exceed the baseline, which suggests that English dialects have systematic differences at the syntactic level. The results are inferior to TEXTCATEGORIZATION, indicating that there are specific words that are predictive of national dialect across domains. This suggests there are systematic differences in the topics of discussion between documents of different origin, likely due to the discussion of specific locations. For example, analysis of our results indicates that (unsurprisingly) the term *Canada* is strongly associated with documents of Canadian origin.

The relatively poor performance of LANGID

Method	Training Domain	Target Domain			
		NATIONAL (2-way)	WEB (3-way)	WEBGOV (3-way)	TWITTER (3-way)
TEXTCATEGORIZATION	NATIONAL	*0.975*	0.287	0.358	0.181
	WEB	0.908	*0.762*	0.811	0.355
	WEBGOV	0.886	0.645	*0.870*	0.415
	TWITTER	0.631	0.573	0.637	*0.773*
NATIVELID	NATIONAL	*0.946*	0.317	0.384	0.101
	WEB	0.794	*0.577*	0.623	0.325
	WEBGOV	0.808	0.507	*0.708*	0.259
	TWITTER	0.508	0.346	0.329	*0.521*

Table 4: Macroaverage F-score for pairwise cross-domain learning. Same-domain results (Table 3) are replicated in *italics* for comparison.

may be due to the small feature set. Lui and Baldwin (2011) select the top 400 features per language over 97 languages, so their feature set consists of 7480 features. We only consider 3 dialects, with a corresponding feature set of 1058 features. Though our features are clearly informative for the task (LANGID results comfortably exceed the baseline), there may be useful information that is lost when a document is mapped into this reduced feature space. LANGID performs exceptionally poorly when applied to TWITTER in a cross-domain setting, because the classifier predicts a minority class 'Australian' for almost all documents. This is likely due to the lack of national corpus training data for 'Australian', as Table 4 suggests that national corpus data are an especially poor proxy for Twitter (a result consistent with the findings of Baldwin et al. (2013)).

The poor performance of the GEOLOCATION is perhaps more surprising, as like TEXTCATEGORIZATION this approach makes use of the full bag-of-words feature set. However, in the geolocation task of Wing and Baldridge (2011), the class space is much larger, and furthermore it is structured; classes correspond to regions of the Earth's surface, and the distance of the predicted region to the goldstandard region is taken into account in evaluation. The national dialect identification task is much more coarse-grained, potentially making it a poor match for geolocation methods.

VARIANTPAIR performs poorly throughout, with results below the random baseline in the cross-domain setting. The key difference between our national dialect identification task and the work of Cook and Hirst (2012) is that they classify entire corpora, whereas we classify individual documents. Documents are much shorter than corpora, and contain less spelling variation because they typically have a single author who is unlikely to choose different spellings of a given word.

8 Conclusion

Our cross-domain classification results strongly suggest that there are characteristics of each national dialect that are consistent across multiple domains. These characteristics go beyond simple topical differences, as representations such as function word distributions, and part-of-speech plus function word bigrams, omit topical information from consideration. Even without topical information, a classifier trained using techniques from native language identification is able to comfortably surpass a random baseline.

In future work, we intend to analyze the features weighted highly by our classifiers to potentially identify previously-undocumented differences between national dialects. Additionally, work on dialect identification might benefit methods for language identification. Prager (1999) finds that modeling Norwegian dialects separately improves language identification performance. In future work, we will examine if similarly modeling English dialects improves language identification.

Acknowledgments

NICTA is funded by the Australian Government as represented by the Department of Broadband, Communications and the Digital Economy and the Australian Research Council through the ICT Centre of Excellence program.

References

Eric Atwell, Junaid Arshad, Chien-Ming Lai, Lan Nim, Noushin Rezapour Asheghi, Josiah Wang, and Justin Washtell. 2007. Which English dominates the World Wide Web, British or American? In *Proceedings of the Corpus Linguistics Conference (CL 2007)*. Birmingham, UK.

Timothy Baldwin, Paul Cook, Marco Lui, Andrew MacKinlay, and Li Wang. 2013. How noisy social media text, how diffrnt social media sources? In *Proceedings of the Sixth International Joint Conference on Natural Language Processing*, pages 356–364. Asian Federation of Natural Language Processing, Nagoya, Japan.

Marco Baroni and Silvia Bernardini. 2004. BootCaT: Bootstrapping corpora and terms from the Web. In *Proceedings of the Fourth International Conference on Language Resources and Evaluation (LREC 2004)*.

Marco Baroni, Silvia Bernardini, Adriano Ferraresi, and Eros Zanchetta. 2009. The WaCky Wide Web: A collection of very large linguistically processed Web-crawled corpora. *Language Resources and Evaluation*, 43(3):209–226.

Julian Brooke and Graeme Hirst. 2012. Robust, lexicalized native language identification. In *Proceedings of COLING 2012*, pages 391–408. The COLING 2012 Organizing Committee, Mumbai, India.

Lou Burnard. 2000. *The British National Corpus Users Reference Guide*. Oxford University Computing Services.

Paul Cook and Graeme Hirst. 2012. Do Web corpora from top-level domains represent national varieties of English? In *Proceedings of the 11th International Conference on Textual Data Statistical Analysis*, pages 281–293. Liège, Belgium.

Corinna Cortes and Vladimir Vapnik. 1995. Support-vector networks. *Machine Learning*, 20:273–297.

Mark Davies. 2009. The 385+ million word Corpus of Contemporary American English (1990–2008+): Design, architecture, and linguistic insights. *International Journal of Corpus Linguistics*, 14(2):159–190.

Franca Debole and Fabrizio Sebastiani. 2005. An analysis of the relative hardness of reuters-21578 subsets. *Journal of the American Society for Information Science and Technology*, 56(6):584–596.

Harris Drucker, Vladimir Vapnik, and Dongui Wu. 1999. Support vector machines for spam categorization. *IEEE Transactions on Neural Networks*, 10:1048–1054.

Jacob Eisenstein, Brendan O'Connor, Noah A. Smith, and Eric P. Xing. 2010. A latent variable model for geographic lexical variation. In *Empirical Methods in Natural Language Processing*, pages 1277–1287. Cambridge, MA, USA.

Dominique Estival, Tanja Gaustad, and Ben Hutchinson. 2007. Author profiling for english emails. In *Proccedings of the 10th Conference for the Pacific Association for Computational Linguistics*, pages 263–272. Melbourne,Australia.

Elizabeth Green and Pam Peters. 1991. The Australian corpus project and Australian English. *International Computer Archive of Modern English*, 15:37–53.

Bo Han, Paul Cook, and Timothy Baldwin. 2012. Geolocation prediction in social media data by finding location indicative words. In *Proceedings of COLING 2012*, pages 1045–1062. The COLING 2012 Organizing Committee, Mumbai, India.

Graeme Hirst and Olga Feiguina. 2007. Bigrams of syntactic labels for authorship discrimination of short texts. *Literary and Linguistic Computing*, 22(4):405–417.

Nancy Ide. 2009. The American National Corpus: Then, now, and tomorrow. In Michael Haugh, editor, *Selected Proceedings of the 2008 HCSNet Workshop on Designing an Australian National Corpus*, pages 108–113. Cascadilla Proceedings Project, Sommerville, MA.

Jennifer Jenkins. 2009. *World Englishes: A resource book for students*. Routledge, London, second edition.

Thorsten Joachims. 1998. Text categorization with support vector machines: learning with many relevant features. In *Proceedings of the 10th European Conference on Machine Learning*, pages 137–142. Chemnitz, Germany.

Adam Kilgarriff. 2001. Comparing corpora. *International Journal of Corpus Linguistics*, 6(1):97–133.

Adam Kilgarriff, Siva Reddy, Jan Pomikálek, and Avinesh PVS. 2010. A corpus factory for many languages. In *Proceedings of the Seventh conference on International Language Resources and Evaluation (LREC 2010)*, pages 904–910. Valletta, Malta.

Moshe Koppel, Jonathan Schler, and Kfir Zigdon. 2005. Automatically determining an anonymous authors native language. *Intelligence and Security Informatics*, 3495:209–217.

Marco Lui and Timothy Baldwin. 2011. Cross-domain feature selection for language identification. In *Proceedings of the 5th International Joint Conference on Natural Language Processing (IJCNLP 2011)*, pages 553–561. Chiang Mai, Thailand.

Marco Lui and Timothy Baldwin. 2012. langid.py: An off-the-shelf language identification tool. In *Proceedings of the 50th Annual Meeting of the Association for Computational Linguistics (ACL 2012) Demo Session*, pages 25–30. Jeju, Republic of Korea.

Frederick Mosteller and David L. Wallace. 1964. *Inference and disputed authorship: The Federalist Papers*. Addison-Wesley, Reading,USA.

Sinno Jialin Pan and Qiang Yang. 2010. A survey on transfer learning. *Knowledge and Data Engineering, IEEE Transactions on*, 22(10):1345–1359.

Yves Peirsman, Dirk Geeraerts, and Dirk Speelman. 2010. The automatic identification of lexical variation between language varieties. *Natural Language Engineering*, 16(4):469–491.

John M. Prager. 1999. Linguini: language identification for multilingual documents. In *Proceedings the 32nd Annual Hawaii International Conference on Systems Sciences (HICSS-32)*. Maui, Hawaii.

John Ross Quinlan. 1993. *C4.5: Programs for Machine Learning*. Morgan Kaufmann, San Mateo, USA.

Randolph Quirk. 1995. *Grammatical and lexical variance in English*. Longman, London.

Stephen Roller, Michael Speriosu, Sarat Rallapalli, Benjamin Wing, and Jason Baldridge. 2012. Supervised text-based geolocation using language models on an adaptive grid. In *Proceedings of the 2012 Joint Conference on Empirical Methods in Natural Language Processing and Computational Natural Language Learning*, pages 1500–1510. Jeju Island, Korea.

Evan Sandhaus. 2008. The New York Times Annotated Corpus. Linguistic Data Consortium, Philadelphia, PA.

Fabrizio Sebastiani. 2002. Machine learning in automated text categorization. *ACM computing surveys (CSUR)*, 34(1):1–47.

Fabrizio Sebastiani. 2005. *Text categorization*, pages 109–129. TEMIS Text Mining Solutions S.A., Italy.

Yanir Seroussi, Fabian Bohnert, and Ingrid Zukerman. 2012. Authorship attribution with author-aware topic models. In *Proceedings of the 50th Annual Meeting of the Association for Computational Linguistics (Volume 2: Short Papers)*, pages 264–269. Association for Computational Linguistics, Jeju Island, Korea.

Serge Sharoff. 2006. Creating general-purpose corpora using automated search engine queries. In Marco Baroni and Silvia Bernardini, editors, *Wacky! Working papers on the Web as Corpus*, pages 63–98. GEDIT, Bologna, Italy.

Efstathios Stamatatos. 2009. A survey of modern authorship attribution methods. *Journal of The American Society for Information Science and Technology*, 60:538–556.

Dolf Trieschnigg, Djoerd Hiemstra, Mariët Theune, Franciska de Jong, and Theo Meder. 2012. An exploration of language identification techniques for the dutch folktale database. In *Proceedings of the LREC workshop on the Adaptation of Language Resources and Tools for Processing Cultural Heritage Objects*.

Peter Trudgill. 1999. Standard English: What it isnt. In Tony Bex and Richard J. Watts, editors, *Standard English: The widening debate*, pages 117–128. Routledge, London.

Peter Trudgill and Jean Hannah. 2008. *International English: A guide to varieties of Standard English*. Hodder Education, London, fifth edition.

Twitter. 2013. New tweets per second record, and how! `https://blog.twitter.com/2013/new-tweets-`

per-second-record-and-how. Retrieved 19 August 2013.

Benjamin P. Wing and Jason Baldridge. 2011. Simple supervised document geolocation with geodesic grids. In *Proceedings of the 49th Annual Meeting of the Association for Computational Linguistics: Human Language Technologies - Volume 1*, HLT '11, pages 955–964. Association for Computational Linguistics, Portland, Oregon, USA.

Sze-Meng Jojo Wong and Mark Dras. 2009. Contrastive analysis and native language identification. In *Proceedings of the Australasian Language Technology Workshop 2009 (ALTW 2009)*, pages 53–61. Sydney, Australia.

Sze-Meng Jojo Wong and Mark Dras. 2011. Exploiting parse structures for native language identification. In *Proceedings of the 2011 Conference on Empirical Methods in Natural Language Processing (EMNLP 2011)*, pages 1600–1610. Association for Computational Linguistics, Edinburgh, Scotland, UK.

Sze-Meng Jojo Wong, Mark Dras, and Mark Johnson. 2012. Exploring adaptor grammars for native language identification. In *Proceedings of the Joint Conference on Empirical Methods in Natural Language Processing and Computational Natural Language Learning 2012 (EMNLP-CoNLL 2012)*, pages 699–709. Association for Computational Linguistics, Jeju Island, Korea.

Yiming Yang and Xin Liu. 1999. A re-examination of text categorization methods. In *Proceedings of the 22nd annual international ACM SIGIR conference on Research and development in information retrieval - SIGIR '99*, pages 42–49. ACM Press, New York, USA.

G. Udny Yule. 1939. On sentence-length as a statistical characteristic of style in prose: With application to two cases of disputed authorship. *Biometrika*, 30:363–390.

Omar F Zaidan and Chris Callison-Burch. 2012. Arabic dialect identification. *Computational Linguistics*, 52(1).

Ying Zhao and Justin Zobel. 2005. Effective and Scalable Authorship Attribution Using Function Words. In *Asia Information Retrieval Symposium*, pages 174–189.

Crowd-Sourcing of Human Judgments of Machine Translation Fluency

Yvette Graham **Timothy Baldwin** **Alistair Moffat** **Justin Zobel**
Department of Computing and Information Systems, The University of Melbourne
{ygraham,tbaldwin,ammoffat,jzobel}@unimelb.edu.au

Abstract

Human evaluation of machine translation quality is a key element in the development of machine translation systems, as automatic metrics are validated through correlation with human judgment. However, achievement of consistent human judgments of machine translation is not easy, with decreasing levels of consistency reported in annual evaluation campaigns. In this paper we describe experiences gained during the collection of human judgments of the fluency of machine translation output using Amazon's Mechanical Turk service. We gathered a large collection of crowd-sourced human judgments for the machine translation systems that participated in the WMT 2012 shared translation task, collected across a range of eight different assessment configurations to gain insight into possible causes of – and remedies for – inconsistency in human judgments. Overall, approximately half of the workers carry out the human evaluation to a high standard, but effectiveness varies considerably across different target languages, with dramatically higher numbers of good quality judgments for Spanish and French, and the reverse observed for German.

1 Introduction

The ability to accurately measure the properties of an object of study, such as a computational system, is fundamental to progress in science. For measurements to be meaningful, they need to be comparable between systems, and to be an accurate proxy for the properties of the systems being studied.

For machine translation (MT), measurement has been a combination of human judgments and automated measurements. With the aim of removing system biases and creating robust comparisons, there has been extensive use of workshops and shared tasks such as the ongoing Workshops on Statistical Machine Translation (WMT) and the NIST Open Machine Translation (OpenMT) evaluations. The basis of system evaluation is generally human judgments, which have also been used to evaluate automatic metrics such as BLEU (Papineni et al., 2001), under the assumption that a metric that correlates strongly with human judgments is more valid than a metric with weak correlation. Human evaluation of MT thus forms the foundation of evaluation in empirical MT, regardless of whether a particular evaluation makes use of human judges or automatic metrics.

The current methodology used for the task of human evaluation in MT is problematic, however, as assessments carried out by expert judges are highly inconsistent. Even when a single expert judge is asked to assess the same pair of translations in two separate sittings, the second judgment is often at odds with the initial one (Bojar et al., 2013). Somewhat paradoxically, and despite the fact that experts are not consistent, when non-experts are employed to do judgments, there is a tendency to give preference to non-experts who demonstrate high agreement with experts.

We have used Amazon's Mechanical Turk service (AMT) to gather human judgments of machine translations. Here we describe the data we have collected, our experiences in gathering this data, and our refinements to the gathering process. In particular, we have carried out a large-scale human evaluation across a range of different assessment configurations. The following assessment dimensions were explored: response scale; question wording; whether to include a reference translation; and deletion of foreign language words from translations. To ensure that the results are not peculiar to a single language pair, we in-

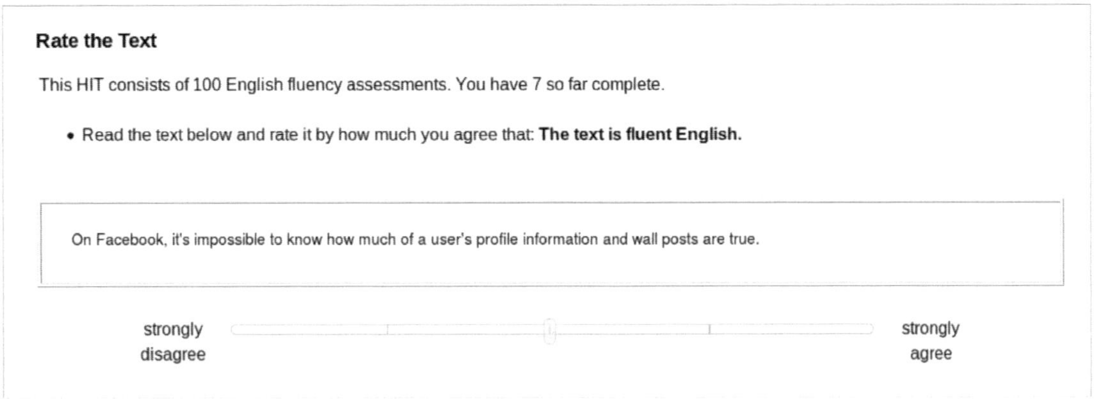

Figure 1: Screen shot for *base* configuration for fluency assessments, including 100 point visual analog scale (VAS), marked but not labeled at 25-50-75.

clude seven language pairs across all participating systems from WMT 2012 (Callison-Burch et al., 2012).

Previous work has shown the advantages of collecting judgments on a continuous rating scale for NLP evaluation (Belz and Kow, 2011) in general, as well as for MT evaluation specifically (Graham et al., 2013), as shown in Figure 1. This approach allows judge-intrinsic quality control to be introduced, so that non-experts can be used, as well as permitting standardization of scores and longitudinal evaluation. We adopt this approach and ask AMT workers to assess the fluency of translations on a continuous rating scale. Since we are primarily concerned with design of the assessment configuration so as to improve the consistency of human judgments, and not with ranking of systems, we limit our assessment to evaluating *fluency*. Graham et al. (2012) suggest *translation quality* should be measured as a hypothetical construct, where measurements that employ more items (dimensions of measurement) as opposed to fewer are considered more valid. Under this criterion, a two-item (fluency and adequacy) scale is more valid than a single-item translation quality measure, further motivating the inclusion of fluency as an assessment item for measurement of translation quality.

Overall, just under half of the Turkers carried out the human evaluation to a standard that met our quality control threshold. In addition, proportions of good quality workers vary considerably from one target language to the next, with dramatically higher proportions of good quality judgments for Spanish and French. The reverse occurs for translation into German, however, where less than one third of completed Human Intelligence Tasks (HITs) were carried out by workers that reached the quality control threshold.

2 Assessment Design

The data we have gathered explores four dimensions of MT quality assessment for fluency: question wording; labeling of the response scale; inclusion of reference translation; and presence of source language words in translations. We first establish a *base configuration* assessment set-up from which seven other configurations are created. Figure 1 shows a screen shot of the base assessment configuration.

For each variant configuration, a single dimension of the base configuration is changed, as shown in Figure 2. The same 100-point continuous response scale was used for all configurations, based on the findings of Graham et al. (2013). All configurations were then applied to seven language pairs. In all cases, instructions and questions were presented to the judges in the target language.

The first dimension of the assessment design we investigate is alternative possible anchor labels of the *visual analog scale* (VAS). The scale shown in Figure 1 is the base assessment configuration, and uses a 100-point *marked VAS* response scale, with tick marks at 25, 50, and 75. Two variants were also explored (the "east" dimension in Figure 2): an unmarked VAS, which omits the markings on the response scale (shown at the top of Figure 3);

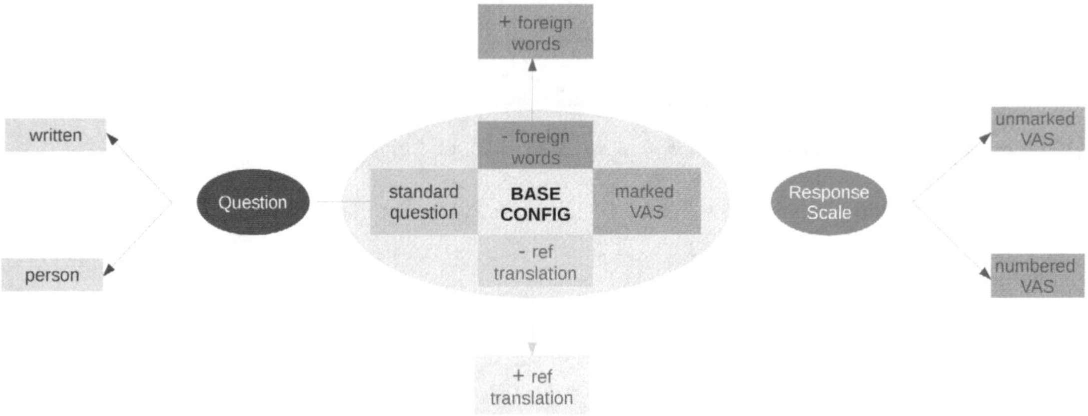

Figure 2: Trialed fluency assessment configurations: base configuration (center); additional assessment configurations diverge from the base on a single dimension.

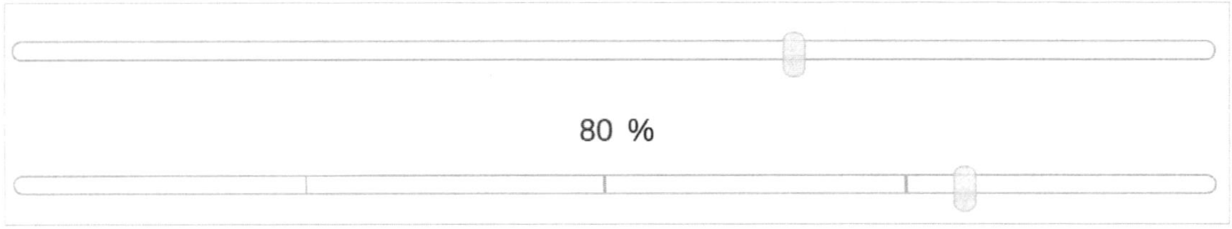

Figure 3: Variant VAS arrangements: unmarked and unlabeled, top; and marked and numbered VAS (100 point scale, marked at 25-50-75, displaying percentage corresponding to slider position), bottom.

and a numbered VAS that provides the judge with the numeric position at which the slider is sitting, a value that smoothly changes when the slider is moved (shown at the bottom of Figure 3).

When asking human judges to assess the fluency of translations, the particular way in which the question is asked is of obvious importance. The data we have collected includes trials of three alternative question wordings and response scale anchor labels (the "west" dimension in Figure 2); the three variants are shown in Table 1. First, the base configuration question (denoted *standard*) is a straightforward Likert declarative statement that directly uses the term "fluent English". But in everyday language usage, the term *fluent* is typically used to describe a person as opposed to expression. Hence, asking the judge whether the person who wrote the text is fluent might make the question more intuitive, and subsequently yield more consistent judgments – the *person* approach listed second in the table. Finally, we choose a wording that simply replaces "fluent" with a phrase more commonly used to refer to language, that is, whether the text is clearly written, denoted in Table 1 as the *written* approach.

The third dimension is whether or not to include a reference translation (the "south" variant in Figure 2). An assessment of fluency independent of adequacy and without a reference translation provides at least one part of an overall evaluation that will not be biased in favor of systems that happen to produce reference-like translations. However, in the past, fluency judgments have generally been carried out with a reference translation present (Callison-Burch et al., 2007). In this part of the evaluation the instructions described the task as assessing automatic translations as opposed to a simple rating of the fluency of the text, since without this context it would be difficult to explain what a reference in fact was. With each translation that was presented a note was displayed on screen to the users as follows: *An equivalent piece of fluent text is provided in gray for your reference.*

The final dimension explored (the "north" variant in Figure 2) is the effect of the presence of source language words in translations. Many of

Configuration	Question	Anchor labels	
		left	right
standard	Read the text below and rate it by how much you agree that: **The text is fluent English**.	strongly disagree	strongly agree
person	Based only on the text below, estimate the extent to which **the person who wrote the text is fluent in English**.	not at all fluent	highly fluent
written	**Is the text in the box below clearly written?**	not at all clear	very clear

Table 1: Alternative wordings for the instructions given to Turkers.

the translations in the data set contain foreign language words, due to MT systems whose response to words that are unknown is to leave them untranslated in the output. The presence of foreign words could be a cause of inconsistency for human judges, however. If, for example, a human judge happens to know the source language, their assessment of a translation containing a foreign word might be more favorable than that of a judge who has no knowledge of the source language. We therefore carried out an assessment with foreign words removed from translations (in the *base* configuration), and a contrasting assessment where foreign words were retained.

3 Data Set

The data set we have gathered consists of approximately 91,000 human judgments of the fluency of translations drawn from the WMT 2012 shared task published data (Callison-Burch et al., 2012). For each of the language pairs German-English, French-English, Spanish-English, Czech-English, English-German, English-French, and English-Spanish 560 system outputs were selected at random across participating systems. To each set of translations, an additional 240 translations were added as same-judge quality-control repeat items, 80 of which were exact repeats (*ask_again*) of a previously assessed translation, another 80 a *bad-reference* item, and the final 80 were reference translations, which should be judged highly by all judges. Thus for each language pair, a set of 800 translations was assessed across the eight different assessment configurations. (We also sought English-Czech judgments, but received a low response rate at AMT.)

Same Judge Repeat Items Control of same-judge repeat items on AMT with the conventional set-up is not straightforward, as a HIT usually consists of a single assessment (whether it be 5 translations or 1 translation per screen). To counter this, we use the unconventional HIT structure described by Graham et al. (2013) and constructed HITs of 100 judgments, so that we can fully control same-judge repeat items. We include a minimum number of 40 intervening judgments between repeat items, making it unlikely that a worker could boost their consistency by simply remembering a previous score.

Distinct Judge Repeat Items Control of distinct judge repeat items on AMT is straightforward, as the requester can specify for a set of HITs that they require a particular number of distinct workers. Since our focus is not on evaluating individual systems, but rather examining consistency of judgments, we specified that two distinct workers should carry out each HIT that we provided.

Worker Reliability We include in the data set for each AMT worker an estimate of their reliability based on score distributions for *bad-reference* pairs (explained below). The reliability estimate is a simplification of the method used in Graham et al. (2013) for quality-control. Instead of applying difference of means tests to *score differences* between that of the first and repeated item, we apply the same test to the mean of raw scores of *bad-reference* pairs.

No judge, when given the same translation to judge twice on a continuous scale (when separated by intervening judgment requests, the approach used in our experiments) can be expected to give precisely the same score for each judgment. A more flexible tool is thus required. We build such a tool by starting with two core assumptions:

A: When a consistent judge is presented with a set of repeat judgments, the mean score for the initial assessments will be neither significantly greater than nor significantly less than the mean score for repeat assessments.

Item A	Item B	MAE	κ_{intra}	κ_{inter}
47.1	47.2	13.3	0.68	0.37

Table 2: Agreement for *ask_again* repeat items for good workers.

Item A	Item B	MoD
26.0	47.3	21.3

Table 3: Agreement for *bad-reference* repeat items for good workers.

B: When a consistent judge is presented with a set of judgments for translations from two distinct systems, one of which is known to be better than the other, the mean score for the better system will be significantly higher than the mean score for the inferior system.

Assumption B is the basis of our reliability estimate, and allows us to distinguish between Turkers who are working carefully from those who are merely going through the motions. Deliberately degraded translations – referred to as *bad-reference* strings – are constructed from systems' translations and placed in to each HIT. Fluency-degraded translations were generated as follows: two words in the translation were randomly selected and randomly re-inserted elsewhere (but not as the initial or final word of the sentence). All translations, from all participating systems, were used to create *bad-reference* pairs, with a random subset used in HITs.

To compute the reliability estimate, *bad-reference* pair scores for a worker's HITS were extracted, a difference of means test undertaken, and the resulting p-value then used as a reliability estimate. A threshold (for example, $p < 0.05$) can then be applied to select the reliable workers. Careless judges have a high p-value, while judges who are both skilled and conscientious have a low p-value. This relationship can be validated by direct inspection of the judgments performed.

4 Judge Consistency

Table 2 shows consistency of human judges for judgments of translations repeated by the same and distinct judges. Mean scores for same judge *ask_again* repeat items show no significant difference. At the same time, mean scores for degraded *bad-reference* translations (Table 3) are significantly lower than for the corresponding system outputs. The Mean Absolute Error, computed as

$$\text{MAE} = \frac{1}{n}\sum_{i=1}^{n} |f_i - y_i| \ , \tag{1}$$

where f_i denotes the prediction (repeated score) and y_i the target (initial score) is 13.3 for *ask_again* items, while Mean of Differences, given by

$$\text{MoD} = \frac{1}{n}\sum_{i=1}^{n} (f_i - y_i) \ , \tag{2}$$

for *bad-reference* repeat items is 21.3. Calculated Kappa coefficients for same- and distinct- judge repeat items are 0.68 and 0.37 respectively when the continuous scores are mapped to two categories: less than or equal to 50; and greater than 50. (Kappa values of 0.0–0.2 represent "slight" agreement; of 0.2–0.4 are "fair"; of 0.4–0.6 are "moderate"; of 0.6–0.8 are "substantial"; and of 0.8–1.0 represent agreements that are "almost perfect".)

5 AMT Lessons

Amazon's Mechanical Turk and other crowd-sourcing services are widely used in NLP to collect data (Snow et al., 2008), with guides available that provide advice on how best to make use of such services (Callison-Burch and Dredze, 2010). Whether engaging with crowd-sourcing services such as AMT as a requester or worker, however, there is some degree of risk, primarily because of the anonymity that is assured by the services. The requester, in providing payment for potentially large volumes of work, is vulnerable to substandard or even robotically completed HITs. In this regard there is a clear sense of "buyer beware" that is part and parcel of using crowd-sourcing services. The worker, on the other hand, earns a relatively low hourly rate, and faces an ongoing risk of having completed HITs declined and of not being reimbursed for diligently completed work. Recently developed online tools provide slightly more power to workers, by enabling requester reviewing and hence allowing workers to identify requesters who too readily reject completed HITs (Irani and Silberman, 2013). And even when workers are paid, rather than volunteers, payment rates are well below the minimum wages that apply in most developed countries (Fort et al., 2011).

Human Ethics Posting HITs on a service such as AMT amounts to research involving humans, and human ethics potentially becomes a concern (Gilles et al., 2011; Fort et al., 2011). Research institutes tend to evolve their own specific human ethics policies for crowd-sourcing tasks. In our particular institution, a two-stage procedure for human ethics approval is in place. An initial stage involves consultation with an advisory group, which functions as a filtering mechanism to determine which applications involving humans need to go through the full ethics application. Our intention to post HITs on AMT was approved at this stage, since material and information collected would not be specifically *about* the subjects.[1] That is, asking AMT workers to assess translations was deemed by the ethics advisory group as research akin to taste-tests or similar market research.

Social Responsibility Besides the issue of personal information, there is an additional ethical concern with regard to payment of workers that remains unresolved in the research community. In non-crowd-sourced research, reimbursing volunteers for work with a small monetary or in-kind reward is common practice and in general is considered ethical. In these experiments the subjects are regarded as volunteers, and the gift or reimbursement is regarded as a gesture of appreciation rather than as payment. With an online service such as AMT, however, the population is mixed: some Turkers may indeed be genuine volunteers, pleased to be able to assist with a research project; and others may be students donating their free time. But almost certainly there are participants – perhaps from developing countries – who rely on their payments as part of their income stream.

It is a human ethics concern if there are large numbers of workers that fall into this last category. Efforts have been made to acquire data about demographics and employment status of workers (Ross et al., 2010; Silberman et al., 2010; Gilles et al., 2011), but little if any of this information is verifiable – in a particularly ironic note, position papers that articulate anti-crowd-sourcing opinions sometimes cite demographics collected through crowd-sourcing as evidence that crowd-sourcing to create datasets is unethical. The service provider itself is probably the only reliable source of information about workers, and even then, there is much that can be hidden behind the screen of Internet anonymity. It can also be argued that, however low the pay rates are compared to minimum wage rates in the country in which the crowd-sourced data is being consumed, to the people carrying out the work, it is better than nothing, and is done voluntarily after full disclosure. Similarly, users of services like AMT observe that if minimum pay rates were to be made compulsory, many of the tasks distributed via crowd-sourcing services would simply be withdrawn, eroding even that modest source of income.

Opportunistic Workers Another issue that arises with crowd-sourcing to create datasets in this regard is that the cloak of anonymity means that there is clear potential for opportunistic workers to attempt to "earn" the payment without doing the work that is required. In some of the literature these workers are referred to as "cheats" (see, for example, Eickhoff and de Vries (2013)) but the reality is that in placing HITs we are seeking to get judgments completed spending as little money as possible; and from the point of view of the workers, their objective is to earn the revenue associated with each HIT spending as little time as possible. That is, both parties to the transaction are seeking to maximize their return. Hence, rather than calling them cheats, we prefer to refer to such workers as being *opportunistic*, or as being *aggressive optimizers*.

Amazon provides some built-in mechanisms to protect requesters from opportunistic workers, and in initial trial HITs we tried some of these restrictions, ultimately retaining some and dropping others. We started with the most conservative restrictions in an attempt to get the best quality data, and applied a *location restriction* according to the target language, in a quest to get native speakers performing the evaluations. We also made use of the *master workers* restriction, which limits workers to a special subset of known (to AMT) high quality workers, at the cost of a slightly higher AMT administration fee. When we applied these restrictions, the response rate was, however, extremely low – possibly due to the combination of the restrictions with too low a payment level. We then reduced the worker restriction from master worker to a 95% previous HIT approval rating. This resulted in a dramatic increase in the response rate for English HITs, but the response

[1] AnonInstitute ethics application reference number 1238934.

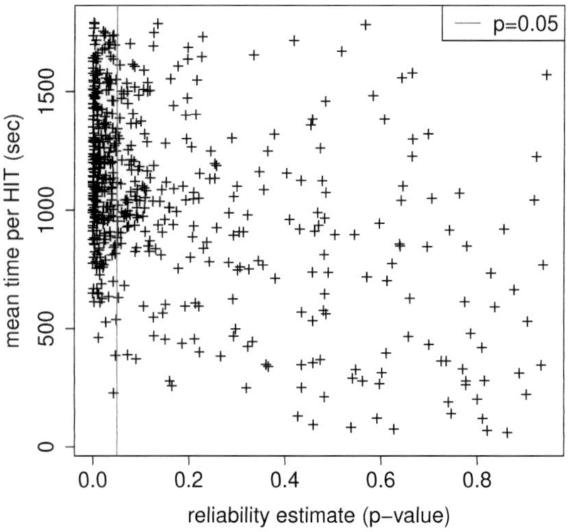

Figure 4: Mean time per 100-translation HIT plotted against workers reliability estimate p-value (lower p-values signify more reliable workers).

rates for the other HITs (restricted to France, Germany, Spain and the Czech Republic, respectively) remained very low. We therefore removed the location restriction for these four languages. The English HITs were location-restricted to US residents throughout the collection process.

The slightly unusual structure of our HITs (each contained 100 judgments) exacerbated the difficulty of deciding what a payment should be. For a HIT of 100 fluency judgments, we set payment at US\$0.50. Based on the time that workers took to complete each hit, this amounted on average to an hourly rate of US\$1.86 when we include all workers, and US\$1.61 for workers who met the quality control threshold (described below).

All but the Czech HITs then proceeded with reasonable response rates. At this level of payment there did not appear to be any group of Czech speakers willing to carry out HITs, and ultimately we dropped the English-Czech language pair from the data collection.

Quality Control One set of opportunistic workers were clearly identifiable due to the unusual structure of our HITs – 100 translations each. The time taken for each HIT ranged from 22 seconds to 1,798 seconds (around 30 minutes). It seems highly unlikely that anyone, no matter how expert, could carry out the task of evaluating a translation on average in 0.22 seconds, and these "workers" made such little effort to pass as human we suspect they may in fact be automated systems. Figure 4 shows for each worker their reliability estimate (as a p value computed over their *bad-reference* pairs, as described in Section 3) versus mean time per HIT (100 translations). Fast HIT completion times almost certainly indicate low quality assessments. For good workers, who met the quality control threshold the average time spent per translation was 10.22s.

Note that the "minimum of 95% approval rating from previous work" requirement was in place throughout our experimentation, including the data plotted in Figure 4. The high number of aggressive optimizers we identified reveals the danger of relying solely on a high previous approval rating. One way in which a worker might manipulate their approval rating is by completing HITs that pay no fee. Presumably, approval of no-fee HITs still results in an increase in a worker's approval rating, and requesters are likely to be less diligent when there is no payment at stake.

Lengthy completion times cannot be used as evidence for good quality work, since no information is available as to what a worker was doing between the time they accepted a HIT and when they submitted it. That is, the workers in the top-right corner of the graph are likely to be a mix of people who sought to obscure their lack of effort by delaying their HIT submission, and people who genuinely spent time on the task, but did not have the necessary knowledge to complete it accurately. Fortunately, a reasonable fraction of workers did meet the quality control threshold of $p < 0.05$.

To avoid rejecting HITs completed by genuine (that is, non opportunistic) workers who were not skilled enough to do the task, we did not decline payments solely on the basis of having a high p-value. Instead, we identified obvious random clickers on the basis of mean scores for *bad-reference* items, for system outputs, and for reference translations. Table 4 shows typical data for the three facets, with worker *D* suspected of being an aggressive optimizer. The HITs from such workers were rejected, and payments declined.

Data Collected Overall, a total of 536 workers generated a total of 91,100 fluency judgments including repeated items. Of these, 49% of workers reached the quality control threshold; they accounted for 57% of the HITs. Four workers com-

Worker	A	B	C	*D*	E	F	G	H	I	J	K	L	M	N
bad-reference	37.7	31.5	19.4	*87.6*	8.5	8.1	3.0	6.6	20.2	7.4	14.2	57.0	50.4	29.3
system	46.5	52.8	41.8	*85.2*	47.0	35.4	16.0	38.0	31.6	33.1	42.5	59.1	66.0	52.7
reference	64.1	92.6	88.8	*81.3*	53.7	42.7	89.7	76.8	92.5	82.4	74.8	60.7	83.9	59.2

Table 4: Mean scores judged by fourteen workers for *bad-reference* items, for system outputs, and for reference translations. Worker *D*'s behavior is sufficiently anomalous that their HITs were rejected.

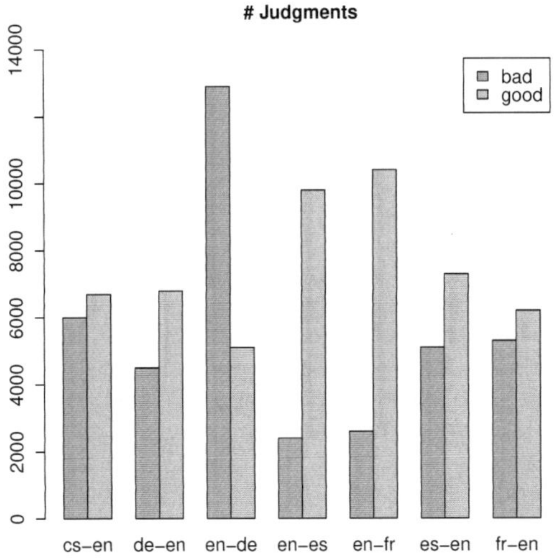

Figure 5: Numbers of judgments by language pair, categorized by whether they reached the desired quality level for *bad-reference* items.

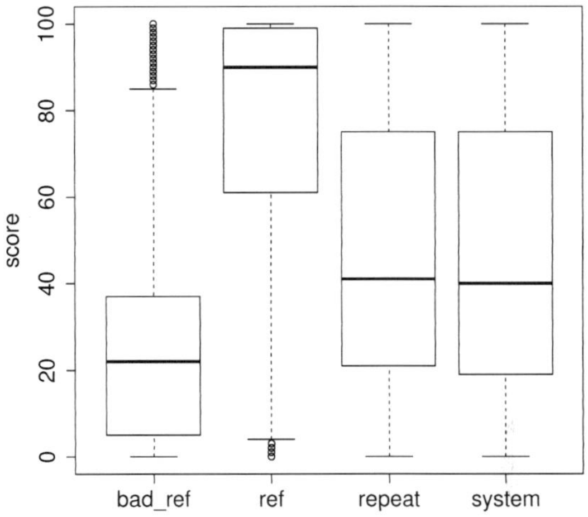

Figure 6: Scores of good workers for (left to right) *bad-reference* degraded translations; reference translations; *ask_again* translations; and normal system outputs.

pleted more than 10 HITs; and one worker completed 50 HITs. Figure 5 shows how the balance between good-quality and bad-quality judgments varied across target languages, with numbers of good French and Spanish judgments far exceeding those of both English and German, and a majority of workers who completed the German task not reaching the quality control threshold. German HITs had a slower response rate, probably due to fewer AMT workers being speakers of German than French, Spanish or English. In total, 28 of the 536 workers had an average HIT completion time of less than 5 minutes, and 17 of those were for German HITs. In addition 3 workers completed HITs for more than one target language; since we had requested native speakers, that was also regarded as being grounds for rejection. The German HITs were targeted by opportunistic workers, but it is interesting that the seemingly equally-tempting Czech HITs were not.

Figure 6 shows the score distributions of the good workers over the four types of item in each HIT, and confirms that the categorization of workers into good and bad yielded the desired outcome.

6 Conclusion

Human evaluation forms the basis upon which all empirical machine translation research is founded, whether it be directly through employing humans to assess the quality of machine translation output or through the use of automatic metrics that have been validated by correlation with human judgments. We have collected a large dataset of human assessments of machine translation system outputs, employing a range of different assessment configurations. This data set will be made public once it has been fully collated and meta-data added to it, and will form a resource for further evaluation of machine translation research.

Acknowledgments This work was supported by the Australian Research Council. Ethics application (number 1238934) submitted November 2012, with outcome of "no approval needed due to the impersonal nature of the material".

References

A. Belz and E. Kow. 2011. Discrete vs. continuous rating scales for language evaluation in NLP. In *Proc. 49th Ann. Meeting of the Association for Computational Linguistics: Human Language Technologies*, pages 230–235, Portland, USA.

O. Bojar, C. Buck, C. Callison-Burch, C. Federmann, B. Haddow, P. Koehn, C. Monz, M. Post, R. Soricut, and L. Specia. 2013. Findings of the 2013 Workshop on Statistical Machine Translation. In *Proc. 8th Wkshp. on Statistical Machine Translation*, pages 1–44, Sofia, Bulgaria.

C. Callison-Burch and M. Dredze. 2010. Creating speech and language data with Amazon's Mechanical Turk. In *Proc. NAACL HLT 2010 Wkshp. on Creating Speech and Language Data with Amazon's Mechanical Turk*, pages 1–12, Los Angeles, USA.

C. Callison-Burch, C. Fordyce, P. Koehn, C. Monz, and J. Schroeder. 2007. (Meta-) evaluation of machine translation. In *Proc. 2nd Wkshp. Statistical Machine Translation*, pages 136–158, Prague, Czech Republic.

C. Callison-Burch, P. Koehn, C. Monz, M. Post, R. Soricut, and L. Specia. 2012. Findings of the 2012 Workshop on Statistical Machine Translation. In *Proc. 7th Wkshp. Statistical Machine Translation*, pages 10–51, Montreal, Canada.

C. Eickhoff and A. P. de Vries. 2013. Increasing cheat robustness of crowdsourcing tasks. *Information Retrieval*, 16(2):121–137.

K. Fort, G. Adda, and K. B. Cohen. 2011. Amazon Mechanical Turk: Gold mine or coal mine? *Computational Linguistics*, 37(2):413–420.

A. Gilles, B. Sagot, K. Fort, and J. Mariani. 2011. Crowdsourcing for language resource development: Critical analysis of Amazon Mechanical Turk overpowering use. In *Proc. 5th Language and Technology Conf.*, Poznań, Poland.

Y. Graham, T. Baldwin, A. Harwood, A. Moffat, and J. Zobel. 2012. Measurement of progress in machine translation. In *Proc. Australasian Language Technology Wkshp.*, pages 70–78, Dunedin, New Zealand.

Y. Graham, T. Baldwin, A. Moffat, and J. Zobel. 2013. Continuous measurement scales in human evaluation of machine translation. In *Proc. 7th Linguistic Annotation Wkshp.*, pages 33–41, Sofia, Bulgaria.

L. Irani and M. S. Silberman. 2013. Turkopticon: Interrupting worker invisibility in Amazon Mechanical Turk. In *Proc. ACM SIGCHI Conf. Human Factors in Computing Systems*, pages 611–620, Paris, France.

K. Papineni, S. Roukos, T. Ward, and W.-J. Zhu. 2001. BLEU: A method for automatic evaluation of machine translation. Technical Report RC22176 (W0109-022), IBM Research, Thomas J. Watson Research Center.

J. Ross, L. Irani, M. S. Silberman, A. Zaldivar, and B. Tomlinson. 2010. Who are the crowdworkers? Shifting demographics in Mechanical Turk. In *CHI'10 Extended Abstracts on Human Factors in Computing Systems*, pages 2863–2872.

M. S. Silberman, J. Ross, L. Irani, and B. Tomlinson. 2010. Sellers' problems in human computation markets. In *Proc. ACM SIGKDD Wkshp. on Human Computation*, pages 18–21, Washington DC, USA.

R. Snow, B. O'Connor, D. Jurafsky, and A.Y. Ng. 2008. Cheap and fast – But is it good? Evaluating non-expert annotations for natural language tasks. In *Proc. Conf. Empirical Methods in Natural Language Processing*, pages 254–263, Honolulu, USA.

The Effect of the Within-speaker Sample Size on the Performance of Likelihood Ratio Based Forensic Voice Comparison: Monte Carlo Simulations

Shunichi Ishihara
Department of Linguistics
Australian National University
shunichi.ishihara@anu.edu.au

Abstract

This study is an investigation into the effect of sample size on a likelihood ratio (LR) based forensic voice comparison (FVC) system. In particular, we looked into how the offender and suspect sample size (or the within-speaker sample size) would affect the performance of the FVC system, using spectral feature vectors extracted from spontaneous Japanese speech. For this purpose, we repeatedly conducted Monte Carlo method based experiments with different sample size, using the statistics obtained from these feature vectors. LRs were estimated using the multivariate kernel density LR formula developed by Aitken and Lucy (2004). The derived LRs were calibrated using the logistic-regression calibration technique proposed by Brümmer and du Preez (2006). The performance of the FVC system was assessed in terms of the log-likelihood-ratio cost (C_{llr}) and the 95% credible interval (CI), which are the metrics of validity and reliability, respectively. We will demonstrate in this paper that 1) the validity of the system notably improves when up to six tokens are included in modelling a speaker session, and 2) the system performance converges with the relative small token number (four) in the background database, regardless of the token numbers in the test and development databases.

1 Introduction

It is well known and accepted that statistical accuracy relies on having a sufficient amount of data. However, in typical forensic voice comparison (FVC) casework, the crime scene recording is often short and contains background noise, which limits the choice of segments that experts can use for the comparison. For example, the word *yes* is one of the most commonly used segments in FVC. However, the number of *yes* tokens we can extract from the offender sample to build his/her model really depends on the recording condition, something that forensic caseworkers cannot control. Thus, we need to know how the performance of an FVC system is influenced by sample size.

The current study employs the Likelihood Ratio (LR) framework, which has been advocated as the logically and legally correct way of analysing and presenting forensic evidence, in the major textbooks on the evaluation of forensic evidence (e.g. Robertson & Vignaux 1995), and by forensic statisticians (e.g. Aitken & Stoney 1991, Aitken & Taroni 2004), and is the standard framework in DNA comparison science. Emulating DNA forensic science, many fields of forensic sciences, such as fingerprint (Neumann et al. 2007), handwriting (Bozza et al. 2008), voice (Morrison 2009) and so on, started adopting the LR framework to quantify evidential strength (= LR).

In order to calculate an LR, we need three sets of speech samples: a set of questioned samples (offender's samples); a set of known samples (suspect's samples); and the background or reference samples. This is because an LR is a ratio of similarity to typicality, which quantifies how similar/different the questioned and the known samples are, and then evaluates that similarity/difference in terms of typicality/atypicality against the relevant background population (i.e. reference samples). Some investigations have been made on how factors such as the size and linguistic compatibility of the background population data can influence LR-based FVC (Kinoshita & Norris 2010, Ishihara & Kinoshita 2008, Kinoshita et al. 2009). Ishihara and Kinoshita (2008), for example, investigated how many speakers are ideally required in the background population data in order to reliably evaluate speech evidence in FVC.

However, to the best of our knowledge, studies focusing on the sample size of the offender and suspect data are conspicuously sparse. Needless to say, the sample size of the offender and suspect data – for example, the number of *yes* tokens we can use in order to build the offender's and suspect's models – has a great affect on the performance of FVC systems.

Thus, this study investigated how the offender and suspect sample sizes (or within-speaker sample size) would influence the performance of an FVC system by employing Monte Carlo simulations (Fishman 1995). In order to answer this question, two experiments: Experiments 1 and 2, were conducted. Detailed explanations of these two experiments are given §4.4.

LRs were estimated using Aitken and Lucy's (2004) MVLR formula (see §4.3). The derived LRs were calibrated using the logistic-regression calibration technique proposed by Brümmer and du Preez (2006) (see §4.5). The performance of the FVC system was assessed in terms of the log-likelihood-ratio cost (C_{llr}) (Brümmer & du Preez 2006) and the 95% credible interval (CI) (Morrison 2011b) (see §4.6).

2 Likelihood Ratio

The LR is the probability that the evidence would occur if an assertion is true, relative to the probability that the evidence would occur if the assertion is not true (Robertson & Vignaux 1995). Thus, the LR can be expressed as Equation 1).

$$LR=\frac{p(E|H_p)}{p(E|H_d)} \quad 1)$$

For FVC, it will be the probability of observing the difference (referred to as the evidence, E) between the offender's and the suspect's speech samples if they had come from the same speaker (H_p) (i.e. if the prosecution hypothesis is true) relative to the probability of observing the same evidence (E) if they had been produced by different speakers (H_d) (i.e. if the defence hypothesis is true). The relative strength of the given evidence with respect to the competing hypotheses (H_p vs. H_d) is reflected in the magnitude of the LR. The more the LR deviates from unity (LR = 1; logLR = 0), the greater support for either the prosecution hypothesis (LR > 1; logLR > 0) or the defence hypothesis (LR < 1; logLR < 0).

For example, an LR of 20 means that the evidence (= the difference between the offender and suspect speech samples) is 20 times more likely to occur if the offender and the suspect had been the same individual than if they had been different individuals. Note that an LR value of 20 does NOT mean that the offender and the suspect are 20 times more likely to be the same person than different people, given the evidence.

The important point is that the LR is concerned with the probability of the evidence, given the hypothesis (either prosecution or defence), which is the province of forensic scientists, while the trier-of-fact is concerned with the probability of the hypothesis (either prosecution or defence), given the evidence. That is, the ultimate decision as to whether the suspect is guilty or not (e.g. the offender and suspect samples are from the same speaker or not) does not lie with the forensic expert, but with the court. The role of the forensic scientist is to estimate the strength of evidence (= LR) in order to assist the trier-of-fact to make a final decision (Morrison 2009: 229).

3 Database, target segment, and speakers

In this study, we used the monologues from the Corpus of Spontaneous Japanese (CSJ) (Maekawa et al. 2000). There are two types of monologues in CSJ: Academic Presentation Speech (APS) and Simulated Public Speech (SPS). Both types were used in this study. APS was recorded live at academic presentations, most of them 12-25 minutes long. SPS contains 10-12 minute mock speeches on everyday topics.

For this study, we focused on the filler /e:/ and the /e:/ segment of the filler /e:to:/. Fillers are a sound or a word (e.g. *um, you know, like* in English) which is uttered by a speaker to signal that he/she is thinking or hesitating. We decided to use these fillers because 1) they are two of the most frequently used fillers (thus many monologues contain at least ten of these fillers) (Ishihara 2010), 2) the vowel /e/ reportedly has the strongest speaker-discriminatory power out of the five Japanese vowels /a, i. u, e, o/ (Kinoshita 2001), and 3) the segment /e:/ is significantly long so that it is easy to extract stable spectral features from this segment. It is also considered that fillers are uttered unconsciously by the speaker and carry no lexical meaning. They are thus not likely to be affected by the pragmatic focus of the utterance. This is another reason we decided to focus on fillers in this study.

For the experiments, we selected our speakers based on five criteria: 1) availability of two non-contemporaneous recordings per speaker, 2) high spontaneity of the speech (e.g. not reading), 3) speaking entirely in standard modern Japanese, 4) containing at least ten /e:/ segments, and 5) availability of complete annotation of the data. Having real casework in mind, we selected only male speakers. This is because they are more likely to commit a crime than females (Kanazawa & Still 2000). These criteria resulted in 236 recordings (118 speakers x 2 non-contemporaneous recordings), and they were used in our experiments.

These 118 speakers (D_{all}) were divided into three mutually-exclusive sub databases; test database (D_{test} = 40 speakers), the background database ($D_{background}$ = 39 speakers) and the development database ($D_{development}$ = 39 speakers). Each speaker of these databases has two recordings which are non-contemporaneous. The first ten /e:/ segments were annotated in each recording. Thus, for example, there are 800 annotated /e:/ segments in the test database (= 40 speakers x 2 sessions x 10 segments). The statistics which are necessary for conducting Monte Carlo simulations were calculated from these databases.

The test database was used to assess the performance of the FVC system. The background database was for a background population, and the development database was for obtaining the logistic-regression weight, which was used to calibrate the LRs of the test database (refer to §4.5 for the detailed explanation of calibration).

4 Experiments

4.1 Features

We used 16 Mel Frequency Cepstrum Coefficients (MFCC) in the experiments as feature vectors. MFCC is a standard spectral feature which is used in many voice-related applications, including automatic speaker recognition. All original speech samples were downsampled to 16KHz, and then MFCC values were extracted from the mid-duration-point of the target segment /e:/ with a 20 ms wide hamming window. No normalisation procedure (e.g. Cepstrum Mean Normalisation) was employed as all recordings were made using the same equipment in CSJ.

4.2 General experimental design

There are two types of tests for FVC: one is the so-called *Same Speaker Comparison* (SS comparison) where two speech samples produced by the same speaker are expected to receive the desired LR value given the same-origin, whereas the other is, *mutatis mutandis*, *Different Speaker Comparison* (DS comparison).

For example, from the 40 speakers of the test database (D_{test}), 40 SS comparisons and 1560 independent (e.g. not-overlapping) DS comparisons are possible.

4.3 Likelihood ratio calculation

The LR of each comparison was estimated using the Multivariate Likelihood Ratio (MVLR) formula, which is one of the standard formulae used in FVC (Ishihara & Kinoshita 2008, Rose 2006, Morrison & Kinoshita 2008, Rose et al. 2004). Although the reader needs to refer to Aitken and Lucy (2004) for the full mathematical exposition of the MVLR formula, this formula estimates a single LR from multiple variables (e.g. 16 MFCC), discounting the correlation among them.

The numerator of the MVLR formula calculates the likelihood (= probability) of evidence, which is the difference between the offender and suspect speech samples, when it is assumed that both of the samples have the same origin (or the prosecution hypothesis (H_p) is true). For that, you need the feature vectors of the offender and suspect samples and the within-group (= speaker) variance, which is given in the form of a variance/covariance matrix. The same feature vectors of the offender and suspect samples and the between-group (= speaker) variance are used in the denominator of the formula to estimate the likelihood of getting the same evidence when it is assumed that they have different origins (or the defence hypothesis (H_d) is true). These within-group and between-group variances are estimated from the background dataset ($D_{background}$). The MVLR formula assumes normality for within-group variance while it uses a kernel-density model for between-group variance.

4.4 Repeated experiments using Monte Carlo simulations

As explained earlier, each speaker has two sets of ten /e:/ segments, and 16 MFCC values were extracted. Thus, we can use a maximum of ten feature vectors to model each session of each speaker. In this study, we randomly generated X feature vectors (X = {2,4,6,8,10}) for each session of each speaker 300 times using the normal distribution function modelled with the mean vector (μ) and variance/covariance matrix (ε) obtained from the original databases ({D_{test}, $D_{background}$, $D_{development}$}).

Figure 1 is an example showing 300 randomly generated first two MFCC values (c1 and c2) from the normal distribution function based on the statistics (μ and ε) obtained from the first session of the first speaker in the test database.

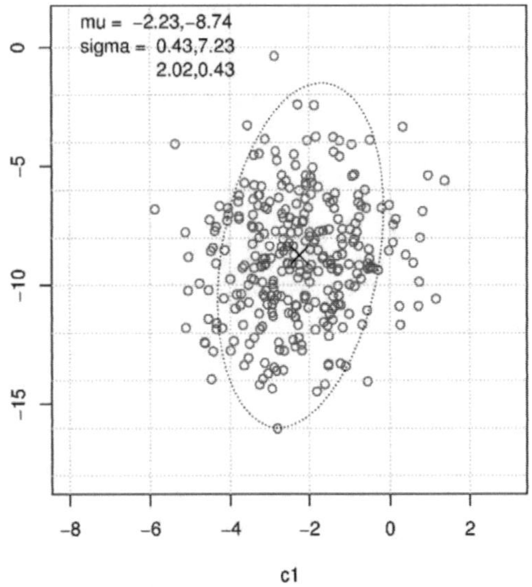

Figure 1: 300 randomly generated values (c1 and c2) from the statistics (μ and ε) obtained from the first session of the first speaker of the test database (only the first and second MFCC) and an ellipse. The cross = μ.

Experiments were repeatedly conducted using randomly generated feature vectors, as explained above. Two experiments: Experiments 1 and 2 were conducted in this study. In Experiment 1, we investigated how the token number (the number of feature vectors) of each speaker's session affects the performance of the FVC system. In Experiment 1, the same token number ({2,4,6,8,10}) was used across the test, background and development databases.

In Experiment 2, Experiment 1 was repeated with different token numbers in the background database ({2,4,6,8,10}) with the token number of the test and development databases kept constant. The aim of Experiment 2 was to investigate how the number of tokens in the background database affects the performance of the FVC system.

4.5 Calibration

A logistic-regression calibration (Brümmer & du Preez 2006) was applied to the derived LRs from the MVLR formula. Given two sets of LRs derived from the SS and DS comparisons and a decision boundary, calibration is a normalisation procedure involving linear monotonic shifting and scaling of the LRs relative to the decision boundary so as to minimise a cost function. The FoCal toolkit [1] was used for the logistic-regression calibration in this study (Brümmer & du Preez 2006). The logistic-regression weight was obtained from the development database.

4.6 Evaluation of performance: validity and reliability

The performance of the FVC system was assessed in terms of its validity (= accuracy) and reliability (= precision) using the log-likelihood-ratio cost (C_{llr}) and the 95% credible intervals (CI) as the metrics of validity and reliability, respectively.

Suppose that you have speech samples collected from two speakers at two different sessions which are denoted as S1.1, S1.2, S2.1, and S2.2, where S = speaker, and 1 & 2 = the first and second sessions (S1.1 refers to the first session recording collected from (S)peaker1, and S1.2 the second session from that same speaker). From these speech samples, two independent (not overlapping) DS comparisons are possible; S1.1 vs. S2.1 and S1.2 vs. S2.2. Further suppose that you conducted two separate FVC tests in the same way, but using two different features (Features 1 and 2), and that you obtained the $\log_{10}$LRs given in Table 1 for these two DS comparisons.

DS comparison	Feature 1	Feature 2
S1.1 vs. S2.1	-3.5	-2.1
S1.2 vs. S2.2	-3.3	0.2

Table 1: Example LRs used to explain the concept of validity and reliability.

Since the comparisons given in Table 1 are DS comparisons, the desired $\log_{10}$LR value would be lower than 0, and the greater the negative $\log_{10}$LR value is, the better the system is, as it more strongly supports the correct hypothesis. For Feature 1, both of the comparisons received $\log_{10}\text{LR} < 0$ while for Feature 2, only one of them got $\log_{10}\text{LR} < 0$. Feature 1 is better not only in that both $\log_{10}$LR values are smaller than 0

[1] https://sites.google.com/site/nikobrummer/focal

(supporting the correct hypothesis) but also in that they are further away from unity ($\log_{10}LR$ = 0) than the $\log_{10}LR$ values of Feature 2. Thus, it can be said that the validity (= accuracy) of Feature 1 is higher than that of Feature 2. This is the basic concept of validity.

Morrison (2011b: 93) argues that classification-accuracy/classification-error rates, such as equal error rate (EER), are inappropriate for use within the LR framework because they implicitly refer to posterior probabilities – which is the province of the trier-of-fact – rather than LRs – which is the province of forensic scientists – and "they are based on a categorical threshholding, error versus non-error, rather than a gradient strength of evidence." In this study, the log-likelihood-ratio cost (C_{llr}), which is a gradient metric based on LR for assessing the validity of the system performance was used. See Equation 2) for calculating C_{llr} (Brümmer & du Preez 2006). In Equation 2), N_{Hp} and N_{Hd} are the numbers of SS and of DS comparisons, and LR_i and LR_j are the LRs derived from the SS and DS comparisons, respectively. If the system is producing desired LRs, all the SS comparisons should produce LRs greater than 1, and the DS comparisons should produce LRs less than 1. In this approach, LRs which support counter-factual hypotheses are given a penalty. The size of this penalty is determined according to how significantly the LRs deviate from the neutral point. That is, an LR supporting a counter-factual hypothesis with greater strength will be penalised more heavily than the ones which are closer to unity, because they are more misleading. The FoCal toolkit[1] was also used for calculating C_{llr} in this study (Brümmer & du Preez 2006). The lower the C_{llr} value is, the better the performance.

$$C_{llr}=\frac{1}{2}\left(\begin{array}{l}\frac{1}{N_{H_p}}\sum_{i\ for H_p=true}^{N_{H_p}}\log_2\left(1+\frac{1}{LR_i}\right)+\\ \frac{1}{N_{H_d}}\sum_{j\ for H_d=true}^{N_{H_d}}\log_2\left(1+LR_j\right)\end{array}\right) \quad 2)$$

Both of the DS comparisons given in Table 1 are the comparisons between S1 and S2. Thus, you can expect that the LR values obtained for these two DS comparisons should be similar as they are comparing the same speakers. However, you can see that the $\log_{10}LR$ values based on Feature 1 are closer to each other (-3.5 and -3.3) than those based on Feature 2 (-2.1 and 0.2). In other words, the reliability (= precision) of Feature 1 is higher than that of Feature 2. This is the basic concept of reliability. As a metric of reliability, we used credible intervals, the Bayesian analogue of frequentist confidence intervals (Morrison 2011b). In this study, we calculated 95% credible intervals (CI) in the parametric manner based on the deviation-from-mean values collected from all of the DS comparison pairs. For example, CI = 1.23 and $\log_{10}LR$ = 2 means that it is 95% certain that it is at least $\log_{10}LR$ =

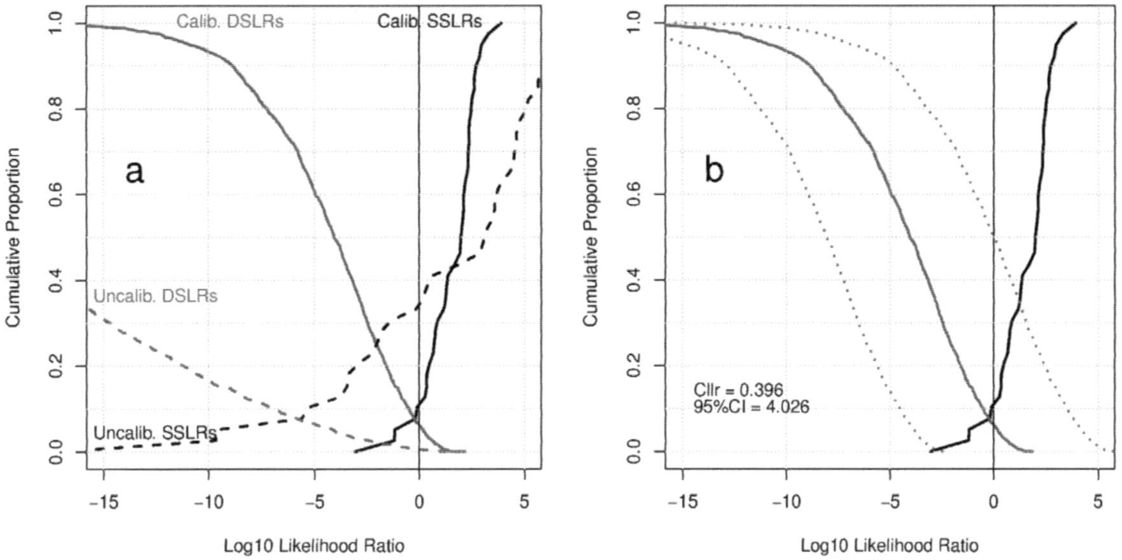

Figure 2: Tippett plot showing the uncalibrated (dashed curves) and calibrated (solid curves) LRs plotted separately for the SS (black) and DS (grey) comparisons (a), and Tippett plot showing the calibrated LRs with ±95% CI band (grey dotted lines) superimposed on the DS LRs (b). X-axis = $\log_{10}LR$; Y=axis = cumulative proportion. C_{llr} value was calculated from the calibrated LRs and CI value was calculated only for the calibrated DS LRs.

0.77 (= 2-1.23) and it is not greater than $\log_{10}$LR = 3.23 (= 2+1.23) for this particular comparison. The smaller the credible intervals, the better the reliability is.

Before presenting the results of Experiments 1 and 2, we conducted an experiment using the original databases (D_{test}, $D_{background}$, $D_{development}$). The results of this experiment are given as Tippett plots in Figure 2 with the C_{llr} and CI values. In these Tippett plots, the $\log_{10}$LRs, which are equal to or greater than the value indicated on the X-axis, are cumulatively plotted, separately for the SS and DS comparisons. Tippett plots graphically show how strongly the derived LRs not only support the correct hypothesis but also misleadingly support the contrary-to-fact hypothesis. In Figure 2a, calibrated and uncalibrated LRs are plotted together in order to show what sorts of effect the logistic-regression calibration brings to the uncalibrated LRs, and in Figure 2b, the calibrated LRs are plotted together with ±CI band on the DS LRs.

Theoretically speaking, the crossing point of the SS and DS LRs should be on $\log_{10}$LR = 0, but you can see the crossing point of the uncalibrated SS and DS LRs are far away from it in Figure 2b. In this circumstance, it is difficult to interpret the given LR appropriately as the theoretical threshold ($\log_{10}$LR = 0) and the obtained threshold ($\log_{10}$LR = ca. -7 in the uncalibrated LRs of Figure 2b) are completely different. A calibration technique needs to be applied in this situation. Please note that the calibrated SS and DS LRs given in Figure 2 are very well calibrated. The C_{llr} value was calculated using these calibrated SS and DS LRs, and it was 0.396. The CI was calculated based on calibrated DS LRs, and it was 4.026.

5 Experimental Results and Discussions

The results of Experiment 1 are graphically presented in Figure 3 in terms of C_{llr} and CI. In Figure 3a, the C_{llr} and CI values obtained from the Monte Carlo simulations (repeated 300 times) are plotted altogether with their mean values for each of the five different token numbers ({2,4,6,8,10}). The numerical values for the mean values are given in Table 2 together with their standard deviation (sd) values. Please note that the same token number was used across the test, background and development databases (test = background = development = {2,4,6,8,10}) in Experiment 1.

What we can observe from Figure 3a and Table 2 is that the validity of the system (C_{llr}) improves as the token number increases whereas the reliability of the system (CI) deteriorates. That is, there is a trade-off between the validity and reliability of the system. The improvement in validity as a function of the token number is non-linear in that there is a large improvement from the token number = {2} to {4} (0.66->0.51)

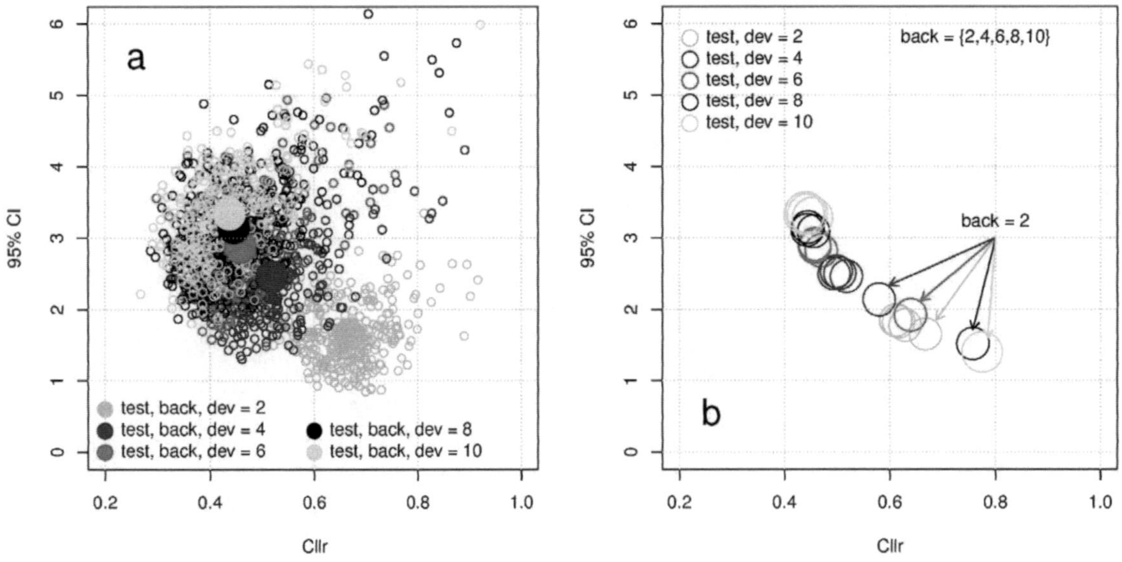

Figure 3: The C_{llr} and CI values of the 300 repeated Monte Carlo simulations are plotted separately for the different token numbers {2,4,6,8,10} with their mean values (large filled circles) (a). The mean C_{llr} and CI values of the 300 repeated Monte Carlo simulations (big empty circles) differing in the token numbers ({2,4,6,8,10}) of the background database (b). X-axis = C_{llr}; Y-axis = CI; test, back and dev = test, background and development databases.

whereas there is not much improvement between the token number = {6} and the token number = {10} (0.45->0.44->0.43). That is, if you have six repeated tokens (e.g. six *yes* tokens for each session of each speaker) in the databases, the performance of the system can be expected to be as good as when you have as many as ten repeated tokens.

	test = background = development =				
	2	4	6	8	10
C_{llr}	0.66	0.51	0.45	0.44	0.43
sd	0.073	0.087	0.091	0.093	0.090
CI	1.65	2.46	2.87	3.14	3.33
sd	0.427	0.629	0.711	0.734	0.700

Table 2: The numerical values of Figure 3a (only mean values).

Another observation that can be made is that the C_{llr} and CI values are more widely scattered when the token number is {6,8,10} than {2,4}. This point can be seen in the sd values given in Table 2 in that, for example, the sd values of the C_{llr} and CI are far smaller when the token number is {2} (0.073 and 0.427, respectively) than when the token number is {10} (0.090 and 0.700, respectively). That is, the performance of the system widely fluctuates when the token number is high (e.g. {6,8,10}).

In Experiment 2, Experiment 1 was repeated five times with the five different token numbers ({2,4,6,8,10}) in the background database. The results of Experiment 2 are given in Figure 3b in which only the mean C_{llr} and CI values are plotted in order to prevent the figure from becoming too crowded. The numerical values of Figure 3b are given in Table 3. For example, the experiment with the token number of {10} in the test and development databases was repeated five times, differing the token number in the background database (background = {2,4,6,8,10}), and then the mean C_{llr} and CI values of these five experiments are plotted in the same colour (gold for the token number of {10} in the test and development databases) in Figure 3b.

We can observe from Figure 3b and Table 3 that each experimental set (e.g. test = development = 8, background = {2,4,6,8,10}) has one result which is very different in performance from the other four results. For example, the results of the token number of {10} in the test and development databases with the token numbers of {4,6,8,10} in the background database are more or less the same (C_{llr} = ca. 0.44 and CI = ca. 3.3) whereas they are significantly better in terms of C_{llr} than the result with the token number of {2} in the background database (= 0.77). In fact, regardless of the token number in the test and development databases, the performance of the system is worse when there are only two repeated tokens in the background database than when there are four or more repeated tokens ({4,6,8,10}) (refer to the arrows given in Figure 3b).

test = dev =	back =	C_{llr}	CI
2	2	0.66	1.65
	4	0.62	1.77
	6	0.61	1.82
	8	0.61	1.84
	10	0.61	1.84
4	2	0.57	2.13
	4	0.51	2.46
	6	0.50	2.50
	8	0.49	2.52
	10	0.49	2.49
6	2	0.63	1.91
	4	0.46	2.82
	6	0.45	2.87
	8	0.45	2.88
	10	0.45	2.91
8	2	0.75	1.51
	4	0.45	3.08
	6	0.44	3.10
	8	0.44	3.14
	10	0.44	3.14
10	2	0.77	1.39
	4	0.45	3.28
	6	0.44	3.33
	8	0.43	3.36
	10	0.43	3.33

Table 3: The numerical values of Figure 3b.

Furthermore, this difference in performance between the token numbers of {4,6,8,10} and that of {2} in the background database becomes greater as the number of tokens used in the test and development databases increases. For example, as can be seen in Table 3, the difference in question is relatively small for the test and development databases = {2} (C_{llr} = 0.66 and CI = 1.65 for the background = {2}; average C_{llr} = 0.61 and average CI = 1.81 for the background = {4,6,8,10}) whereas it is far larger for the test and development databases = {10} (C_{llr} = 0.77 and CI = 1.39 for the background = {2}; average C_{llr} = 0.43 and average CI = 3.32 for the background = {4,6,8,10}).

As far as the C_{llr} values are concerned, the performance never deteriorates as the size increases from the background = {4} to {10}. Whereas there are some very small fluctuations in performance in terms of the CI values from the background = {4} to {10}. The reasons for these fluctuations are not clear at this stage.

The results of Experiment 2 tell us that, if you have four repeated tokens (e.g. four *yes* tokens for each session of each speaker) in the background database, the system can achieve as good a performance as when you have ten repeated tokens. However, if you have only two repeated tokens in the background database, it will result in an underperformance of the system in comparison to when you have four or more repeated tokens.

6 Conclusions and Future Directions

This study investigated how the offender and suspect sample sizes (or the within-speaker sample size) influences the performance of an FVC system. In order to answer this question, two experiments based on Monte Carlo simulations: Experiments 1 and 2, were conducted.

In Experiment 1, five different token numbers ({2,4,6,8,10}) were used in the databases to see how the performance of the system would be influenced by the token number. The results demonstrated that 1) there was a trade-off between the validity (C_{llr}) and reliability (CI) of the system; 2) there was a large improvement in the validity between the token number = {2} and the token number = {4} whereas no large improvement was observed from the token number = {6} to the token number = {10}. That is, if we have six repetitions of the target segment/word (e.g. *yes*), the system validity is almost as good as when we have ten repetitions.

In Experiment 2, Experiment 1 was repeated by changing the token number ({2,4,6,8,10}) of the background database while keeping the same token number for the test and development databases. The results of Experiment 2 demonstrated that regardless of the token number in the test and development databases, the system with the token number = {2} in the background database significantly underperformed in accuracy when compared to the systems with the token number = {4,6,8,10}, of which the performances were very similar. The results of Experiment 2 also demonstrated that the above-mentioned discrepancy in performance between two repeated tokens ({2}) and four or more repeated tokens ({4,6,8,10}) becomes wider as the token number of the test and development databases increases.

These results suggest that when we compile a database which can be used as background population data, we do not need many repetitions in the database as a model based on four repeated tokens can achieve very similar results as one based on ten repeated tokens. However, if we have only two repeated tokens in the background database, we need to be aware that the performance will be compromised, even if you have many repetitions in the test and development databases.

In this study, we mainly focused on the token numbers of the test and background databases. However, it goes without saying that the token number of the development database is also important to the performance of a system. We need to look into this point as well.

In this study, although some other techniques are available for the estimate of LRs, the MVLR formula was used. For example, Morrison (2011a) reported that the procedures based on the Gaussian Mixture Model – Universal Background Model (GMM-UBM) outperformed those based on MVLR procedures, and that the GMM-UBM resulted in an improvement in both the validity and reliability (without trade-offs between them). Since the GMM-UBM is another popular way of estimating LRs in FVC, it is important to investigate the relationship between its performance and the sample size as well.

Acknowledgments

The author appreciates the very detailed comments and suggestions made by the three anonymous reviewers.

References

Aitken CGG & D Lucy 2004 'Evaluation of trace evidence in the form of multivariate data' *Journal of the Royal Statistical Society Series C-Applied Statistics* 53: 109-122.

Aitken CGG & DA Stoney 1991 *The Use of Statistics in Forensic Science* Ellis Horwood New York; London.

Aitken CGG & F Taroni 2004 *Statistics and the Evaluation of Evidence for Forensic Scientists* Wiley Chichester.

Bozza S, F Taroni, R Marquis & M Schmittbuhl 2008 'Probabilistic evaluation of handwriting evidence: Likelihood ratio for authorship' *Journal of the Royal Statistical Society: Series C (Applied Statistics)* 57(3): 329-341.

Brümmer N & J du Preez 2006 'Application-independent evaluation of speaker detection' *Computer Speech and Language* 20(2-3): 230-275.

Fishman GS 1995 *Monte Carlo: Concepts, Algorithms, and Applications* Springer New York.

Ishihara S 2010 'Variability and consistency in the idiosyncratic selection of fillers in Japanese monologues: Gender differences' *Proceedings of the Australasian Language Technology Association Workshop 2010*: 9-17.

Ishihara S & Y Kinoshita 2008 'How many do we need? Exploration of the population size effect on the performance of forensic speaker classification' *Proceedings of Interspeech 2008*: 1941-1944.

Kanazawa S & MC Still 2000 'Why men commit crimes (and why they desist)' *Sociological Theory* 18(3): 434-447.

Kinoshita Y 2001 *Testing Realistic Forensic Speaker Identification in Japanese: A Likelihood Ratio Based Approach Using Formants* Unpublished Ph.D. thesis, the Australian National University.

Kinoshita Y, S Ishihara & P Rose 2009 'Exploring the discriminatory potential of F0 distribution parameters in traditional forensic speaker recognition' *International Journal of Speech Language and the Law* 16(1): 91-111.

Kinoshita Y & M Norris 2010 'Simulating spontaneous speech: Application to forensic voice comparison' *Proceedings of the 13th Australasian International conference on Speech Science and Technology*: 26-29.

Maekawa K, H Koiso, S Furui & H Isahara 2000 'Spontaneous speech corpus of Japanese' *Proceedings of the 2nd International Conference of Language Resources and Evaluation*: 947-952.

Morrison GS 2009 'Forensic voice comparison and the paradigm shift' *Science & Justice* 49(4): 298-308.

Morrison GS 2011a 'A comparison of procedures for the calculation of forensic likelihood ratios from acoustic-phonetic data Multivariate kernel density (MVKD) versus Gaussian mixture model-universal background model (GMM-UBM)' *Speech Communication* 53(2): 242-256.

Morrison GS 2011b 'Measuring the validity and reliability of forensic likelihood-ratio systems' *Science & Justice* 51(3): 91-98.

Morrison GS & Y Kinoshita 2008 'Automatic-Type Calibration of Traditionally Derived Likelihood Ratios: Forensic Analysis of Australian English vertical bar o vertical bar Formant Trajectories' *Proceedings of Interspeech 2008*: 1501-1504.

Neumann C, C Champod, R Puch-Solis, N Egli, A Anthonioz & A Bromage-Griffiths 2007 'Computation of likelihood ratios in fingerprint identification for configurations of any number of minutiae' *Journal of forensic sciences* 52(1): 54-64.

Robertson B & GA Vignaux 1995 *Interpreting Evidence: Evaluating Forensic Science in the Courtroom* Wiley Chichester.

Rose P 2006 'Technical forensic speaker recognition: Evaluation, types and testing of evidence' *Computer Speech and Language* 20(2-3): 159-191.

Rose P, D Lucy & T Osanai 2004 'Linguistic-acoustic forensic speaker identification with likelihood ratios from a multivariate hierarchical random effects model: A "non-idiot's Bayes" approach' *Proceedings of the 10th Australian International Conference on Speech Science and Technology*: 492-497.

Noise in Speech-to-Text Voice: Analysis of Errors and Feasibility of Phonetic Similarity for Their Correction

Hanna Suominen
NICTA / Locked Bag 8001,
Canberra ACT 2601, Australia
The Australian National University
University of Canberra
hanna.suominen@nicta.com.au

Gabriela Ferraro
NICTA / Locked Bag 8001,
Canberra ACT 2601, Australia
The Australian National University
gabriela.ferraro@nicta.com.au

Abstract

In Australian healthcare, failures in information flow cause over one-tenth of preventable adverse events and are tangible in clinical handover. Regardless of a good verbal handover, anything from two-thirds to all of this information is lost after 3–5 shifts if notes are taken by hand or not taken. Speech to text (SST) and information extraction (IE) have been proposed for taking the notes and filling in a handover form with extrapolated evaluations from related studies promising over 90 per cent correctness for both STT and IE. However, this cascading evokes a fruitful methodological challenge: the severe implications that errors may have in clinical decision-making call for superiority in STT; the correctness percentage measured in a peaceful laboratory is decreased to 77 by noise in clinical practise; and the STT errors multiply when cascaded with IE. We provide an analysis of STT errors and discuss the feasibility of phonetic similarity for their correction in this paper. Our data consists of one hundred simulated handover records in Australian English with STT recognising 73 per cent of the 7, 277 words (1 h 8 min 5 s) correctly. In text relevant to the form, 836 unique error types are present. The most common errors include inserting *and*, *in*, *are*, *arm*, *is*, *a*, *the*, or *am* ($5 \leq n \leq 94$), deleting *is* ($n = 17$), and substituting *and*, *obs are*, *2*, *he with in*, *also*, *to*, or *and she* ($7 \leq n \leq 11$), respectively. Eighteen per cent of word substitutions sound exactly the same as the correct word and 26 per cent have a similarity percentage above 75. This encourages using phonetic similarity to improve STT.

1 Introduction

Fluent *information flow* is important in any information-intensive area of decision making, but critical in healthcare. Clinicians are responsible for making decisions with even life-and-death impact on their patients' lives. The flow is defined as links, channels, contact, or communication to a pertinent person or people in the organisation (Glaser et al., 1987). In Australian healthcare, failures in this flow are associated with over one-tenth of preventable adverse events (ACS, 2008; ACS, 2012). Failures in the flow are tangible in *clinical handover*, that is, when a clinician is transferring professional responsibility and accountability, for example, at shift change (AMA, 2006). Regardless of verbal handover being accurate and comprehensive, anything from two-thirds to all of this information is lost after three to five shifts if no notes are taken or they are taken by hand (Pothier et al., 2005; Matic et al., 2011).

There is a proposal to use a semi-automated approach of *speech to text* (STT) and *information extraction* (IE) for taking the handover notes (Suominen et al., 2013). First, a STT (a.k.a. speech recognition) engine converts verbal information into written, free-form text. Then, an IE system fills out a handover form by automatically identifying relevant text-snippets for each slot of the form. Finally, this pre-filled form is given to a clinician to proof and sign off.

The semi-automated approach evokes an STT challenge. First, the correctness of STT is challenged by background noise, other people's voices, and other characteristics of clinical practise that are far from a typical setting in a peaceful office. Second, the STT errors multiply when cascaded with IE. Third, correctness in cascaded STT and IE needs to be carefully evaluated as excellent, because of the severe implications that errors may have in clinical decision-making. In summary, the original voice (i.e., information) in the big noise from clinical setting and STT errors needs to be heard.

Motivated by this challenge, we provide an analysis of STT errors and discuss the feasibility of *phonetic similarity* for their correction in this paper. Phonetic similarity (PS, a.k.a phonetic distance) addresses perceptual confusion between speech sounds and is used to improve STT (Mermelstein, 1976). To illustrate **phonetically similar words**, *PS measures can be seen as the **rites** of **righting writing**, that is **right**.*

The rest of the paper is organised as follows: In Section 2, we provide background for clinical STT and IE. In Section 3, we describe our simulated handover data, STT methods, PS measures, and analysis methods. In Section 4, we present the results of the error analysis and discuss the feasibility of phonetic similarity for error correction. In Section 5, final conclusions and directions for future work are given.

2 Background

In clinical STT, different engines give comparable results and can reach over 90 per cent of the words being correct. A comparison on the same dataset shows the mean correctness percentages of 85–86; 85–87; and 90–93 for Dragon Medical 3.0; L&H Voice Xpress for Medicine 1.2, General Medicine; and IBM ViaVoice 98, General Medicine, respectively (Devine et al., 2000). The dataset consists of four medical report entries (two progress notes, one assessment summary, and one discharge summary) and twelve US English male physicians.

Only 30–60 min tailoring to a given voice improves the correctness percentage up to 99 but in a preliminary evaluation of STT with minimal tailoring, Australian English, six simulated handover cases (over 1,200 words of continuous free-form text), and Dragon Medical 11.0, the percentage is 79, 64, and 54 for a native male physician, native female nursing scientist, and Spanish-accented female nurse, respectively (Suominen et al., 2013). The percentages for tailored STT originate from experiments on the aforementioned four medical report entries and twelve US English male physicians; 47 emergency-department charts and two US English physicians (Zick and Olsen, 2001); and 206 surgical pathology reports, seven Canadian English pathologists, a researcher with an accent (Al-Aynati and Chorneyko, 2003).

However, these correctness percentages, measured in peaceful laboratory settings, are challenged by noise in clinical practise. On eight voices, a total of about 3,600 typical short anaesthesia comments in Danish, and with noise being present, only 77 per cent of words are correct (Alapetite, 2008).

The review (Meystre et al., 2008) discusses 174 studies from 1995 to 2008 on clinical IE. It concludes that the quality of these systems has gradually improved, exceeding the F1-measure (i.e., the harmonic mean of the proportion of slots that the system filled correctly and the proportion of snippets that the system extracted from those it should have extracted) of 90 per cent in several cases. These systems mostly focus on chest and other types of radiography reports, echocardiogram reports, discharge summaries, and pathology reports. Their typical tasks include extracting codes; enriching or structuring the content and utility of the electronic health record, especially to support computerised decision-making; surveillance; supporting research; de-identification of clinical text; and terminology management.

3 Materials and Methods

3.1 Materials

The dataset of 100 simulated handover records used in this study was created as follows.

First, a senior researcher in clinical language processing (i.e., HS) imagined an *Australian medical ward*. With an aim for balance in patient types, she created simulated profiles of 25 *cardiac*, 25 *neurological*, 25 *renal*, and 25 *respiratory patients* of the ward. Each imaginary *profile* included a photo from a free-to-use gallery, name, age, admission story, in-patient time, and the familiarity of this patient to the nurses giving and receiving the handover (Fig. 1).

Second, a registered nurse with over twelve years experience from clinical nursing was hired to create nursing-handover records for the hundred profiles as *written, free-form text records*, *structured forms*, and *spoken free-form text records* (Fig. 1, Table 1). She spoke Australian English as a second language and was originally from Philippines. In the creative writing task, HS guided her to write realistic reports in the role of the nurse giving the handover. In the structuring task, HS guided her to use these written, free-text records to identify text snippets relevant to the slots of the handover form by using *Knowtator* (Ogren, 2006). The handover form was developed in collaboration with HS and nurse. It was based on international standards and practical experiences. The identification task was multi-class classification, that is, each word belonged to precisely one or none of the slots. In the speaking task, HS guided the nurse to read the written, free-text records out loud in the role of the nurse giving the handover. The digital recorder and microphone were *Olympus WS-760M* (200 AUD) and *Olympus ME52W* (lapel, noise cancelling, 15 AUD), previously shortlisted as producing a superior percentage of correct words in STT (i.e., up to 79) (Suominen et al., 2013) .

3.2 STT Methods

Dragon Medical 11.0 was used to convert the audio files to written, free-form text records. Audio files were converted from stereo to mono tracks and from WMA to WAV files on *Audacity 2.0.3*. Dragon was initialised for the *Age* of *22-54 years* and *Accent* of *Australian English*, and tailored to the nurse's voice by her reading the document of *The Final Odyssey* using the aforementioned recorder and microphone (3,893 words, 29 min 22 s). Tailoring was left minimal since it could limit comparability with other studies and might not be feasible for every clinician in practise.

Dragon *vocabularies* of *general*, *medical*, *nursing*, *cardiology*, *neurology*, and *pulmonary disease* were compared. The *SCLITE scoring tool of the Speech Recognition Scoring Toolkit 2.4.0* was used to analyse correctly recognised, substituted, inserted, and deleted words. The reference standard in all comparisons consisted of the original written reports (i.e., not transliterations by hand) where punctuation was removed and capitalisation was not considered as a distinguishing feature.

The vocabulary resulting in the best correctness (i.e., *nursing* with both highest mean (73%) and lowest standard deviation (SD, 7%) of correct words, Fig. 2) was chosen for the error analysis. In 74 out of 100 cases, this vocabulary gave the largest number of correct words. With 25 cardiac (neurological) [respiratory] patients, the matching vocabulary (i.e., cardiology, (neurology), and [pulmonary disease]) gave more correct words than any other vocabulary only 3 (4) [0] times. The matching vocabulary gave more correct words than the nursing vocabulary only 4 (3) [6] times.

Name: Leila Sonya Da Silva
Age: 34 years
Admission story: Leila has difficulties to control her diabetes. Her blood sugars tend to climb up too high but in the morning, the values are too low. Her diabetes was diagnosed when she was 6. She suffers from hypertension too but has had no medication to it yet.
At medical ward: She has been at the ward for a day. She is new both to you and the next nurse.

Leila sonya Da silva, bed 5, 34 under Dr Liu, came in for management of her diabetes. With history of type 1 DM since childhood and HPN. She is still for referral to the diabetic educator and she is self caring with her own BGLS and insulin. Her insulin is on a sliding scale insulin and on variable dose so just ask the doctor for the next dose depending on her blood sugar. Her BGL trend used to be high during the AM.so still need the team to review for that.Her BP is not so bad and of a high normal range and still for review.otherwise she is pretty much self caring and ambulant and there are no other problems noted.

Heading	*Slots*
Introduction	Room, Bed, Dr, Name, Age, Gender, Allergy, Admission reason/diagnosis, Chronic condition, Problem history
My shift	Status, Contraption, Activities of daily living, Input/diet, Output/diuresis/ bowel movement, Wounds/skin, Risk management, Other observation
Medication	Medicine, Dosage, Status
Appointment	Description, Place, Time, Status, Clinician
Future	Goal/task to be completed/ expected outcome, Alert/warning/abnormality, Care/discharge/transfer plan

Figure 1: A profile, report, and form structure

Table 1: Descriptive statistics of the records, words (w), and inside words (i)

Patient type (n)	cardiac (25)	neurological (25)	renal (25)	respiratory (25)	*All* (100)
Record length					
Min–Max [w]	19–162	26 – 106	29–149	31–209	19–209
Mean (SD) [w]	70 (37)	60 (22)	71 (33)	83 (39)	71 (34)
Min–Max [s]	17–89	16 – 60	16–77	20–97	16–97
Mean (SD) [s]	44 (19)	38 (13)	36 (17)	46 (18)	41 (17)
n of w's (uniq.)	1,795 (556)	1,545 (500)	1,818 (496)	2,119 (604)	7,277 (1,304)
Top 1 (n)	and (95)	and (64)	and (88)	and (100)	and (347)
Top 2 (n)	he (59)	is (60)	is (72)	is (69)	is (256)
Top 3 (n)	for (58)	he (54)	he (69)	on (63)	he (243)
Top 4 (n)	is (55)	she (38)	in, she (46)	he (61)	in (170)
Top 5 (n)	the, with (43)	in (35)		with (51)	for (163)
Top 6 (n)		with (34)	the (38)	in (49)	with (162)
Top 7 (n)	in (40)	on (33)	with (34)	for (43)	she (151)
Top 8 (n)	to (32)	for (31)	came (32)	she (42)	on (141)
Top 9 (n)	of (30)	to (29)	for (31)	the (37)	the (138)
Top 10 (n)	came (27)	came (24)	to (30)	to (33)	to (124)
n of i's (uniq.)	1,140 (447)	1,006 (397)	1,086 (408)	1,305 (483)	4,547 (1,106)
Top 1 (n)	he (57)	he (52)	he (63)	and (51)	he (220)
Top 2 (n)	for (47)	she (35)	she (39)	he (48)	she (139)
Top 3 (n)	and (26)	for (25)	and (34)	she(40)	and (131)
Top 4 (n)	bed, she (25)	dr (22)	bed, is (24)	for (27)	for (118)
Top 5 (n)		and, old (20)		dr (25)	dr (88)
Top 6 (n)	dr (23)		to (23)	is, on, to (20)	to (84)
Top 7 (n)	to (22)	bed, to (19)	old, yrs (21)		bed (80)
Top 8 (n)	the (21)				is (76)
Top 9 (n)	her, old (18)	yrs (17)	all (20)	room (18)	old (72)
Top 10 (n)		her, is (16)	for (19)	of (16)	all, her (61)

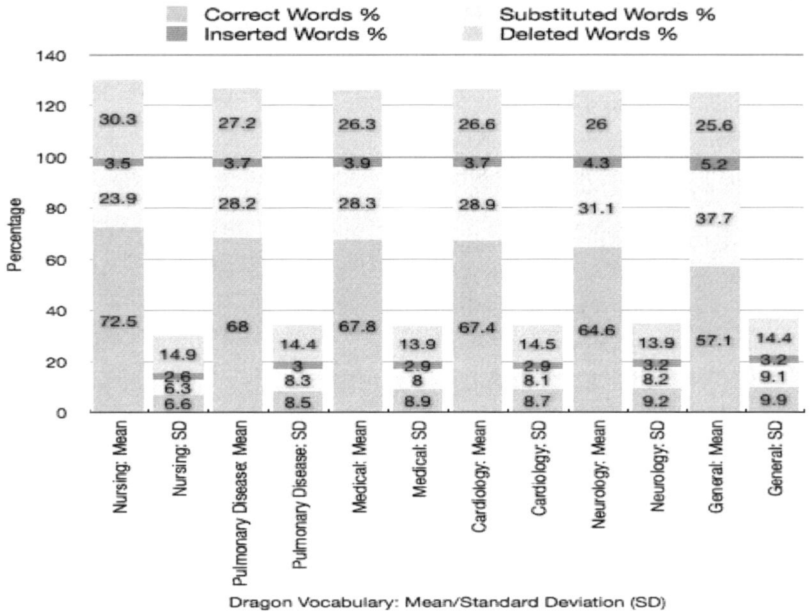

Figure 2: STT with different vocabularies: mean and SD over the 100 records

3.3 PS Measures

Measuring PS is relevant in speech processing, spelling correction, dialectometry, historical distance between sounds, and many other contexts. PS measures quantify the similarity between speech forms (e.g., words) on the basis of their sounds. Usually they consist of two steps (Kondrak, 2002): First, *words are transcribed into their phonetic representation*. Second, a *weighted* or *unweighted edit-distance* is applied to calculate the similarity between the transcriptions. Recent approaches weight the edit distance by hand on the basis of linguistic knowledge (Kondrak, 2000) or automatically using learning algorithms (Mann and Yarowsky, 2001; Kondrak, 2002; Mackay and Kondrak, 2005).

We calculated *PS of substitutions errors* from a STT engine. Similarly to other studies (Kaki et al., 1998; Jeong, 2004; Pucher et al., 2007), our hyphotesis was that substitutions that sound similar to the reference standard can be solved by applying a correction metric that combines a generator of sound-alike words with principles for distributional semantics. In other words, a good correction candidate was a word that sounds similar to the reference standard and fullfills its usage context. As a first step towards the creation of such correction metric, we implemented a procedure for selecting *(quasi-)homonym substitutions* (i.e., sound (almost) the same but have different meaning) based on phonetic distance.

We built a simple PS measure, which *combines a sound-alike algorithm with edit distance*. To transcribe the words into a phonetic representation, we used the *Double Metaphone* (DMetaphone) phonetic encoding algorithm (Philips, 2000) which is part of the *Methaphone* family (Philips, 1990). We chose DMetaphone, because it approximates accented English from Slavic, Germanic, French, Spanish, among others languages. DMetaphone returned for each word an aproximation of its sound instead of a sequence of phonemes. It translated each consonant into a limited set of characters where similar sounds are represented by the same character (e.g., *b* and *p* both sound like *p*). To calculate the similarity between the encoded words, we applied the unweighted edit-distance. This computed the minimum number of edit operations (i.e., substitutions, insertions, and deletions) required to transform an encoded word into another.

3.4 Analysis Methods

We used *content analysis* (Stemler, 2001) to analyse STT errors quantitatively and qualitatively. The correct, substituted, inserted and deleted words were defined by the SCLITE scoring tool.

For the PS discussion, we performed two experiments. First, we computed PS for *single-word substitutions* (e.g., *four–for*), in which the first word is the STT word and the second word is from the reference standard. Each word was encoded into its DMetaphone value using the *Apache Commons Metaphone* utility. The edit distance between the encoded words was calculated using the open source *Simmetric* library from Sheffield University. Second, we computed PS for *multi-word substitutions* (e.g., *doctors signed–dr san*). Because DMetaphone is designed to encode a single word at a time, each word in a multi-word concept was individually encoded into its metaphone value, encoded words were combined as sequences, and the edit distance was used to calculate the similarity between the sequences.

In all analyses and experiments, we used the entire dataset and the subset that affects the IE system (i.e., *inside* refers to text identified as relevant to the slots of the handover form).

4 Results and Discussion

Fifteen per cent (18%) of all unique substitutions (unique inside substitutions) sound exactly the same as in the reference standard and 23 per cent (26%) have a similarity score above 75 per cent (Tables 2&3). Consequently, substitutions with a high PS value can be considered as candidates for error correction.

In text relevant to the handover form, 836 unique error types are present (Table 2). The most common of them include inserting *and*, *in*, *are*, *arm*, *is*, *a*, *the*, or *am* ($5 \leq n \leq 94$), deleting *is* ($n = 17$), and substituting *and*, *obs are*, *2*, *he with in*, *also*, *to*, or *and she* ($7 \leq n \leq 11$), respectively.

Five types of substitution errors are present:

1. proper names;
2. singular vs. plural forms;
3. use of abbreviations in the reference standard and complete forms in STT;
4. systematic differences between the reference standard and STT (e.g., Australian (reference) vs. US (STT) spelling and writing

Table 2: Correct, substituted, inserted, and deleted single-words
These descriptive statistics also include cases where STT deleted (inserted) a word (i.e., white space is computed as a word). In the top substitutions, the first word is the STT word and the second from the reference standard.

	Correct words	Substituted words	Inserted words	Deleted words
All (Inside)	5,270 (3,237)	1,685 (1,132)	2,111 (1,541)	322 (178)
	Unique correct	Unique substitutions	Unique insertions	Unique deletions
All (Inside)	839 (710)	1,187 (827)	449 (371)	154 (93)
Inside	Top correct (n)	Top substitutions (n)	Top insertions (n)	Top deletions (n)
1	he (178)	years yrs (48)	and (210)	is (20)
2	she (134)	in and (22)	is (136)	are (13)
3	for (112)	one 1 (17)	in (106)	and (11)
4	dr (87)	also obs (12)	she (71)	s (8)
5	and (80)	to 2 (12)	are (58)	obs (6)
6	old (71)	and he (1)	all (45)	of (5)
7	to (70)	he his (9)	arm (44)	bed (4)
8	bed (64)	also are (7)	for (43)	her (4)
9	all (56)	ambien ambulant (6)	the (37)	4 (3)
10	the (55)	ambulating ambulant (6)	he (35)	all (3)
11	stable (54)	antibiotics abs (6)	that (34)	fbc (3)
12	is (52)	desilva de (5)	a (27)	for (3)
13	her (50)	for 4 (5)	her (19)	got (3)
14	of (44)	hypertension hpn (5)	eats (15)	he (3)
15	on (38)	in nil (5)	on (15)	silva (3)
16	pain (33)	she he (5)	also (14)	the (3)
17	with (31)	tomorrow tom (5)	am (12)	to (3)
18	his (27)	ultrasound us (5)	does (11)	a (2)
19	self (27)	and nil (4)	bed (10)	hdx (2)
20	caring (26)	george jorge, his he, is are, is obs, is s, iv ivabs, lee li, p prn, x xray (4)	s (10) to (10)	normal (2) review(2)

numbers as digits (reference) vs. letters (STT)); and

5. misspelling/typos in the reference standard (e.g., *feeling* vs. *feelling* or *arrhythmia* vs. *arrythmia*).

Substitutions and insertions are the most common error types, both in all data and within text identified as relevant to the slots of the handover form. The majority of the top insertions and deletions corresponds to functional words, (lexemes with little semantic meaning such as determiners, prepositions, auxiliary verbs and pronouns).

According to our PS measure, for the set of all word substitutions, 23 per cent have a similarity percentage above 75 and in 15 per cent of these highly similar cases the STT and reference words sound exactly the same (Tables 3&4). When experimenting with the set of inside substitutions, 26 per cent have a similarity percentage above 75 and in 18 per cent of these highly similar cases the STT and reference words sound exactly the same. Thus, around a fourth of the substitution errors can be considered as candidates for their correction.

A proper name is included in 24 per cent of substitutions and 3 per cent of them sound exactly the same (e.g., *Lane* vs. *Laine* or *Lee* vs. *Li*). Correcting this is critical in the healthcare context. Different spellings of the same word are not uncommon (e.g., *Johnson* vs. *Johnsson* or *organised* vs. *organized*). Aproximately 2 per cent of the substitutions that sound the same are due the difference between singular and plural forms of the same lemma (e.g., *investigation* vs. *investigations* or *fibrosis* vs. *fibroses*).

As expected, the number of substitutions that sound similar is quite low (Table 4). Only 14 per cent of single-word substitutions are minimally 75 per cent similar. For multi-word substitutions, the

Table 3: Top errors within inside words
- refers to a single white space and the total number of incorrect multi-words is 1,204 and 836 of them are unique

STT	*reference*	*n*	*STT*	*reference*	*n*
and	-	94	in the	nil -	4
years	yrs	48	iv antibiotics	ivabs -	4
in	-	25	lee	li	4
are	-	21	x ray	xray -	4
-	is	17	-	fbc	3
arm	-	11	and	he	3
in	and	11	and there is	- - -	3
is	-	11	antibiotics	abs	3
a	-	9	arm she	- -	3
also -	obs are	8	ii	2	3
to	2	8	is	s3	
and she	he -	7	is a	- -	3
the	-	7	kinsey	kenzie	3
am	-	5	lane and	laine -	3
hypertension	hpn	5	our	-	3
-	of	4	she	he	3
ambulating -	ambulant and	4	tomorrow	tom	3
and she is	- - -	4	ultrasound	us	3

top similarity percentage is 72. After removing instances that contained an empty column, 651 unique substitution types are present in the data.

For PS from 0.74 to 0.50, the single-word substitutions are still phonetically close to the reference (e.g., *cause* vs. *course*, *weeks* vs. *weak*, and *from* vs. *for*) which suggest that they might be also considered as secondary correction candidates in future experiments. When PS is below 0.5, errors are heterogeneous, meaning that some of them still sound a bit similar (e.g., *bed* vs. *the*) but others sounds completely different (e.g., *energies* vs. *physiotherapist*), and should not be taken into account for their correction based on this PS approach. Fifty per cent of the substitution errors occur with words shorter than 4 characters. These short words are obviously more difficult for STT than longer words.

Not all substitutions that sound similar to the reference should be considered as potential candidates for error correction. For example, errors due to abbreviations, typos, and spelling variations represent 9 per cent of the errors, and are not strictly speaking STT errors. This is because the original written records, and not careful transliterations by hand, were used as a reference standard. The use of abbreviations in the writing environment and the use of the complete form in STT seems natural for people but creates an inconsistency in the error analysis. For example, the nurse is always using *yrs* when writing instead of *year*, *obs* instead of *observations*, *his K* instead of *his potassium*, among others.

5 Conclusion and Future Work

A detailed error analysis is a crucial step in the development of pipeline applications (i.e., applications that cascade methods) similar to the one described in this paper. We have found that a substantial amount of STT errors occurs with words that are phonetically similar to each other. Consequently, using an error correction method based on PS seems appropriate in reducing the error rate.

As the first step towards the correction method, we have assessed a PS measure that calculates the similarity between words. This component will be used in the future as a post-processing method to select errors for their correction. Single-word substitutions are more suitable for this post-processing than insertion and deletion errors. However, we address the inserted and deleted words indirectly via the multi-word substitution and white-space analyses (Tables 2–4).

Based on the presented analysis, the correction method will take into account the following four characteristics:

Table 4: Examples of the sound-alike substitutions

Analysis	*STT*	*reference*	*phoneSim*
Single-word	Gaylor	Gayler	1.0
	dialyses	dialysis	1.0
	results	result	1.0
	harrowed	Harrod	1.0
	cord	GORD	1.0
	ambulance	ambulant	1.0
	arrhythmia	arrythmia	1.0
	Lane	Laine	1.0
	doctors	doctor	1.0
	ambulating	ambulant	1.0
	wheelie	wheely	1.0
	years	yrs	1.0
	and/ even	endone/ eventhough	0.75
	heart/ relater	heartburn/ later	0.75
	every/ state	everytime/ stent	0.75
	menders/ arrive	Mendez/ arrived	0.75
Multi-word	george desilva s	jorge de silva	0.72
	in ampulla	and ambulant	0.72
	aspergilloses are she	aspergillosis he	0.71
	blanford	plan for	0.71
	can assume	cannot seem	0.71
	coronae idd sees	coronary artery disease	0.71
	you ve am	if all	0.71
	flexing	clexane	0.71
	one keay	wound care	0.71
	do explained	explain	0.70
	endo p r n	endone prn	0.70
	haemodialyses am	heamodialysis	0.70
	racquel saw iris date dino	raquel soares caetano	0.68
	this orders	disorders	0.66
	cystic fibroses and	cyctic fibrosis	0.66

1. detection and correction of errors in proper names;
2. difference between single-word and multi-word errors;
3. spelling correction strategies; and
4. grammar checking to ensure correctness.

Even though only one-fourth of all substitution errors could be considered as correction candidates, every corrected word is one less potential error in clinical decision-making.

Acknowledgments

NICTA is funded by the Australian Government through the Department of Communications and the Australian Research Council through the ICT Centre of Excellence Program. NICTA is also funded and supported by the Australian Capital Territory, the New South Wales, Queensland and Victorian Governments, the Australian National University, the University of New South Wales, the University of Melbourne, the University of Queensland, the University of Sydney, Griffith University, Queensland University of Technology, Monash University and other university partners. We acknowledge the contribution of Maricel Angel, RN in creating our dataset as a NICTA employee.

References

ACSQHC, Australian Commission on Safety and Quality in Health Care, 2008. *Windows into Safety and Quality in Health Care,* `goo.gl/wB0XZ1`.

ACSQHC, Australian Commission on Safety and Quality in Health Care, 2012. *The OSSIE Guide to Clinical Handover Improvement,* `goo.gl/IvS7dc`.

M Al-Aynati and K Chorneyko. 2003. Comparison of voice-automated transcription and human transcription in generating pathology reports. *Archives of Pathology and Laboratory Medicine*, 127(6):721–5.

A Alapetite. 2008. Impact of noise and other factors on speech recognition in anaesthesia. *International Journal of Medical Informatics*, 77(1):68–77.

AMA, Australian Medical Association, 2006. *Safe Handover: Safe Patients,* `goo.gl/9U8wjm`.

E Devine, S Gaehde, and A Curtis. 2000. Comparative evaluation of three continuous speech recognition software packages in the generation of medical reports. *Journal of the American Medical Informatics Association: JAMIA*, 7(5):462–8.

S Glaser, S Zamanou, and K Hacker. 1987. Measuring and interpreting organizationalculture. *Management Communication Quarterly*, 1(2):173–98.

Minwoo Jeong. 2004. Using higher-level linguistic knowledge for speech recognition error correction in a spoken q/a dialog. In *Proceedings of the HLT-NAACL special workshop on Higher-Level Linguistic Information for Speech Processing*, pages 48–55.

S Kaki, E Sumita, and H Iida. 1998. A method for correcting errors in speech recognition using the statistical features of character co-occurrence. In *Proceedings of the 36th Annual Meeting of the Association for Computational Linguistics and 17th International Conference on Computational Linguistics - Volume 1*, ACL '98, pages 653–7, Stroudsburg, PA, USA. Association for Computational Linguistics.

G Kondrak. 2000. A new algorithm for the alignment of phonetic sequences. In *Proceedings of the 1st North American chapter of the Association for Computational Linguistics conference*, NAACL 2000, pages 288–95, Stroudsburg, PA, USA. Association for Computational Linguistics.

G Kondrak. 2002. Determining recurrent sound correspondences by inducing translation models. In *Proceedings of the 19th international conference on Computational linguistics - Volume 1*, COLING '02, pages 1–7, Stroudsburg, PA, USA. Association for Computational Linguistics.

W Mackay and G Kondrak. 2005. Computing word similarity and identifying cognates with pair hidden Markov models. In *Proceedings of the Ninth Conference on Computational Natural Language Learning*, CONLL '05, pages 40–7, Stroudsburg, PA, USA. Association for Computational Linguistics.

G Mann and D Yarowsky. 2001. Multipath translation lexicon induction via bridge languages. In *Proceedings of the second meeting of the North American Chapter of the Association for Computational Linguistics on Language technologies*, NAACL '01, pages 1–8, Stroudsburg, PA, USA. Association for Computational Linguistics.

J Matic, P Davidson, and Y Salamonson. 2011. Review: bringing patient safety to the forefront through structured computerisation during clinical handover. *Journal of Clinical Nursing*, 20(1–2):184–9.

P Mermelstein. 1976. Distance measures for speech recognition, psychological and instrumental. *Pattern Recognition and Artificial Intelligence*, 116:374–88.

S Meystre, G Savova, K Kipper-Schuler, and J Hurdle. 2008. Extracting information from textual documents in the electronic health record: a review of recent research. review. *Yearbook of Medical Informatics*, pages 128–44.

P Ogren. 2006. Knowtator: a protégé plug-in for annotated corpus construction. In *Proceedings of the 2006 Conference of the North American Chapter of the Association for Computational Linguistics on Human Language Technology*, pages 273–5, Morristown, NJ, USA. Association for Computational Linguistics.

L Philips. 1990. Hanging on the Metaphone. *Computer Language*, 7(12 (December)).

L Philips. 2000. The Double Metaphone search algorithm. *C/C++ Users Journal*, 18(5), June.

D Pothier, P Monteiro, M Mooktiar, and A Shaw. 2005. Pilot study to show the loss of important data in nursing handover. *British Journal of Nursing*, 14(20):1090–3.

M Pucher, A Türk, J Ajmera, and N Fecher. 2007. Phonetic distance measures for speech recognition vocabulary and grammar optimization. In *Proc. 3rd congress of the Alps Adria Acoustics Association, Graz.*

S Stemler. 2001. An overview of content analysis. *Practical Assessment, Research & Evaluation*, 7(17).

H Suominen, J Basilakis, M Johnson, P Sanchez, L Dawson, L Hanlen, and B Kelly. 2013. Preliminary evaluation of speech recognition for capturing patient information at nursing shift changes: accuracy in speech to text and user preferences for recorders. In *Proceedings of the 4th International Louhi Workshop on Health Document Text Mining and Information Analysis*, Sydney, NSW, Australia.

R Zick and J Olsen. 2001. Voice recognition software versus a traditional transcription service for physician charting in the ed. *The American Journal of Emergency Medicine*, 19(4):295–8.

Examining the Impact of Coreference Resolution on Quote Attribution

Tim O'Keefe
tokeefe@
it.usyd.edu.au

Kellie Webster
kweb3773@
uni.sydney.edu.au

James R. Curran
james@
it.usyd.edu.au

ə-lab, School of Information Technologies
University of Sydney
NSW 2006, Australia

Abstract

Quote attribution is the task of identifying the speaker of each quote within a document. While recent research has established large-scale corpora for this task, these corpora are not yet consistent in the way they handle candidate speakers, and many of the reported results rely on gold standard annotations of both entities and coreference chains.

In this work we evaluate three quote attribution systems with automatically produced candidate speakers and coreference chains. We perform these experiments over four separate corpora, which allows us to determine how coreference resolution effects quote attribution, and to use the task as an extrinsic evaluation of three coreference systems.

1 Introduction

News articles are often driven by the quotes that appear within them. Approximately 32% of the tokens in the Sydney Morning Herald Corpus (SMHC) (Pareti et al., 2013) appear within a quote. Ignoring the attributed nature of this text can result in incorrectly assigning text to a document's author, rather than to the speaker the author attributes it to. Quote attribution is thus important for applications such as information retrieval, opinion mining, media monitoring, and others.

Early research into quote attribution and quote extraction was largely rule-based, as there was no large-scale data available. Several more recent studies (Elson and McKeown, 2010; O'Keefe et al., 2012; He et al., 2013; Pareti et al., 2013) have addressed this with corpora covering both news articles and literature. However, despite the importance of candidate speakers to this task, work thus far has treated candidates speakers inconsistently. Elson and McKeown (2010) include automatically identified named entities and common nouns, but do not include pronominal references or attempt coreference, which they state is problematic due to the domain (literature). He et al. (2013) include automatically identified named entities with limited gold-standard coreference, but do not include pronouns or common nouns. The SMHC (Pareti et al., 2013) includes gold-standard named entities and pronouns, as well as gold-standard coreference, but does not include common noun candidates. Finally the PARC (Pareti, 2012) is intended to cover attribution more generally, and so does not include any candidate speakers except for those that have attributed text.

Our work addresses the problem of inconsistent candidates within these corpora by separately aligning the output of three coreference resolution systems, Stanford (Lee et al., 2011), Reconcile (Stoyanov et al., 2010), and a naive baseline system, with the gold-standard speaker annotations. We can then evaluate the quote attribution methods from O'Keefe et al. (2012) with a set of speakers that have been identified in a more consistent manner across attribution methods and corpora. O'Keefe et al. note that one of the primary factors confounding their evaluation was that the set of candidates was not consistent, which our work addresses.

Our second main contribution is that we use quote attribution as an extrinsic evaluation for coreference resolution. Intrinsic evaluation of coreference is known to be problematic (Luo, 2005; Stoyanov et al., 2009) and for this reason, Mitkov et al. (2007) proposes extrinsically evaluating it by measuring its impact on downstream processes. Additionally we are able to gauge the impact of coreference resolution on quote attribution in literature, which is a domain that has not been studied in the work on coreference thus far.

2 Background

The first work to use large-scale data and machine learning for this task was the work of Elson and McKeown (2010) (hereafter referred to as EM2010). Their system uses a binary classifier to produce a probability that each of 15 candidates is the speaker, and returns the candidate with the highest probability. For data they build a corpus of direct quotes from 19th century literature, which includes both proper nouns and common nouns as candidate speakers, with the former identified using the Stanford NER system, and the latter identified through their own method. They do not identify pronouns and only perform coreference on the NEs, using a simple system.

Following on from EM2010, was the work of O'Keefe et al. (2012). They note that EM2010 had used some features that relied on gold standard information about previous decisions, which O'Keefe et al. replaced with features using predicted information and a sequence decoding step. They also evaluated their method on two other corpora, one that they build from Sydney Morning Herald[1] news articles (SMHC), and another over Wall Street Journal[2] news articles (PARC) that was introduced in Pareti (2012). They found that removing the gold standard features had a large impact on accuracy, and that their sequence labelling approaches could recover some of that lost accuracy. Later work by Pareti et al. (2013) extended the SMHC to include indirect and mixed quotes, though their focus was on quote extraction.

While the work of O'Keefe et al. (2012) and Pareti et al. (2013) was mainly focused on news articles, He et al. (2013) focused on literature. They developed a model that treated the task similarly to EM2010, though they considered it to be a ranking problem. As part of their work they introduced a new corpus which covers the entirety of the novel *Pride & Prejudice*. While their work outperformed the previous work on literature by EM2010, their system was very slow, so they did not provide a full comparison.

2.1 Coreference resolution

Coreference resolution (e.g. Pradhan et al. (2011)) is the task of partitioning mentions (typically noun phrases) into equivalence classes which refer to the same real world entity. It has largely been framed in terms of anaphoric links; that is, clusters of coreferential mentions are formed by determining whether a particular mention anaphorically points to another preceding it in the text (its antecedent). Both supervised and unsupervised models have been proposed.

The first competitive learning based system is described in Soon et al. (2001). A binary classifier was trained to determine whether pairs of mentions were coreferential, based on 12 features which considered surface level details such as string matching and heuristically determined morphosyntatics. Its feature set was expanded in Ng and Cardie (2002) to include the role of syntactic constraints and modification on coreference. Various works (Bengtson and Roth, 2008; Stoyanov et al., 2010; Stoyanov and Eisner, 2012) have expanded this feature set further.

Ng and Cardie (2002) also proposed ranking potential coreference links. Where Soon et al. assigned the closest positively classified mention as the antecedent of an active mention, ranking approaches define a window for candidate selection and return the most probable candidate within the window. Systems can either incorporate ranking as a post-processing stage which forms clusters based on pairwise probabilities (Ng and Cardie, 2002; Stoyanov et al., 2010; Denis and Baldridge, 2008), or they can rank during clustering (Rahman and Ng, 2009).

Stanford's system (Lee et al., 2011) achieved the best result in the CoNLL 2011 shared task and remained competitive in CoNLL2012 using a simple, unsupervised classifier. It captures global consistency constraints by having cluster level modelling, which it achieves by having a series of sieves that each read the document and expand clusters. The sieves are arranged in order of decreasing precision, such that mentions with a high chance of being coreferential are clustered first, which allows more difficult mentions to use more information from the expanded clusters.

Research into quote attribution has ignored the impact that these different approaches could have, and the four large-scale corpora that exist for quote attribution all include some gold-standard information about either the mentions or the coreference chains. Thus the goal of our work is to use consistent coreference methods across the different corpora, in order to evaluate the effect of coreference on quote attribution. This also allows us to

[1] `http://www.smh.com.au`

[2] `http://www.wsj.com`

Corpus		SMHC	PARC	LIT	P&P
Documents		965	2,280	11	1
Tokens		601k	1,139k	407k	144k
Quotations		6,705	9,961	3,486	1,692
Entities	Proper	Gold	Gold	Auto	Auto
	Pronouns	Gold	Gold	-	-
	Common	-	Gold	Auto	-
Coref	Proper	Gold	-	Auto	Gold
	Pronouns	Gold	Gold	-	-
	Common	-	-	-	-

Table 1: Comparison of the four corpora in terms of both size, and the candidate speakers included.

evaluate the coreference methods extrinsically.

3 Corpora

In this work we perform experiments over two corpora containing news articles and two corpora containing works of fiction.

3.1 Sydney Morning Herald Corpus (SMHC)

The original version of the SMHC (O'Keefe et al., 2012) covered all of the direct quotes from 965 articles from the 2009 Sydney Morning Herald. The quotes were extracted automatically, and their speakers were annotated by one of 16 annotators, 11 of whom were employed using the website Freelancer[3], while the remaining 5 were expert annotators. 400 of the documents were double annotated, with raw agreement on the speakers of 98.3%. Later work by Pareti et al. (2013) extended the SMHC by adding indirect and mixed quotes, which was performed by a single annotator.

The candidate speakers for this corpus consist of gold-standard annotations of NEs and pronouns, which were completed as part of a separate research project (Hachey et al., 2013). Both the NEs and the pronouns were manually merged into coreference chains. Annotating a candidate as being the correct speaker of a quote in this corpus involves linking to the *coreference chain*, rather than a specific mention. This corpus does not include any common noun references to entities.

3.2 Penn Attribution Relations Corpus (PARC)

Our next corpus was introduced in Pareti (2011, 2012) and covers 2,280 articles from the Wall Street Journal. Pareti's work includes more general forms of attributable text than we are interested in, so we use just the assertions, as they correspond to quotes. This corpus was built semi-automatically from the Penn Discourse TreeBank (Prasad et al., 2006), which does not include all quotes, so it is not yet fully annotated. Pareti estimates that 30-50% of the corpus is unannotated, which means that there are many articles where legitimate quotes are missed.

As this corpus is not specifically designed for quote attribution, it does not come with any candidate speakers, with the exception of the text that each quote is attributed to. O'Keefe et al. (2012) use the BBN pronoun coreference and entity type corpus (Weischedel and Brunstein, 2005), although with automatically coreferred pronouns. This gives them gold-standard named entities, pronouns, and common nominal references, but only coreference for pronouns. To align Pareti's speakers (called *source*) O'Keefe et al. used the first BBN entity that was a subspan of Pareti's *source* annotations, and where no BBN entity matched, they inserted Pareti's *source* itself as an additional mention. The quotes from Pareti's annotations with an implicit source cannot be automatically linked to any entity, so they were ignored.

3.3 Columbia Quoted Speech Attribution Corpus (LIT)

The LIT corpus was introduced by Elson and McKeown (2010) and constituted the first large-scale corpus of quote attribution. It partially covers 7 short stories and chapters from 4 novels from 19th century fiction. The corpus was annotated using Amazon's Mechanical Turk[4], with three annotations per quote. Disagreements were settled by taking a majority vote, and in their original work, quotes with three-way disagreement were discarded, along with cases of non-dialogue text. Later work (O'Keefe et al., 2012) re-annotated the cases of three-way disagreement and filled in other gaps in the corpus, such that the annotated parts of each text were contiguous.

EM2010 found candidate speakers by identifying NEs with the Stanford NE tagger, and common nouns through patterns looking for a determiner, an optional modifier, and a head noun. They use their own system to link NEs with similar names, though they do not attempt any coreference on

[3] http://www.freelancer.com

[4] http://www.mturk.com/

the common nouns. They do not find pronouns, as they consider coreference to be part of the attribution system's job. In their results over LIT, O'Keefe et al. (2012) did identify pronouns, and used a simple rule-based method to link them to either NEs or common nouns.

3.4 Pride and Prejudice Corpus (P&P)

The final corpus that we use in this work is the corpus introduced by He et al. (2013). This corpus was annotated by an English Major and covers the entirety of the novel *Pride & Prejudice* by Jane Austen. It contains 1,260 quotes, which were extracted automatically.

He et al. also found candidate speakers by using the Stanford NER system, along with a manual preprocessing step where they grouped proper nominal references into sets of aliases for each character. They consider a correct attribution to be from a quote to a character, rather than to a textually-grounded mention of a character. As such, their candidate characters are two proper noun references before and two after each quote, as long as those proper nominal references are within the set of aliases that they manually defined. Since they are trying to explicitly link quotes to characters, they do not consider common or pronominal references as candidates, though they do use them as features. Note that the set of characters that they can attribute quotes to is closed, and does not include any unnamed characters.

3.5 Corpus Comparison

Table 1 shows a comparison of the four corpora. The largest in terms of documents, tokens, and number of quotations is the PARC, although it is worth noting that it is not yet fully annotated. The LIT corpus is also not fully annotated, although as the direct quotations were extracted automatically we know that there are 2,416 quotes that are missing their speakers. The other two corpora (SMHC and P&P) are fully annotated and so give a fair indication of the density of quotes. For this table we only counted quotes where a speaker was given.

In terms of candidate speakers the table shows considerable variance amongst the corpora. All the corpora include proper nominal candidates, although only the SMHC and PARC include gold standard proper nominals. Pronouns and common nominals are more mixed, with only the PARC including gold-standard candidates from these two categories. Coreference information is even less consistent, with the SMHC including gold-standard coreference for the two categories of candidates it contains and P&P including gold-standard coreference for its automatically identified named entities. LIT includes only automatic coreference of named entities, while PARC only includes gold-standard coreference of pronouns.

System	MUC-6		CoNLL-2011	
	MUC	B^3	MUC	B^3
Stanford	*78.2*	*73.8*	59.6	68.9
Reconcile	66.4	70.8	-	-

Table 2: Performance of Stanford and Reconcile on standard test sets using standard evaluation metrics. Results using gold cf. automatically detected mentions are indicated in italics.

4 Coreference Systems

The three coreference resolution systems that we use are Stanford's CoreNLP package (Raghunathan et al., 2010), Reconcile (Stoyanov et al., 2010), and a naive baseline system. By using Stanford and Reconcile we can evaluate the two main types of systems, as they are unsupervised and supervised respectively. The naive system is included for comparison. It performs NE coreference using simple string-matching of NEs found with Stanford's NE tagger, and coreference of pronouns by linking them to the most recent gender-matching antecedent. The naive baseline does not include common noun mentions. We experimented with a fourth system, CherryPicker (Rahman and Ng, 2009), but are unable to include results using CherryPicker as it crashed frequently.

Intrinsic evaluation of coreference resolution is difficult and even the relative performance of different systems can be hard to determine since system performance may be quoted on different corpora, using different evaluation metrics and even in different environments (e.g. the use of gold vs. automatically detected mentions). All of these effects can be seen in Table 2, with results using gold mention boundaries indicated in italics.

In this work we attempt to run all systems with minimal deviation from their default settings. However, since these systems were built for newswire, their architecture is not designed to scale to the longer texts from P&P and LIT, which forced us to make some changes. There were also some further issues that are detailed below.

Stanford

Stanford's mention spans are by design longer than the other two systems, and include overlapping mentions. We greedily kept the smaller mention of any overlapping pair, and retained the non-overlapping fragments from the longer mention as separate mentions. Some fragments and boundary tokens contained extraneous information, which we removed. We also removed the part of any mention following a comma or WH word, so as to retain the head NP. The default setting where all preceding mentions are potential antecedents was kept for the newswire corpora, but for LIT and P&P, a threshold of 100 sentences was used.

Reconcile

Due to memory constraints, the longer of the LIT texts and the training set of P&P were processed in 500 paragraph chunks.

5 Quote Attribution

Given a set of candidate speakers and a quote, quote attribution is the task of determining which of the candidates is the speaker of the quote. We note that for this task it is possible to consider a correct attribution to be either to a textually-grounded mention of an entity (called the *source* of the qoute), or to an entire coreference chain. In many cases the *source* will be a pronoun or common noun, that does not provide much information on its own. Other cases will include no explicit source, such as paragraph-long direct quotes. While our systems consider individual mentions as candidates, we consider a correct attribution to be to a whole coreference chain, meaning that the system can return the wrong textually-grounded mention, but still be considered correct if that mention is clustered with the *source*.

As the focus of this work is on evaluating the impact of coreference resolution on quote attribution, we do not propose any new approaches. Instead we use three of the systems from O'Keefe et al. (2012), namely the rule-based system, a simple binary classifier (called *no sequence* in O'Keefe et al.), and a CRF. All of these systems use the preprocessing described in O'Keefe et al., and all are evaluated using accuracy.

Rule-based

The rule-based system works by returning the candidate speaker that is nearest to either the quote or a speech verb, as long as that candidate is in the paragraph the verb or quote is in, or any preceding it. Speech verbs are identified using the list from Elson and McKeown (2010), and must be found in the same sentence as the quote. If a speech verb is found then the candidate nearest the verb is returned, otherwise it is the candidate nearest the quote. Though this system is very simple, O'Keefe et al. found that it worked about as well as machine learning approaches.

Binary classifier

The binary classifier assigns a binary probability of *speaker* vs. *not speaker* for up to 15 candidate speakers that are mentioned in the paragraph the quote is in or any preceding it. The final decision on which of the 15 candidates is the speaker is made by returning the candidate with the highest *speaker* probability. We use the maximum entropy learner from scikit learn[5]. While this method makes use of machine learning, there is no decoding step to ensure a sensible sequence of speakers, nor is there direct competition for probability mass between candidates. The advantage of this method is that it is able to generate many training instances, as there are effectively up to 15 training instances per quote, rather than the single instance that would be present for a model involving direct competition for probability mass.

Conditional Random Field (CRF)

The final quote attribution method that we use is a CRF which, similarly to the binary classifier, chooses between up to 15 candidate speakers. The difference with the CRF is that it includes a decoding step, and so can forego good local decisions about particular quotes in order to achieve a better sequence of decisions for all of the quotes. It includes a class labelling scheme where the candidates are numbered according to their ordinal position preceding the quote. This labelling scheme forces the candidates to compete for probability mass, although it reduces the number of training instances available to the classifier, and increases the number of features that are considered at each decision point.

6 Speaker Alignment

In order to evaluate the effect of coreference on quote attribution we first align the gold-standard

[5] `http://scikit-learn.org`

	SMHC			PARC			LIT			P&P		
	Rule	Bin	CRF	Rule	Bin	CRF	Rule	Bin	CRF	Rule	Bin	CRF
Naive	70	73	72	63	65	68	44	46	37	60	62	54
Stanford	68	78	76	80	82	83	40	48	40	44	56	53
Reconcile	69	76	76	77	80	81	37	50	37	45	51	45
Gold	74	78	75	87	92	92	54	54	50	54	62	57

Table 3: Quote attribution results using the source-based alignment method. The gold results use the candidates that come with the corpora.

speaker annotations with the automatically generated coreference chains. These alignment methods erase the gold-standard speaker annotation from each quote and replace it with one of the automatically generated coreference chains, so that the quote attribution methods can learn and predict using predicted coreference chains only. Quotes whose speakers could not be aligned are considered incorrect, as no correct attribution is possible.

Source-based alignment

Not all the corpora have gold-standard coreference chains, so our first alignment method aligns the textually-grounded source of each quote with a mention from the automatic coreference chains. Since speaker predictions are to whole coreference chains, any mention in the automatic coreference chain would then be considered correct. Consider the following example:

> "It doesn't seem the numbers are there yet, but I will continue to build my case," Senator Xenophon said.

The textually-grounded source of this quote is 'Senator Xenophon', so the source-based alignment works by finding the automatic coreference chain that includes 'Senator Xenophon' as a mention. This aligned coreference chain would then be considered the speaker.

While all of the corpora include some annotations of which mention best represents the speaker, there are some individual quotes where these annotations are not included. For these cases we align the automatic coreference chain with the mention from the gold-standard speaker's coreference chain that is nearest to the quote.

Canonical mention-based alignment

Two of our data sets, SMHC and P&P, include full coreference between the labelled gold-standard mentions, and have annotations of which gold-standard chain represents the speaker. For these two corpora, rather than considering the source of the quote, we use the canonical mention from the speaker's gold-standard coreference chain. We can then align the canonical mention with a mention from the automatic coreference chains, and again consider any mention from that chain to be the correct speaker. The gold-standard canonical mention will normally be mentioned early in a document, and will be an unambiguous reference to the real-world entity.

	SMHC			P&P		
	Rule	Bin	CRF	Rule	Bin	CRF
Naive	51	54	52	34	47	41
Stan.	40	47	46	32	43	33
Recon.	39	45	43	37	50	38

Table 4: Quote attribution results using the canonical-based alignment method.

7 Results

7.1 Quote attribution

The results in Tables 3 and 4 demonstrate that quote attribution is more successful over news than it is over literature, which agrees with O'Keefe et al. (2012). This is likely due to a number of factors, including the upstream processes being trained over news, the length of the documents, the formality of the text, and that journalists need to clearly identify who is speaking, while authors of fiction have more artistic freedom.

In all but one case the simple binary model outperformed the rule-based approach. This indicates that while the task may appear reasonably straightforward, there is still significant value in using large-scale data to learn a model. In particular some of the gains in literature were as high as 13 percentage points.

While the binary model performed well, the CRF model was somewhat inconsistent. On news text with the source-based alignment method the CRF did nearly as well as and sometimes better than the binary model, and better than the rule-based model. However with the literature text the CRF performed poorly. We found that this was due to some quotes not having a correct speaker within the set of 15 candidates that the learner considered. In these cases the CRF marks the quotes as not having a speaker, however, as these cases tend to cluster together in long dialogue chains in the literature corpora, the CRF learned that it is extremely likely to transition from not having a speaker to not having a speaker. This meant that if the CRF predicted that a single quote had no speaker then it would tend to predict that a number of subsequent quotes had no speaker. By contrast, the rule-based method and the binary model are forced to choose a speaker, and so do not suffer from this problem.

Across all of the corpora the gold-standard results were at least as good, if not better than the results using automatic coreference. This indicates that coreference systems are not over-clustering their results. The most surprising of the gold standard results is on PARC, where they are far better than the automatic results, despite PARC not including full coreference. The reason for this is that the PARC quotes must be attributed to entities within the same sentence as the quote. Both Stanford and Reconcile will tend to produce more mentions than the PARC gold standard, which can confuse the classifier, and Naive will produce no common nominal mentions, so all three automatic systems will perform substantially worse than the gold standard, despite potentially having more coreference information.

7.2 Extrinsic evaluation

Before discussing the results of our extrinsic evaluation, we would first like to note a weakness of our approach. In our framework if any coreference system outputs a single chain containing all mentions, it would score perfectly, as any predicted speaker would be the chain containing the correct mention. While this is not ideal, Vilain et al. (1995)'s MUC F-score has a similar problem, so, as they do, we simply note that this evaluation can not be considered independently of other metrics.

Table 5 shows the number of quotes whose speaker had no corresponding mention in the automatic coreference chains. For the source-based alignment the naive approach had a large number

	SMHC	PARC	LIT	P&P
Source				
Naive	352	656	214	0
Stanford	19	45	6	0
Reconcile	22	25	13	0
Canonical				
Naive	367			0
Stanford	285			0
Reconcile	297			0

Table 5: Number of gold speakers without a corresponding mention in the automatic coreference chains, for both the source and canonical-based alignment methods.

of misses, which is mostly due to the naive system not handling common noun references. This problem is not as severe in the canonical-based alignment, which will in most cases be a proper nominal reference, which the naive method can detect. Interestingly, there were no mentions that could not be aligned in P&P, although it is worth noting that P&P does not include quotes whose speakers are only referenced with common nouns.

For the source-based alignment results in Table 3, we note that in almost all cases the coreference systems were able to help the quote attribution systems when compared to the naive baseline. This result is particularly true of the learned methods, which may also be learning some amount of coreference themselves (as noted by Elson and McKeown (2010)). The rule-based system did not benefit as much, and in some cases performed worse, which was a consequence of the large number of common noun candidates, which often appeared between a quote and its speaker.

With the canonical-based alignment (Table 4) the naive coreference was actually better for quote attribution on the SMHC than the coreference systems, while the P&P results show that Reconcile with the simple binary model outperformed the other combinations. In some respects this is counter to intuition, as the coreference systems are designed for news text and appeared to produce poor results for literature. As noted earlier, the coreference systems tended to over-cluster mentions that shared a family name, even if they had distinct honorifics, which for P&P caused the systems to over-cluster the Bennets, who do most of the talking. This actually causes the quote attribution results to go up, as the alignment methods are imperfect. The naive system does not make the mistake of over-clustering based on family name, and so performs worse with this metric.

The poor results by Stanford and Reconcile on the SMHC are largely caused by their tendency to avoid clustering common nominal mentions with proper nominal mentions. This means that while the correct choice will be a chain containing a proper nominal mention, the quote attribution systems using the candidates from Stanford and Reconcile will have a number of candidate chains that contain only common nominal mentions. As there are no features that allow the quote attribution systems to distinguish these chains from any other chains, they are not able to avoid choosing them. While fixing this problem would be straightforward, it does illustrate that naive use of coreference systems can hurt performance.

8 Coreference Error Analysis

In order to understand some of the problems that were occurring with the coreference systems, we examined some of the main cases of errors. The first problem we identify is that there are a large number of chains with a single mention whose token is POS tagged as a pronoun. Reconcile had the largest number of these with 13,938 (35% of the extracted pronouns) on LIT and 5,501 (33% of the pronouns) on P&P. This is consistent with the result in Kummerfeld and Klein (2013) which finds a large number of missing mentions from Reconcile's output. This problem is particularly acute for quote attribution, as there are a large number of quotes that are directly attributed to a pronoun.

Stanford does better on this problem, having only 1,238 singleton pronouns on LIT and 361 on P&P, of which only 154 and 43, are gendered. Stanford deterministically assigns pronouns to the closest compatible mention in the preceding three sentences and it seems that this is a better way of modelling pronoun discourse. This is in line with Denis and Baldridge (2008)'s claim that the resolution of the different mention types could be more successfully handled with a series of classifiers. However, of these 1,238, 549 are forms of 'you', which suggests that Stanford's discourse sieve needs to be extended to handle the complexities of literature beyond newswire and the conversational data in OntoNotes (Pradhan et al., 2011).

Another major source of errors that we see when manually inspecting the data is conflation of chains corresponding to characters which share a family name, such as the 'Miss Bennet's' and their parents from P&P. To quantify this, we extract all the honorifics within a chain and report cases where a chain is assigned more than one honorific. For Stanford 1.7% of the mentions in LIT and 10.0% of the mentions in P&P are in chains with mixed honorifics, with the majority of the clashes coming from chains including honorifics for both genders. Reconcile makes a similar number of errors with 1.9% of mentions in LIT and 9.9% of mentions in P&P containing clashing honorifics.

9 Conclusions

In this work we addressed the problem of inconsistent candidate speakers within quote attribution corpora. To achieve this we ran three coreference resolution systems over the four corpora, and aligned the gold-standard speakers with chains produced by the coreference systems. This allowed us to more consistently compare the results of three quote attribution methods across the corpora, and additionally provided a more realistic setting for evaluating those methods.

We were also able to use quote attribution as an extrinsic evaluation of coreference resolution. While the speaker alignment methods make it possible to cheat the task, the results are nonetheless informative, and give an indication of how well coreference resolution performs in the literature domain, which has not been assessed with other metrics due to a lack of annotated data.

Future work will include examining the effect of quote extraction on these results, so that the full pipeline effect can be measured. It will also include investigation of features for quote attribution that utilise the information provided by coreference systems. In particular, the number and type of mentions within coreference chains clearly has an impact on the likelihood of them representing a speaker. Lastly, we suggest that coreference systems could be improved by ensuring that honorifics are consistent.

Acknowledgements

O'Keefe was supported by a University of Sydney Merit scholarship and a Capital Markets CRC top-up. This work was supported by ARC Discovery grant DP1097291 and the Capital Markets CRC Computable News project.

References

Eric Bengtson and Dan Roth. 2008. Understanding the value of features for coreference resolution. In *Proceedings of the Conference on Empirical Methods in Natural Language Processing*, pages 294–303. Association for Computational Linguistics.

Pascal Denis and Jason Baldridge. 2008. Specialized models and ranking for coreference resolution. In *Proceedings of the Conference on Empirical Methods in Natural Language Processing*, pages 660–669. Association for Computational Linguistics.

David Elson and Kathleen McKeown. 2010. Automatic attribution of quoted speech in literary narrative. In *Proceedings of the Association for the Advancement of Artificial Intelligence Conference on Artificial Intelligence*, pages 1013–1019.

Ben Hachey, Will Radford, Joel Nothman, Matthew Honnibal, and James R. Curran. 2013. Evaluating entity linking with Wikipedia. *Artificial Intelligence*, 194(0):130–150.

Hua He, Denilson Barbosa, and Grzegorz Kondrak. 2013. Identification of speakers in novels. In *Proceedings of the 51st Annual Meeting of the Association for Computational Linguistics*, pages 1312–1320. Association for Computational Linguistics.

Jonathan K. Kummerfeld and Dan Klein. 2013. Error-driven analysis of challenges in coreference resolution. In *Proceedings of the Conference on Empirical Methods in Natural Language Processing*.

Heeyoung Lee, Yves Peirsman, Angel Chang, Nathanael Chambers, Mihai Surdeanu, and Dan Jurafsky. 2011. Stanford's multi-pass sieve coreference resolution system at the CoNLL-2011 shared task. In *Proceedings of the Fifteenth Conference on Computational Natural Language Learning: Shared Task*, pages 28–34. Association for Computational Linguistics.

Xiaoqiang Luo. 2005. On coreference resolution performance metrics. In *Proceedings of the conference on Human Language Technology and Empirical Methods in Natural Language Processing*, pages 25–32. Association for Computational Linguistics.

Ruslan Mitkov, Richard Evans, Constantin Orsan, LeAn Ha, and Viktor Pekar. 2007. Anaphora resolution: To what extent does it help NLP applications? In *Anaphora: Analysis, Algorithms and Applications*, pages 179–190. Springer.

Vincent Ng and Claire Cardie. 2002. Improving machine learning approaches to coreference resolution. In *Proceedings of the 40th Annual Meeting on Association for Computational Linguistics*, pages 104–111. Association for Computational Linguistics.

Tim O'Keefe, Silvia Pareti, James R. Curran, Irena Koprinska, and Matthew Honnibal. 2012. A sequence labelling approach to quote attribution. In *Proceedings of the 2012 Joint Conference on Empirical Methods in Natural Language Processing and Computational Natural Language Learning*, pages 790–799. Association for Computational Linguistics.

Silvia Pareti. 2011. Annotating attribution relations and their features. In *Proceedings of the fourth workshop on Exploiting Semantic Annotations in Information Retrieval*, pages 19–20. ACM.

Silvia Pareti. 2012. A database of attribution relations. In *Proceedings of the Eighth International Conference on Language Resources and Evaluation*, pages 3213–3217.

Silvia Pareti, Tim O'Keefe, Ioannis Konstas, James R. Curran, and Irena Koprinska. 2013. Automatically detecting and attributing indirect quotations. In *Proceedings of the 2013 Conference on Empirical Methods in Natural Language Processing*. Association for Computational Linguistics.

Sameer Pradhan, Lance Ramshaw, Mitchell Marcus, Martha Palmer, Ralph Weischedel, and Nianwen Xue. 2011. CoNLL-2011 shared task: Modeling unrestricted coreference in OntoNotes. In *Proceedings of the Fifteenth Conference on Computational Natural Language Learning*.

Rashmi Prasad, Nikhil Dinesh, Alan Lee, Aravind Joshi, and Bonnie Webber. 2006. Annotating attribution in the Penn Discourse TreeBank. In *Proceedings of the Workshop on Sentiment and Subjectivity in Text*, pages 31–38.

Karthik Raghunathan, Heeyoung Lee, Sudarshan Rangarajan, Nathanael Chambers, Mihai Surdeanu, Dan Jurafsky, and Christopher Manning.

2010. A multi-pass sieve for coreference resolution. In *Proceedings of the 2010 Conference on Empirical Methods in Natural Language Processing*, pages 492–501. Association for Computational Linguistics.

Altaf Rahman and Vincent Ng. 2009. Supervised models for coreference resolution. In *Proceedings of the 2009 Conference on Empirical Methods in Natural Language Processing*, pages 968–977. Association for Computational Linguistics.

Wee Meng Soon, Hwee Tou Ng, and Daniel Chung Yong Lim. 2001. A machine learning approach to coreference resolution of noun phrases. *Computational linguistics*, 27(4):521–544.

Veselin Stoyanov, Claire Cardie, Nathan Gilbert, Ellen Riloff, David Buttler, and David Hysom. 2010. Coreference resolution with reconcile. In *Proceedings of the ACL 2010 Conference Short Papers*, pages 156–161. Association for Computational Linguistics.

Veselin Stoyanov and Jason Eisner. 2012. Easy-first coreference resolution. In *Proceedings of the 24th Internation Conference on Computational Linguistics 2012*.

Veselin Stoyanov, Nathan Gilbert, Claire Cardie, and Ellen Riloff. 2009. Conundrums in noun phrase coreference resolution: Making sense of the state-of-the-art. In *Proceedings of the Joint Conference of the 47th Annual Meeting of the ACL and the 4th International Joint Conference on Natural Language Processing of the AFNLP*, pages 656–664. Association for Computational Linguistics.

Marc Vilain, John Burger, John Aberdeen, Dennis Connolly, and Lynette Hirschman. 1995. A model-theoretic coreference scoring scheme. In *Proceedings of the 6th Conference on Message Understanding*, pages 45–52. Association for Computational Linguistics.

Ralph Weischedel and Ada Brunstein. 2005. BBN pronoun coreference and entity type corpus. *Linguistic Data Consortium, Philadelphia.*

Multi-Objective Optimization for Clustering of Medical Publications

Asif Ekbal **Sriparna Saha**
Indian Institute of Technology
Patna, Bihar, India
asif@iitp.ac.in
sriparna@iitp.ac.in

Diego Mollá
Department of Computing
Macquarie University, Sydney
NSW 2109, Australia
diego.molla-aliod@mq.edu.au

K Ravikumar
Indian Institute of Technology
Patna, Bihar, India
ravi.mc12@iitp.ac.in

Abstract

Clustering the results of a search can help a multi-document summarizer present a summary for evidence based medicine (EBM). In this work, we introduce a clustering technique that is based on multi-objective (MOO) optimization. MOO is a technique that shows promise in the areas of machine learning and natural language processing. In our approach we show how MOO based semi-supervised clustering technique can be effectively used for EBM.

1 Introduction

Evidence Based Medicine (EBM) urges the medical doctor to incorporate the latest clinical evidence available at point of care (Sackett et al., 1996). However, the amount of published clinical evidence is enormous. PubMed,[1] for example, indexes over 23 million citations, and the amount is growing every day. There are systematic reviews such as Cochrane's reviews that distill and summarize the information relevant to a particular topic, but often the doctor needs to access the primary literature, especially for cases that are rather infrequent and do not have systematic reviews dedicated to them, when dealing with particular segments of the population, or when the patient has simultaneous conditions ("comorbidity"). A search to PubMed can easily return hundreds of results, and finding specific information from that sea of information is time-consuming.

To help the doctor's need to find the evidence, it has been proposed to cluster the search results according to the different topics present in the clinical answer (Shash and Mollá, 2013). The motivation for this is that answers to a clinical question usually have several distinct parts, each of which is backed by a distinct set of published evidence. For example, as shown in Figure 1, the documents that answer the clinical inquiry *which treatments work best for hemorrhoids?* published in the Journal of Family Practice[2] can be grouped into three clusters, one for each suggested treatment (excision, hemorrhoidectomy, rubber band ligation).

Which treatments work best for hemorrhoids?

1. Excision is the most effective treatment for thrombosed external hemorrhoids. [11289288] [12972967] [15486746]
2. For prolapsed internal hemorrhoids, the best definitive treatment is traditional hemorrhoidectomy. [17054255] [17380367]
3. Of nonoperative techniques, rubber band ligation produces the lowest rate of recurrence. [1442682] [16252313] [16235372]

Figure 1: PubMed IDs of documents relevant to the answer to a clinical question.

We therefore propose to cluster all the documents relevant to a clinical query into clusters. Given a collection of clinical questions, the documents of each question represent a separate clustering task. In this paper, we present a method that uses multi-objective optimization techniques to cluster the results.

Section 2 gives a brief survey of clustering in general and within EBM. Section 3 introduces the general framework for the multi-objective optimization techniques that we use. Section 4 details the particular approach that we use to integrate multi-objective optimization techniques for clustering. Section 5 presents and discuss the results, and section 6 concludes this paper.

2 Brief Survey of Clustering

Document clustering is an unsupervised machine learning task that focuses on grouping similar doc-

[1] http://www.ncbi.nlm.nih.gov/pubmed

[2] http://www.jfponline.com

uments into clusters (Andrews and Fox, 2007). It has been used in a wide range of tasks such as Web search (Di Marco and Navigli, 2013), topic detection and tracking (Rajaraman and Tan, 2001), training data expansion for supervised classification (Karystinos and Pados, 2000), and multi-document summarization (Wang et al., 2008).

Document clustering has also been used within the domain of EBM. For example, Pratt and Fagan (2000) clustered search results corresponding to a user query. Lin and Demner-Fushman (2007) grouped MEDLINE citations into clusters based on interventions extracted from the document abstracts. Lin et al. (2007) used *K*-Means clustering to group PubMed query results. And Shash and Mollá (2013) used *K*-Means clustering to recover the original clusters used to determine the references relevant to clinical queries.

3 Formulation of Clustering as a Multi-objective Optimization Problem

Most of the existing clustering techniques are based on a single criterion which reflects a single measure of goodness of a partitioning. However, a single cluster quality measure is seldom equally applicable for different kinds of data sets with different characteristics. Hence, it may become necessary to simultaneously optimize several cluster quality measures that can capture different data characteristics. In order to achieve this, the problem of clustering a data set has been posed as one of multiobjective optimization (MOO) (Deb, 2001) in literature. Therefore, the application of sophisticated metaheuristic multiobjective optimization techniques seems appropriate and natural.

Determining the appropriate number of clusters from a given data set is an important consideration in clustering. For this purpose, and also to validate the obtained partitioning, several cluster validity indices have been proposed in the literature. The measure of validity of the clusters should be such that it will be able to impose an ordering of the clusters in terms of their goodness. In the literature there exists many cluster validity indices, that can be grouped mainly in two types: external and internal. In external validity indices, the true partitioning information (provided by user) is utilized while validating a particular partition. But in unsupervised classification, it is often difficult to generate such information. Because of this reason, external validity indices are rarely used to validate partitionings. Some common examples of such indices include *Minkowski scores* (Jiang et al., 2004) and *F-measures* (Saha and Bandyopadhyay, 2013). Internal validity indices rely on the intrinsic structure of the data. Most of the internal validity indices quantify how good a particular partitioning is in terms of the compactness and separation between clusters:

Compactness: This type of indices measures the proximity among the various elements of the cluster. One of the commonly used measures for compactness is the variance.

Separability: This particular type of indices is used in order to differentiate between two clusters. Distance between two cluster centroids is a commonly used measure of separability. This measure is easy to compute and can detect hyperspherical-shaped clusters well.

Some well-known internal cluster validity indices are the BIC-index (Raftery, 1986), CH-index (Caliński and Harabasz, 1974), Silhouette-index (Rousseeuw, 1987), DB-index (Davies and Bouldin, 1979), Dunn-index (Dunn, 1973), XB-index (Xie and Beni, 1991), PS-index (Chou et al., 2002), and I-index (Maulik and Bandyopadhyay, 2002). Maulik and Bandyopadhyay (2002) show the effectiveness of I-index and XB-index compared to the other indices in determining the appropriate number of clusters from the data sets. Being guided by these observations we use these two cluster validity indices as the two objective functions in our proposed multiobjective clustering technique. However it is to be noted that the proposed algorithm is very general, and can be applicable with any sets of cluster validity indices. These objectives are not conflicting to each other, and their (I-index and XB-index) goals are to minimize cluster compactness and maximize cluster separation. But while XB-index maximizes minimum distance between any two cluster centroids, I-index maximizes maximum distance between any two cluster centroids. This difference helps them to determine different sets of clusters from a data set.

3.1 I-Index

The I-index (Maulik and Bandyopadhyay, 2002) is defined in the following equation:

$$I(K) = (\frac{1}{K} \times \frac{\mathcal{E}_1}{\mathcal{E}_K} \times D_K)^p \qquad (1)$$

where K is the number of clusters. Here

$$\mathcal{E}_K = \sum_{k=1}^{K} \sum_{j=1}^{n_k} d_e(\overline{c}_k, \overline{x}_j^k) \qquad (2)$$

and

$$D_K = \max_{i,j=1}^{K} d_e(\overline{c}_i, \overline{c}_j) \qquad (3)$$

where $\overline{c}_j$ denotes the centroid of the jth cluster and $\overline{x}_j^k$ denotes the jth point of the kth cluster. The number n_k is the total number of points present in the kth cluster. The value of K for which I-index takes its maximum value is considered as the appropriate number of clusters.

The index I is a composition of three factors, namely $\frac{1}{K}$, $\frac{\mathcal{E}_1}{\mathcal{E}_K}$ and D_K. The first factor attempts to reduce index I as the value of K is increased. The second factor is the ratio of $\mathcal{E}_1$ and $\mathcal{E}_K$. While the former remains constant for a given data set, the later decreases with increase in K. Hence, because of this term, index I gradually increases as $\mathcal{E}_K$ decreases. This, in turn, denotes that formation of more numbers of compact clusters would be encouraged. Finally, the third factor, D_K, measures the maximum separation between two clusters over all possible pairs of clusters. This increases proportionally with the value of K. However, the ultimate value of this factor can exceed the maximum separation between two points in the data set. Thus, the three factors are found to compete with and balance each other critically. The power p is used to control the contrast between the different cluster configurations. In this paper, we set the value of p to 2.

3.2 XB-Index

The second objective function used in the clustering algorithm is the XB-index. This is one of the widely used internal cluster validity indices in the literature. In 1991, Xie and Beni (1991) developed this cluster validity index (XB-index) which is again based on two properties: compactness and separation. As per the definitions the numerator quantifies the compactness of the partitioning while the denominator quantifies the separation between clusters. Separation is measured based on the Euclidean distance between the cluster centroids. In principle, in order to attain a good partitioning, the compactness value should be minimum and the separation should be maximum. Therefore, in order to obtain a desirable partitioning, the value of XB-index should be minimized after varying the number of clusters in the range, $k = 1, \ldots, K_{max}$. Let K cluster centroids be represented by $\overline{c}_i$ where $1 \leq i \leq K$ and $[u_{ij}]_{K \times n}$ denote the membership matrix for the data. Then the XB-index is defined by the following equation:

$$XB(K) = \frac{\sum_{i=1}^{K} \sum_{j=1}^{n} u_{ij}^2 \|\overline{x}_j - \overline{c}_i\|^2}{n(\min_{i \neq k} \|\overline{c}_i - \overline{c}_k\|^2)} \qquad (4)$$

Thus the two objective functions used for clustering are $f_1 = I$ and $f_2 = \frac{1}{XB}$. The clustering algorithm will attempt to maximize these two indices.

3.3 Multi-Objective Optimization

Multi-objective optimization can be formally stated as follows: find the vector $\overline{x}^* = [x_1^*, x_2^*, \ldots, x_n^*]^T$ of decision variables that simultaneously optimize M objective values

$$\{f_1(\overline{x}), f_2(\overline{x}), \ldots, f_M(\overline{x})\}$$

while satisfying user-defined constraints, if any.

An important concept in MOO is that of domination. Within the context of a maximization problem, a solution $\overline{x_i}$ is said to dominate $\overline{x_j}$ if $\forall k \in 1, 2, \ldots, M$, $f_k(\overline{x_i}) \geq f_k(\overline{x_j})$ and $\exists k \in 1, 2, \ldots, M$, such that $f_k(\overline{x_i}) > f_k(\overline{x_j})$. Among a set of solutions P, the nondominated set of solutions P' are those that are not dominated by any member of the set P. The nondominated set of the entire search space S is called the globally Pareto-optimal set or Pareto front. In general, a MOO algorithm outputs a set of solutions not dominated by any solution encountered by it.

These notions can be illustrated by considering an optimization problem with two objective functions — say, f_1 and f_2 — with five different solutions, as shown in Figure 2. In this example, solutions 3 and 5 dominate all the other three solutions 1, 2 and 4; solutions 3 and 5 are non-dominating to each other, because whereas 5 is better than 3 with respect to f_1, 3 is better than 5 with respect to f_2. Therefore, the Pareto front is made of solutions 3 and 5.

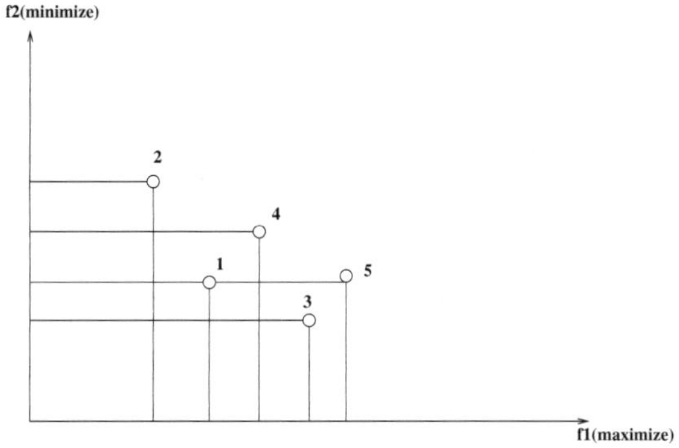

Figure 2: Example of dominance and Pareto optimal front.

4 Proposed Method of Multi-Objective Clustering

This section describes the multi-objective clustering technique, *AMOSA-clus*, in detail. This technique uses AMOSA (Bandyopadhyay et al., 2008) as the underlying optimization strategy. A short description of AMOSA is also provided in this section.

4.1 String Representation and Population Initialization

In *AMOSA-clus* clustering, centroid-based real-encoding is used. Here each member of the archive is encoded as a string that represents the coordinates of the centroids of the partitions. Each string has a different length. Let us assume string i represents the centroids of K_i clusters and the dimension of the data space is d, then the string has length l_i where $l_i = d * K_i$. For example, in the case of two-dimensional space, the string

$$< 12.3\ 1.4 \quad 22.1\ 0.01 \quad 0.0\ 15.3 \quad 10.2\ 7.5 >$$

represents four cluster centroids:

$$(12.3, 1.4), (22.1, 0.01), (0.0, 15.3), (10.2, 7.5)$$

An important point of string encoding is that each centroid is regarded to be indivisible. This means at the time of mutation if we will insert a new centroid all the dimensional values have to be inserted and if we want to delete a centroid all the dimensional values have to be deleted. The number of centroids, K_i, encoded in a string i is chosen randomly between two limits K_{min} and K_{max}. The value is determined using the following equation:

$$K_i = (rand()\text{mod}(K_{max} - 1)) + 2 \qquad (5)$$

Here, $rand()$ is a function returning a random integer number, and K_{max} is the upper-limit of the number of clusters. The minimum number of clusters is assumed to be 2. The number of whole clusters present in a particular string of archive can therefore vary in the range of two to K_{max}. The K_i cluster centroids represented in a string are some randomly selected distinct points from the data set.

4.2 Assignment of Points to Different Clusters and Objective Function Computations

The computation of the objective functions is done in two steps. The first step concerns with the assignment of n points (where n is the total number of points in the data set) to different clusters. In the second step, we compute our two cluster validity indices, XB-index (Xie and Beni, 1991) and I-index (Maulik and Bandyopadhyay, 2002), and use them as two objective functions of the string. Thereafter we simultaneously optimize the two objective functions using the search capability of AMOSA.

4.2.1 Assignment of Points to Different Clusters

In *AMOSA-clus*, the assignment of points to different clusters is done based on the minimum distance based criterion in a similar way as is done in an iteration of the *K*-means clustering algorithm. In particular, any point j is assigned to a cluster k whose centroid has the minimum distance to j. That is:

$$k = argmin_{i=1,\ldots K} d(\overline{x}_j, \overline{c}_i) \qquad (6)$$

K denotes the total number of clusters, $\overline{x}_j$ is the jth data point, $\overline{c}_i$ is the centroid of the ith cluster and $d(\overline{x}_j, \overline{c}_i)$ denotes some distance measure between the data point $\overline{x}_j$ and cluster centroid $\overline{c}_i$.

After assigning all the points to different clusters, the cluster centroids represented in a particular string of the archive are updated by the average of the points which are in a single cluster:

$$\overline{c}_i = \frac{\sum_{j=1}^{n_i} (\overline{x}_j^i)}{n_i}, \quad 1 \leq i \leq K \qquad (7)$$

Where n_i is the number of points in cluster i and $\overline{x}_j^i$ is the jth point of the ith cluster.

4.3 Search Operators

As mentioned earlier the proposed clustering technique uses a multiobjective simulated annealing based technique as the underlying optimization technique. As a simulated annealing step, we need to introduce mutation operations. We introduce three:

Mutation 1: In this mutation each cluster centroid is changed by some small amount. The Laplacian distribution is used in order to generate some completely random numbers. Here each cluster centroid represented in a string is modified with a random variable which is drawn using a Laplacian distribution,

$$p(\epsilon) \propto e^{-\frac{|\epsilon - \mu|}{\delta}}$$

The magnitude of perturbation is measured using the scaling factor δ and μ is the old value at the position which is to be mutated. The scaling factor δ is generally set equal to 1.0. By using the Laplacian distribution a value near the old value is generated and the old value is replaced with the newly generated value. This is applied individually to all the dimensions of a particular centroid if it is selected for mutation.

Mutation 2: This mutation operation is used to reduce the size of the string. A cluster centroid is generated at random and selected to be deleted from the string. This is done to decrease the number of cluster centroids encoded in the string by 1. Cluster centroids are considered to be indivisible. This means as a result of deleting a particular cluster centroid, all the dimensional values are removed.

Mutation 3: This mutation is for incrementing the number of clusters by 1. One new centroid is inserted in the string, and so the number of cluster centroids encoded in the string is incremented by 1. As the cluster centroids are indivisible, all the dimensional values of the centroid, selected randomly, are inserted into the string.

For example, let the string $< 3.5\ 1.5 \quad 2.1\ 4.9 \quad 1.6\ 1.2 >$ represent three cluster centroids in a 2-d plane $(3.5, 1.5)$, $(2.1, 4.9)$, and $(1.6, 1.2)$.

1. For mutation type 1, let position 2 be selected randomly. Then, each dimension of $(2.1, 4.9)$ will be changed by some values generated using the Laplacian distribution.
2. If mutation type 2 is selected, a centroid will be removed from the string. Let centroid 3 be selected for deletion. Then, after deletion, the string will look like $< 3.5\ 1.5 \quad 2.1\ 4.9 >$.
3. In case of third mutation, a new centroid will be added to the string. Let the randomly chosen point from the data set to be added to the string be $(9.7, 2.5)$. After inclusion of this centroid, the string looks like $< 3.5\ 1.5 \quad 2.1\ 4.9 \quad 1.6\ 1.2 \quad 9.7\ 2.5 >$.

In order to generate a new string any one of the above-mentioned mutation types is applied to each string. We have associated equal probability with each of these mutation operations. Thus in 33% cases mutation 1, in 33% cases mutation 2 and in 33% cases mutation 3 take place.

4.4 Selecting a Single Solution from the Pareto Optimal Front

Any multi-objective optimization technique produces a set of non-dominated solutions on its final Pareto optimal front (Deb, 2001). Each of these non-dominated solutions corresponds to a complete assignment of clusters to the data set. In the absence of additional information, any of those solutions can be selected as the optimal solution. But sometimes the user can have labelled information for some portions of the dataset. In this section we describe a process of semi-supervised clustering where, for every question, a portion of the documents are already clustered. This could happen, for example, when someone wants to update some known evidence with further evidence gathered via a document search process. The known information can be used to select one of the non-dominated solutions from the final Pareto front.

In our experiments, we use cluster entropy to determine the best solution from the Pareto front. Cluster entropy is calculated based on the cluster precision, that is the ratio of elements retrieved from a particular source cluster. Thus, to compute the entropy of cluster i, we first determine how many data points from each source cluster j appear in cluster i, relative to the size of cluster i:

$$p_{ij} = \frac{m_{i,j}}{m_i} \tag{8}$$

Then the entropy of cluster i is:

$$Entropy(i) = -\sum_j p_{i,j} \times log_2 p_{i,j} \quad (9)$$

The entropy measure of the clusters generated for a particular data set is the weighted sum of the entropies of all clusters for that data set. Here the weight is the ratio of the cluster size relative to the total number of data points present in the data set.

For every non-dominated solution, the entropy values of the training set are computed, and the solution with lowest (best) entropy is selected. For the results presented in this paper we have chosen a training set of 10% of the total data points.

Let us take an example. Suppose that we have four questions, each one with five documents. The set of documents is:

$$S = \begin{array}{l} \{\{a, b, c, d, e\}, \{f, g, h, i, j\}, \\ \{k, l, m, n, o\}, \{p, q, r, s, t\}\} \end{array}$$

We apply the *AMOSA-clus* clustering technique on these four questions separately. For the sake of this example, for each question we select one document as the training set. Let us assume there is a total of N solutions on the final Pareto front. Based on each of these N solutions, we assign a class label to this training document. Now the entropy value is computed for this one document for each solution. The solution with *minimum entropy* value is selected as the optimal solution. Now the centers encoded in this solution are used to assign class labels to the remaining four documents. Next *AMOSA-clus* is applied on the second question and the same procedure is repeated to calculate the overall entropy for the second question. In this way the *AMOSA-clus* clustering technique is applied for all the questions and the same procedures are repeated to compute the final results.

4.5 The SA Based MOO Algorithm: AMOSA

Archived multi-objective simulated annealing (AMOSA) (Bandyopadhyay et al., 2008) is an efficient MOO version of the simulated annealing (SA) algorithm. Simulated annealing is a search technique for solving difficult optimization problems, which is based on the principles of statistical mechanics (Kirkpatrick et al., 1983). Although the single objective version of SA has been quite popular, its utility in the multi-objective case was limited because of its search-from-a-point nature. Recently Bandyopadhyay et al. (2008) developed an efficient multi-objective version of SA called AMOSA that overcomes this limitation.

The AMOSA algorithm incorporates the concept of an archive where the non-dominated solutions seen so far are stored. Two limits are kept on the size of the archive: a hard or strict limit denoted by *HL*, and a soft limit denoted by *SL*. Given $\gamma > 1$, the algorithm begins with the initialization of a number $(\gamma \times SL)$ of solutions each of which represents a state in the search space. The multiple objective functions are computed. Each solution is refined by using simple hill-climbing and domination relation for a number of iterations. Thereafter the non-dominated solutions are stored in the archive until the size of the archive increases to *SL*. If the size of the archive exceeds *HL*, a single-linkage clustering scheme is used to reduce the size to *HL*. Then, one of the points is randomly selected from the archive. This is taken as the current-pt, or the initial solution, at temperature $T = Tmax$. The current-pt is perturbed/mutated to generate a new solution named new-pt, and its objective functions are computed. The domination status of the new-pt is checked with respect to the current-pt and the solutions in the archive. A new quantity called amount of domination, $\Delta dom(a, b)$ between two solutions a and b is defined as follows:

$$\Delta dom(a, b) = \prod_{i=1, f_i(a) \neq f_i(b)}^{M} \frac{f_i(a) - f_i(b)}{R_i} \quad (10)$$

where $f_i(a)$ and $f_i(b)$ are the ith objective values of the two solutions, R_i is the corresponding range of the objective function and M is the number of objective functions. Based on domination status different cases may arise viz., accept the (i) new-pt, (ii) current-pt, or, (iii) a solution from the archive. Again, in case of overflow of the archive, clustering is used to reduce its size to *HL*. The process is repeated *iter* times for each temperature that is annealed with a cooling rate of $\alpha(< 1)$ till the minimum temperature $Tmin$ is attained. The process thereafter stops, and the archive contains the final non-dominated solutions.

In order to reduce the temperature, we have used geometric cooling: $T_{k+1} = \alpha \times T_k$ where α is the cooling rate. We have used $\alpha = 0.9$ in the current paper. We use AMOSA as the underlying MOO technique in this work because of its improved performance over some other well-known MOO algorithms especially for three or more objectives (Bandyopadhyay et al., 2008).

5 Results

Below we present the results based on a random partition of 276 clinical questions from the corpus by Mollá and Santiago-Martínez (2011). Each question has an average of 5.89 documents. The corpus is based on the material from the Clinical Inquiries section of the Journal of Family Practice. The data set has information about the question, the answer, and the documents that are relevant to each part of the answer, as illustrated in the example of Figure 1. The documents of each of the answer parts determines a cluster. The *AMOSA-clus* clustering technique is therefore applied on each question individually. The average entropy value of all the questions is then calculated. The parameters of the *AMOSA-clus* clustering technique are as follows: *SL*=100 *HL*=50, *iter*=50, *Tmax*=100, *Tmin*=0.0001 and cooling rate $\alpha = 0.9$.

Table 1 compares the entropy results for clustering using *AMOSA-clus* with a fixed and variable number of clusters. We experimented with two cluster measures of document distance: Euclidean distance, and cosine distance. The cosine distance is computed as 1-cosine similarity. Strictly speaking this is not a distance metric but it is included to compare with the results presented by Shash and Mollá (2013), who reported optimal results by using *K*-means with this use of the cosine distance, and which we also include in the table as the baseline.[3] We include the Euclidean distance since this is the standard metric used for *K*-means clustering and is also reported by Shash and Mollá (2013). All the results reported in the table, included the *K*-means baseline, are based on the same partition of 276 questions from the corpus developed by Mollá and Santiago-Martínez (2011).

Each document is represented as a vector of *tf.idf* values based on stemmed and lowercased words, with stop words removed.

5.1 Finding the Number of Clusters

The training set includes information about the actual number of clusters. We have used this information to test *AMOSA-clus*' ability to determine the optimal number of clusters, by implementing two variants: *AMOSA-clus1* performs clustering by fixing the number of clusters to the number provided by the corpus, whereas *AMOSA-clus2* automatically determines the optimal number of clusters.

[3]Our baseline is a replication of the original paper's experiment and the results are different.

Table 2: Measure of the error of number of clusters of *AMOSA-clus2* and a number of popular methods.

Method	Error
AMOSA-clus2 Cosine	1.90
AMOSA-clus2 Euclidean	1.91
$k = 1$	3.91
$k = 2$	2.14
$k = 3$	2.38
$k = 4$	4.61
Rule of Thumb	2.56
Cover	1.98

AMOSA-clus2 is executed on each question by varying the number of clusters in a range between 2 and $\sqrt{n}$ where n is the number of documents per question, and using the above mentioned indices I-index and XB-index to determine the best solution. The average number of clusters identified by this procedure for each question is 2.51 and 2.34, respectively, with cosine and Euclidean distance measurements. The average number of clusters in the actual annotated set is 2.38. Since entropy is based on cluster precision, a larger number of clusters will naturally lead to a better value of entropy, reaching a perfect zero when there are as many clusters as documents. Consequently, we can only rely on the Euclidean metric (with average 2.34 clusters) to assess the efficacy of the automatic selection of number of clusters. We observe that the results of *AMOSA-clus2* using the Euclidean metric is slightly better than *AMOSA-clus1*, which gives some evidence that the proposed *AMOSA-clus2* technique to determine the number of clusters is promising.

Next we have compared the generated number of clusters with the known number of clusters using the mean of the squares of the errors:

$$error = \frac{\sum_i (target_i - predicted_i)^2}{\#\ of\ questions} \quad (11)$$

Table 2 compares the error in the generation of numbers of clusters between *AMOSA-clus2* and a set of heuristics widely used in the literature: fixed number of clusters ($k = 1, 2, 3, 4$), the Rule

Table 1: Average Entropy values obtained by two variants of *AMOSA-clus* and a baseline *K*-means clustering technique for whole XML files; here *AMOSA-clus1*: *AMOSA-clus* with fixed number of clusters, *AMOSA-clus2*: *AMOSA-clus* with variable number of clusters, *K*-means: *K*-means with fixed number of clusters; best: entropy value of the solutions selected by the procedure described in Section 4.4; average: average entropy of all the solutions present on the final Pareto front.

Distance Measure	*AMOSA-clus1*		*AMOSA-clus2*		*K*-means (baseline)
	best	average	best	average	
Euclidean	0.190	0.249	0.177	0.235	0.240
Cosine	0.187	0.231	0.177	0.230	0.237

of Thumb ($k = \sqrt{n/2}$) (Mardia et al., 1979), and the cover method (Can and Esen A. Ozkarahan, 1990). We observe that the error of *AMOSA-clus2* is lowest in both distance measures, cosine and Euclidean. We conducted a Wilcoxon signed-rank test and observed that the differences in the squared errors between the *AMOSA-clus2* variants and the cover method are statistically significant.

5.2 Semi-supervised Setting

Each *AMOSA-clus1* and *AMOSA-clus2* has been run both in a semi-supervised setting and a fully unsupervised setting. In the semi-supervised setting, the information of 10% of the documents relevant to a question is used to select the best non-domimant solution from the Pareto front as described in Section 4.4. The entropy reported in the *best* column of Table 1 indicates the entropy values after disregarding the 10% documents used to select the solution. In the unsupervised setting, we report the average of all solutions of the Pareto front and is presented in the *average* column. We observe that the semi-supervised approach produces a better (lower) entropy, and a Wilcoxon signed-rank test reveals that the difference with respect to the baseline *K*-means clustering method is statistically significant. The results of the unsupervised setting also have a statistically significant difference with the baseline, though we can observe that the difference is much lesser and in one case it is worse.

6 Conclusions

We have presented a novel approach for clustering documents that is based on the use of multi-objective optimization (MOO), for the task of splitting the documents relevant to the answer of a clinical question into each of the answer parts. The MOO approach is based on a variant of Archived Multi-Objective Simulated Annealing (AMOSA) that we call *AMOSA-clus*, which uses cluster-based evaluation indices as the objectives to optimize. Even though the results do not show an improvement over a baseline of *K*-means reported in the literature, a semi-supervised variant shows an improvement over the baseline. Our experiments show the effectiveness of the use of MOO techniques for this clustering task in particular. Given the generality of the approach proposed, it is reasonably to conclude that these MOO techniques would be useful in a general clustering setting.

We have experimented with a variant that uses the known cluster numbers, and another variant that automatically determines the optimal number of clusters. The good results of the option with automatic number of clusters show the promising potential of this approach.

The improvement of results by using MOO techniques are highly encouraging. Further work can be done in several fronts. First of all, further experiments are required to improve the efficacy of the automatic selection of the number of clusters. Also, it is desirable to test whether *AMOSA-clus* improves the results in other clustering applications such as the ones briefly mentioned in Section 2. In our experiments we used the *I* and XB indices as the objective functions to optimise due to their general popularity. It would be interesting to test the use of other combinations of cluster validity indices, or even to build a MOO system that uses a larger selection of them.

Within the area of multi-document summarization, further work will focus on the determination of techniques of extraction or generation of topic labels that could be used for the generation of the final summaries.

References

Nicholas O. Andrews and Edward A. Fox. 2007. Recent Developments in Document Clustering. Technical report, Virginia Tech.

Sanghamitra Bandyopadhyay, Sriparna Saha, Ujjwal Maulik, and Kalyanmoy Deb. 2008. A simulated annealing based multi-objective optimization algorithm: AMOSA. *IEEE Transactions on Evolutionary Computation*, 12(3):269–283.

R. B. Caliński and J. Harabasz. 1974. A dendrite method for cluster analysis. *Comm. in Stat.*, 3:1–27.

Fazli Can and Esen A. Ozkarahan. 1990. Concepts and Effectiveness of the Cover-Coefficient-Based Clustering Methodology for Text Databases. *ACM Transactions on Database Systems*, 15(4):483–517.

Chien-Hsing Chou, Mu-Chun Su, and Eugene Lai. 2002. Symmetry as a new measure for cluster validity. In *2nd WSEAS Int. Conf. on Scientific Computation and Soft Computing*, pages 209–213. Crete, Greece.

David L. Davies and Donald W. Bouldin. 1979. A cluster separation measure. *IEEE Transactions on Pattern Analysis and Machine Intelligence*, 1:224–227.

Kalyanmoy Deb. 2001. *Multi-objective Optimization Using Evolutionary Algorithms*. John Wiley and Sons, Ltd, England.

Antonio Di Marco and Roberto Navigli. 2013. Clustering and Diversifying Web Search Results with Graph-Based Word Sense Induction. *Computational Linguistics*, 39(3):709–754, November.

J. C. Dunn. 1973. A fuzzy relative of the ISODATA process and its use in detecting compact well-separated clusters. *Journal of Cybernetics*, 3:32–57.

Daxin Jiang, Chun Tang, and Aidong Zhang. 2004. Cluster analysis for gene-expression data: A survey. *IEEE Trans. Knowledge Data Eng.*, 16:1370–1386.

G N Karystinos and D A Pados. 2000. On overfitting, generalization, and randomly expanded training sets. *IEEE transactions on neural networks / a publication of the IEEE Neural Networks Council*, 11(5):1050–7, January.

S. Kirkpatrick, C. D. Gelatt, and M. P. Vecchi. 1983. Optimization by simulated annealing. *Science*, 220:671–680.

Jimmy J. Lin and Dina Demner-Fushman. 2007. Semantic clustering of answers to clinical questions. In *AMIA Annual Symposium Proceedings*.

Yongjing Lin, Wenyuan Li, Keke Chen, and Ying Liu. 2007. A Document Clustering and Ranking System for Exploring {MEDLINE} Citations. *Journal of the American Medical Informatics Association*, 14(5):651–661.

Kanti V. Mardia, John T. Kent, and John M. Bibby. 1979. *Multivariate Analysis*. Academic Press, London.

Ujjwal Maulik and Sanghamitra Bandyopadhyay. 2002. Performance evaluation of some clustering algorithms and validity indices. *IEEE Transactions on Pattern Analysis and Machine Intelligence*, 24(12):1650–1654.

Diego Mollá and Maria Elena Santiago-Martínez. 2011. Development of a Corpus for Evidence Based Medicine Summarisation. In *Proceedings of the Australasian Language Technology Workshop*.

Wanda Pratt and Lawrence Fagan. 2000. The Usefulness of Dynamically Categorizing Search Results. *Journal of the American Medical Informatics Association*, 7(6):605–617.

A. Raftery. 1986. A note on Bayes factors for log-linear contingency table models with vague prior information. *Journal of the Royal Statistical Society*, 48(2):249–250.

Kanagasabi Rajaraman and Ah-Hwee Tan. 2001. Topic Detection, Tracking, and Trend Analysis Using Self- Organizing Neural Networks. In *PAKDD '01 Proceedings of the 5th Pacific-Asia Conference on Knowledge Discovery and Data Mining*, pages 102–107, London. Springer-Verlag.

Peter J. Rousseeuw. 1987. Silhouettes: A graphical aid to the interpretation and validation of cluster analysis. *J. Comp App. Math*, 20:53–65.

David L Sackett, William M Rosenberg, Jamuir Gray, R Brian Haynes, and W Scott Richardson. 1996. Evidence Based Medicine: What it is and what it isn't. *BMJ*, 312(7023):71–72.

Sriparna Saha and Sanghamitra Bandyopadhyay. 2013. A generalized automatic clustering algorithm in a multiobjective framework. *Appl. Soft Comput.*, 13(1):89–108.

SF Shash and D Mollá. 2013. Clustering of Medical Publications for Evidence Based Medicine Summarisation. In *Artificial Intelligence in Medicine*, pages 305–309.

Dingding Wang, Shenghuo Zhu, Tao Li, Yun Chi, and Yihon Gong. 2008. Integrating Clustering and Multi-document Summarization to Improve Document Understanding. In *Proceedings of the 17th ACM conference on Information and knowledge management*, pages 1435–1436.

Xuanli Lisa Xie and Gerardo Beni. 1991. A validity measure for fuzzy clustering. *IEEE Transactions on Pattern Analysis and Machine Intelligence*, 13:841–847.

A Study: From Electronic Laboratory Notebooks to Generated Queries for Literature Recommendation

Oldooz Dianat, Cécile Paris, and Stephen Wan
CSIRO Computational Informatics
Sydney, Australia
firstname.lastname@csiro.au

Abstract

Relating one's research to the vast body of scientific knowledge is a difficult task; the sheer volume of literature makes it difficult to keep up-to-date with scientific developments. Particularly when research is on-going, keeping track of related work is especially important to avoid an unintended duplication of effort. We outline a novel approach to this problem that uses the text in an Electronic Laboratory Notebook (ELN) as a representation of an experimental context in the field of Chemistry. The contribution of this work is to situate the literature recommendation task within the context of the user's experimental information needs. We find that our approach to transform the ELN text into queries for use with PubMed is able to recover a subset of user bibliographies. We find that alternative methods for query generation that capture both scientific terminology and salient terms in the ELN complement each other.

1 Introduction

Identifying the relationship between one's research and the ever growing body of scientific knowledge is a time-consuming and laborious task. The sheer volume of existing literature makes it difficult to stay up-to-date with new scientific developments. Furthermore, this task is continual: this relationship must be revisited periodically so that one can avoid unintended overlaps with work published in parallel.

To help keep up with advances by our scientific peers, we can use a number of tools to provide continual exposure to newly published work. These can range from collaborative bibliography tools with a social network component, for example, the Mendeley application[1]. However, such tools do not have a mechanism to capture the information needs of a researcher that might change on a daily or weekly basis due to the outcomes of experiments.

In this work, we recognise the increasing use of Electronic Laboratory Notebooks (ELNs) in our research environments to capture a representation of research as it progresses. As part of the project described in this paper, we introduce the novel use of the text in the ELNs as a representation of the user's context—specifically, their current experimental context—that provides insights on their information needs. Our aim is to devise a system to transform this context into queries for a scientific literature search engine, and then suggest references that may be relevant.

This paper describes the initial exploration in generating queries from the on-going experimental context as represented in ELNs. In this work in progress, we investigate the effectiveness of different types of information extracted from ELN content for the purposes of suggesting relevant literature.

The ability to suggest references in the context of reading an ELN entry is potentially useful in many contexts. Indeed, in our user study, we noted that users often mentioned the need to identify relevant literature based on content from the ELN entry. For example, a doctoral student may have identified closely related work to scope the thesis, but may nevertheless want to monitor the literature to ensure that the scoping remains novel. Using our approach, as she writes up her daily work in the ELN, our system would look for and suggest related work to read, reducing the risk that recently published work that is closely related goes by unnoticed.

We conducted our studies with the LabTrove

[1] http://www.mendeley.com/

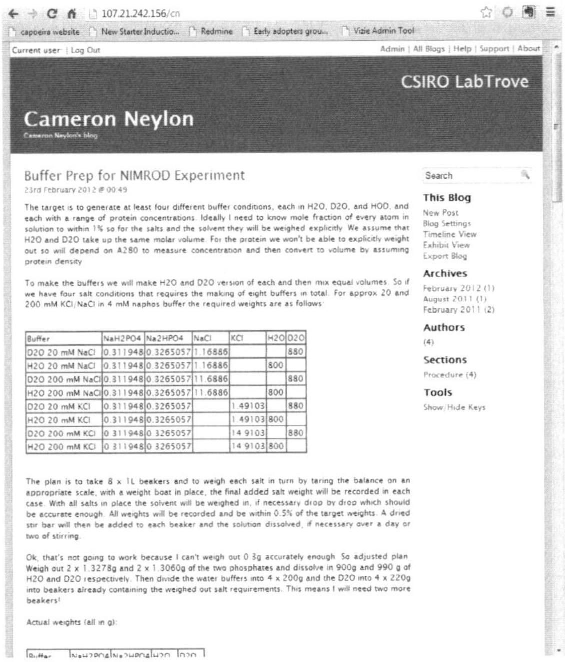

Figure 1: A LabTrove blog entry by Cameron Neylon during his affiliation with the University of Southampton. (Reproduced with permission from Cameron Neylon.)

tool[2] (Milsted et al., 2013), an ELN based on open source webblog software. LabTrove, designed by the University of Southampton, has been designed with Chemistry researchers in mind, allowing them to post daily updates about their research outcomes. Although we focus on chemistry ELN entries in this work, LabTrove is potentially more widely usable by other researchers in the experimental sciences. A screenshot of the LabTrove interface is presented in Figure 1.

Ideally, we would conduct user studies to evaluate the effectiveness of the suggested references for a knowledge discovery task; however, the time required for such a study makes this approach prohibitive for exploratory research. In lieu of such studies, we describe the extent to which generated queries can reconstruct the bibliographies of users, a slightly different scenario to knowledge discovery. An instance of the LabTrove ELN was in use at the chemistry department in the University of New South Wales. Users of LabTrove at the university that were interested in collaborating with us were identified by the university library which helps to host the ELN. The users provided access to their LabTrove entries and their research bibliographies.

[2]http://www.labtrove.org/

Figure 2: Automatically detected chemical entities and suggested PubMed references are shown after the main blog entry.

This study is based on the blogs and bibliographies of three users. Finding additional data was difficult given our recruiting constraints. Nevertheless, we are able to report on preliminary findings that indicate the extent to which the different query generation methods are able to reconstruct the gold standard bibliographic information. This provides insights as to the strengths and weaknesses of the different approaches to query generation when used for this scenario. We find that alternative methods that capture both scientific terminology and salient terms in the ELN complement each other.

In the remainder of this report, we present an overview of the system in Section 2. We describe the data used in this study in Section 3. The algorithms for generating queries from ELN content are described in Section 4. We present our evaluation of different query generation methods in Section 5. We discuss the results obtained and outline future work in Section 6. Section 7 describes related work in suggesting scientific literature and evaluating these query generation methods. We finish with concluding remarks in Section 8.

2 A System Description

We have deployed a version of LabTrove with our code to provide extra linked data at the university for the participants who have volunteered to trial. To provide links to relevant scientific literature from the ELN entries, we instrumented Lab-

Trove such that, as an ELN user reads a blog entry (that he or she is entitled to read), a list of automatically detected chemical entities are presented following the main text entry. These entities are detected using the OSCAR tool for Named Entity Recognition in chemistry literature (version 4 (Jessop et al., 2011)). For a description of earlier OSCAR versions, see Corbett and Murray-Rust (2006) and Corbett et al. (2007)).[3]

In this deployed version, to automatically suggest scientific literature, we use the chemical named entities as queries which are sent to the PubMed Entrez Application Programming Interface (API). This API provides references from the PubMed repository of scientific literature, bibliographic details and abstracts for references matching the query.

We modified the blog display page to provide extra linked data. A screenshot of the CSIRO plugin is presented in Figure 2. Within the interface, the user can decide whether or not to view extra linked data that we have associated with the blog text (clearly indicating, for legal reasons, that this is added data, kept separate to the author's original entry).

The linked data includes relevant chemical properties which are obtained by sending the chemical named entities as queries to the ChemSpider[4] web services maintained by the Royal Chemistry Society. Our plugin for LabTrove also suggests scientific publications retrieved from the PubMed API to help show what existing literature may be relevant to blog content. The user can request suggested references triggering the on-demand retrieval of search results from PubMed. These are presented alongside the list of detected chemical entities. Any user clickthrough data is stored in a log to allow for automatic tuning of the algorithms.[5]

3 The LabTrove Users and their Data

We used the blog posts of 3 users who provided matching bibliographies for their blogs, refered to hereafter as L, R and D.[6] An overview of the descriptive statistics of the users' ELN blogs is presented in Table 1. The users belong to the same research group and share the same research supervisor. The supervisor is known to be a strong advocate for the use of ELNs, and the group uses the ELN on a regular basis within their research meetings.

user	num of posts
L	571
R	148
D	1078

Table 1: Number of posts for our three users.

In our user study, we found that the main use of the ELN was to record and archive daily experimental data. The ELN is also used, however, for a number of other research tasks, such as:

1. Experimentation in using the ELN itself;
2. Archiving supporting research documents like reference files;
3. Archiving draft publication files; and
4. Record iterations of thesis structure and argument.

As such, the text collection are a heterogeneous collection. In this preliminary investigation, we assume that each blog (containing a series of entries) is about a single research goal and that the user has a single bibliographic file against which we can compare suggested references. However, in reality, not all of the blog entries are related to an overarching research goal that might subsume a series of experiments. Indeed, a blog may span multiple research goals, each deserving a separate set of bibliographic recommendations.

4 Query Generation

In our system design, the suggestion of references from ELN blog entries would ideally perform the following broad steps:

1. Represent the user's experimental context as a query;
2. Retrieve scientific publications to suggest (for this user context);
3. Filter candidate suggestions; and
4. Present the suggestions to the user.

[3]The OSCAR tools is run every night to process new ELN entries.

[4]www.chemspider.com

[5]This is a feature to be explored in future work.

[6]A fourth user, W, also provided a bibliography. However, the bibliography was relatively small and did not have a substantial overlap with PubMed references.

To simplify our investigation of suggesting references, in this work, we consider steps 1, 2 and 4 of the problem. We do not include any filters (step 3) to vet the suggestions against a list of references representing the user's prior reading history. Although such a filter would undoubtedly be useful (we return to this point in Section 6), our focus here is in characterising the transformation process from ELN content to query formulation.

For this investigation, we used four approaches for creating queries from the ELN content, specifically:

1. Chemical entities in a single ELN post;
2. The title of a single ELN post;
3. Salient terms from a single post; and
4. Overlapping terms from adjacent posts.

The first method has been deployed for the participants to trial. In this paper, however, we investigate the pros and cons of all methods.

Each method provides an ordered list of candidate query terms. However, the complete set of candidate query terms may be too restrictive to retrieve results. To determine the final set of query terms resulting from each of the four approaches, we use a filtering method for query terms which we refer to here as *iterative back-off*. This filter identifies the largest query set that retrieves results from PubMed. Essentially, the approach, outlined in Algorithm 1, continually drops the least ranked candidate until a non-null set is returned by the PubMed API. In this way, results are as specific as possible.

```
Data: Set of unique words, W
Result: Set of query words, Q where Q ⊂ W
Initialisation;
Q ← W;
Results ← pubmed(Q);
while Results is empty do
    WeakItem ← min_q(score(q) : for q in Q);
    Q ← Q \ WeakItem;
    Results ← pubmed(Q);
end
return Q;
```

Algorithm 1: The algorithm for iteratively trying queries until a non-null result is obtained from PubMed.

As a parameter, this filter requires a scoring function, $score(q)$, defined for each set of candidate terms. This function is used for sorting purposes. In the remainder of this section, we describe the four methods and the relevant scoring functions.

4.1 Chemical Entities in a Single ELN Post

Intuitively, chemical knowledge related to the user's current work may be useful in the query generation process. A starting point for this is to identify which words and phrases are in fact part of chemistry terminology and then to use these as queries. For each post in an ELN blog, the OSCAR tool provides a list of chemical entities referenced in the text.

Each of these entities has an associated confidence score from OSCAR. For the iterative back-off, we use this confidence score to sort the list of query candidates (based on chemical entities) in reverse order.

4.2 The Title of a Single ELN Post

As an alternative to using chemical terms as indicators of the experimental focus of a blog post, we can also use the words from the title. Title words are generally chosen to reflect the focus of the blog. Indeed this heuristic is used in text summarisation approaches to suggest keywords (Edmundson, 1969).

For each post, we retrieve the title, identify the words, and remove stopwords.[7] We use the relative placement within the title as a scoring mechanism for the iterative back-off method.

4.3 Salient Terms from a Single Post

To rank unique words (except for stopwords) based on their salience in the text we use one of two standard weighting methods: (1) Term Frequency (TF), or (2) Term Frequency with an Inverse Document Frequency factor (TF.IDF) (for an overview of Information Retrieval methods including TF and TF.IDF, see Manning et al. (2008).)

A priori, it is unclear as to which weighting method will be best, and so we test both variants in this work. The words with a high TF can be interpreted as an indicator of the content of the document. However, some words like "water" may occur often in the user's ELN blog. This could

[7] In the remaining methods, we define words as space delimited tokens with all non-alphanumeric characters replaced by space.

signify that it is a less important reactant in the experiment since it is a common substance used in all the user's experiments. This may be captured by the TF.IDF weighting.

Given a particular weighting scheme, to find the candidate list of query terms, we obtain a reverse sort of the unique words in the text (after removing stopwords) and then apply the iterative back-off approach to obtain a query set.

4.4 Overlapping Terms from Adjacent Posts

In this method, we try to make use of more context to find suggested literature. The intuition is that additional contextual information, for example the wider research goal of the user, will help provide better query terms. For example, in some ELN blogs, results for control conditions might be written up in a separate entry to the results for the test conditions for the independent variable. Using content from more than one LabTrove blog entry may thus provide additional experimental context.

We start by considering the preceding post to the post in question, using a Markov assumption that this captures the relevant experimental context. We compile unique words for both post_i and post_{i-1}. We then take the intersection of these two sets. In this particular study, the list is assumed to be unranked (or tied). However, one could also employ a weighting scheme like TF or TF.IDF to rank the words. To help make the query more specific, we also only keep queries that are longer than 2 words.

We hypothesise that any experimental context that is useful in generating a query will be repeated in the adjacent posts. The advantage to this approach is its simplicity, we do not need to employ computationally expensive methods to identify in advance the set of posts in a blog that corresponds to a single research goal. We borrow from work in multi-document summarisation (for example, see Barzilay et al. (1999)) which treats words mentioned in multiple texts (in this case, both posts) as being particularly important in capturing background information.

5 Evaluation

In this investigation, we are interested in testing different query generation methods that are based on the experimental context found in the ELN blog. Although we intend for the suggestion of new literature to be presented during a knowledge discovery task, for simplicity, we examine the effects of the query generation methods on a bibliography reconstruction task for each of the three participant's blogs.

We do note, however, this ground truth version of "relevance" is limited for two reasons. Firstly, the bibliography is not exhaustive: that is, it does not evaluate the ability to count related articles outside the bibliography as useful suggestions and so it may miss relevant work (which is, in a way, the point of suggesting references). Secondly, the bibliography may also be too broad, containing not only work related to the central focus of the blog (or the user's core research), but any literature that the user deemed worth curating. While the evaluation of suggested literature based on bibliographies is not a perfect fit with the knowledge discovery application, it does allow us to study the query generation methods using intrinsic methods.

As an additional constraint in this work, we limit our investigations to PubMed which only contains a subset of research in the Analytical Chemistry, namely those to do with the Life Sciences. Research documented in the ELN that lies outside of this domain cannot be evaluated in this work.

Because of these limitations, the absolute value of the recall and precision metrics is not the focus of the study. Our aim is not to reconstruct the bibliographies. We use the metrics simply to rank the different query generation methods under review in this work.

5.1 Preparing the Bibliography Gold Standards

We used the three bibliographies volunteered by the users: L, R and D. The bibliographic files required preprocessing to convert them into sets of PubMed references, against which we compare our suggested references. The bibliographies were originally provided in EndNote format. Each EndNote file was converted into plain text, where each bibligraphic entry was transformed into a reference, one reference per line.[8]

We wrote a Python script to use the article title and date from the reference as search parameters in PubMed. Those entries that retrieved a corresponding PubMed identifier were kept and stored in a gold standard set for evaluation.

[8]We used a free evaluation copy of EndNote X6.0.1 (Bld 6599) for this conversion.

5.2 Procedure

We now describe the procedure for computing the suggested references that we wish to evaluate. For this study, we computed a set of references for each approach described above.

For each user blog, we compiled a suggested bibliography by using the following procedure:

1. For each blog entry in the blog, find suggested references (max 100) for the blog entry, using one of the above query generation procedures;

2. Take the union of all suggested references (excluding duplicates) and compare these to the user bibliography.

We repeated this procedure with each method for query generation outlined above. For each application of this procedure, we obtain a set of suggested PubMed unique identifiers. We compare these to the gold standard bibliographic sets (one for each user) of PubMed identifiers, and measure performance using the standard Information Retrieval (IR) metrics of recall and precision (for an overview of IR evaluation, see Salton and McGill (1983)).

5.3 Experiment Results

In this section, we provide the raw results from our evaluations against user bibliographies. As highlighted above, given the limitations of this evaluation framework, we are primarily interested in using the relative values to rank our query generation methods and to understand how they may be improved. The recall results are presented in Table 2 and the precision scores are presented in Table 3.

Note that the precision scores are very low because the suggested references are the union of the suggested references for each blog. We note however that Parra and Brusilovsky (2009) also report precision scores in similar ranges, indicating that other researchers have found the problem of literature recommendation to be a difficult problem with regard to precision. We list the precision results here for completeness but base our rankings on recall results, since this indicates the ability to find any relevant results. Due to the small sample size, we are unable to report significance. However, the rankings are still useful in determining which query generation methods show the most promise for further development.

Method	L	R	D	Ave.
OSCAR4	3.4%	2.3%	2.4%	2.7%
Expt.	6.9%	0.2%	3.2%	3.4%
Title	3.2%	3.2%	4.0%	3.7%
TF.IDF	5.1%	1.6%	4.4%	3.7%
TF	8.6%	1.3%	7.3%	5.7%

Table 2: Recall scores (expressed as a percentage) for each method used independently. Legend: Columns show the recall scores for the three blogs and the average recall. "Expt." stands for experimental context.

Method	L	R	D	Ave.
Title	0.2%	0.2%	0.1%	0.2%
TF.IDF	0.1%	0.3%	0.2%	0.2%
Expt.	0.4%	0.1%	0.2%	0.2%
OSCAR4	0.2%	0.7%	0.1%	0.3%
TF	0.4%	0.2%	0.2%	0.3%

Table 3: Precision scores (expressed as a percentage) for each method used independently. Legend: Columns show the precision scores for the three blogs and the average recall. "Expt." stands for experimental context.

We find that, with regard to recall, the best method for suggesting references is based on the Salience (TF) method using term frequencies for choosing keywords.

To determine if the approaches are complementary in nature, we combine them to see the effect on recall. If the margin of improvement is large enough, this suggests that relevant references being retrieved are not overlapping, and that the approaches can usefully be combined. We present the recall results in Table 4 (with precision results in Table 5 presented for completeness).

We find that the best result overall is indeed to use all approaches, for which we see an average recall of 9.3%. This represents almost 60% increase in recall over the best performing single method (Salience TF) which achieved a recall of 5.7% on average. Note however that this combined result is only marginally better than the slightly less complex combination which uses the Title, OSCAR4 and Salience (TF), which obtains a recall of 9.2%.

6 Discussion and Future Work

There are a two research avenues we would like to pursue: (1) improving the methods for query generation, (2) conducting further experimentation on

Method	L	R	D	Ave.
M1	5.9%	5.3%	5.7%	5.6%
M2	11.3%	6.0%	10.2%	9.2%
M3	11.5%	6.0%	10.5%	9.3%

Table 4: Recall scores (expressed as a percentage) for method used in combination. Legend: Columns show the recall scores for the three blogs and the average recall. M1: Title, OSCAR4 methods; M2: M1 with TF; M3: M2 with Experimental Context.

Method	L	R	D	Ave.
M1	0.2%	0.3%	0.0%	0.2%
M2	0.2%	0.2%	0.1%	0.2%
M3	0.2%	0.2%	0.1%	0.2%

Table 5: Precision scores (expressed as a percentage) for method used in combination. Legend: Columns show the precision scores for the three blogs and the average recall. M1: Title, OSCAR4 methods; M2: M1 with TF; M3: M2 with Experimental Context.

performance.

In this study, we found that the Salience (TF) method is the best approach, which accords well with textbook approaches to generic query generation. However, it is interesting to note that using chemical entities retrieves a complementary set of references to the Salience (TF) method, as evidenced by the gain in recall performance as we combine these approaches.

Better methods for incorporating chemistry domain information might still be possible, perhaps by using the IDF approach to model which chemical entities are salient across the entire blog and thus across the experimental context. In addition, we can experiment with the use of the chemical named entities detected by the OSCAR tool that describe chemical processes.

Implementation of a larger experimental context method was not overly successful. Recall that our hypothesis was that what was common between two adjacent posts would be important. Even when using the experimental context with other methods (M3), we only observed a slight benefit.

There are a number alternative approaches to using a larger experimental context. Perhaps it might be the differences and not the similarities between the posts that are more useful as query terms for retrieving literature.

We could also take a different approach to capturing the research goals of the student as captured by the blog. It may be the case that more than one post is required for this purpose, or that the simple adjacency of posts is not sufficient for capturing the context of the overaching research goals in general. If the latter, we could first segment the blog into portions, where each portion represents a linguistically coherent set of text describing laboratory tasks that correlates to some larger research goal. We could then generate a query for each segment. For this task, we might employ text segmentation approaches which use dramatic changes in vocabulary to signify a new topical segment (for example, see Hearst (1994) as the seminal work in such text segmentation approaches). This might also hopefully improve recall since retrieval would be based on segments and not blog posts.

Interestingly, the evaluation results suggest that the blogs might themselves be different. For example, the suggested references for ELN Blog R consistently under-performs compared to Blog L and D. This could be because there are fewer entries in Blog R. As we are using only three blogs (limited by the number of bibliographies we were provided), our results might be heavily affected by the individual variations in the blogs. Ideally, we would repeat this experiment with a larger number of blogs to gain a more stable impression of the strengths and weaknesses of the various query generation methods.

We can also employ post-processing methods on both the query generation and literature retrieval processes. Query expansion methods (for example, see Jones et al. (2006)) could help select additional search terms for the set of query terms selected after the iterative back-off process. In addition, for a real knowledge discovery scenario, we could filter the retrieved references that the user is already aware of.

The evaluation task presented here simply looked at strict comparisons against user bibliographies. As described in Section 5, this approach does not have the ability to reward relevant articles that do not belong to the gold standard. One avenue for future research is to explore methods like those described in (Büttcher et al., 2007) to handle unknown documents for which we have no relevance judgements.[9]

[9]We thank the anonymous reviewers for this suggestion.

We could also consider a looser evaluation which examines articles commonly cited by the suggested references, as is done in (Jha et al., 2013). This would allow the ability to detect older seminal articles that we may not be able to recover using generated queries if that seminal work uses vocabulary that is different to contemporary research. Appropriately handling these by counting them as matched if one or more suggested references cite them may help provide a better understanding of the performance of the system.

Finally, we are now collecting user interface data with which to conduct user studies. By analysing cases where the user clicked the PubMed links based on the abstract of the suggested reference, we may be able to learn if the system is able to present useful recommendation in a real research context.

7 Related Work

Representing the user's context as part of an information need is an open research question. In related work by Wan and Paris (2008), the user's reading context was used to summarise Wikipedia text[10]. Similar methods have been used for summarising scientific literature to capture the user's context (Mei and Zhai, 2008).

There are a number of related works sharing the same motivation of helping researchers keep in touch with current scientific developments. Research in automatically generating literature surveys focuses on generating the text of the survey using summarisation methods (for example, see Mohammad et al. (2009)). However, that work does not tackle the problem of suggesting the references themselves. In work by Jha et al. (2013), articles are retrieved from a query provided by the user and a survey is generated from these. The authors used a results expansion method that adds certain cited references from the retrieved articles. Although they also retrieve references, our problem is different in that we have to automate the query generation from some textual documents representing the user's experimental context.

The work described here is more akin to link creation, where we postulate a link from an ELN entry to an article. In most link creation work, there is a pre-existing list of potential candidates to link to. For example, in work on linking Wikipedia pages, the candidate pages are the existing wikipedia pages whose title occurs in the potential linking page (for example, see Milne and Witten (2008)). In our case, such a correspondence between the linking page and the potential link target does not exist.

Previous work has examined the problem of recommending articles to users, but this has usually been performed using topic modelling approaches to identify similarities amongst articles (Wang and Blei, 2011), or else capitalising on social and collaborative networks for sharing publications like CiteULike[11], Mendeley[12] and Bibsonomy[13] where suggestions are based on collaborative filtering methods (for example, see Bogers and Van den Bosch (2008) and Parra and Brusilovsky (2009)). In these works, the evaluations have opted for task-based user studies (Parra and Brusilovsky, 2009).

8 Conclusions

In this work, we explore the problem of using electronic laboratory notebooks to suggest literature to a researcher. The aim is to help researchers keep abreast of scientific developments whilst their work is continuing. We use the notebook entries to generate queries which are sent to PubMed to retrieve scientific literature. In this paper, we presented recall and precision results when comparing against lists of references known to be relevant, which we source from the bibliography files of the ELN users. We find that our combined method for query generation, using both traditional information retrieval methods and chemistry NER achieves 60% improvement over the best performing single method, using term frequency methods. This suggests that the methods presented in this paper are the first steps towards utilising the user's experimental context to suggest literature for a knowledge discovery task.

9 Acknowledgements

We thank the Digital Libraries Division of the UNSW for supporting this work. We appreciate the help of Brynn Hibbert and his students L, R, W and D for kindly sharing their blog data and bibliographies. Finally, we thank Cameron Neylon for allowing us to reproduce content from his LabTrove blog for demonstration purposes.

[10] www.wikipedia.org

[11] www.citeulike.org

[12] www.mendeley.com

[13] www.bibsonomy.org

References

Regina Barzilay, Kathleen R. McKeown, and Michael Elhadad. 1999. Information fusion in the context of multi-document summarization. In *Proceedings of the 37th conference on Association for Computational Linguistics*, pages 550–557, Morristown, NJ, USA. Association for Computational Linguistics.

Toine Bogers and Antal Van den Bosch. 2008. Recommending scientific articles using citeulike. In *Proceedings of the 2008 ACM conference on Recommender systems*, pages 287–290. ACM.

Stefan Büttcher, Charles L. A. Clarke, Peter C. K. Yeung, and Ian Soboroff. 2007. Reliable information retrieval evaluation with incomplete and biased judgements. In *Proceedings of the 30th annual international ACM SIGIR conference on Research and development in information retrieval*, SIGIR '07, pages 63–70, New York, NY, USA. ACM.

Peter Corbett and Peter Murray-Rust. 2006. High-throughput identification of chemistry in life science texts. In *Proceedings of the Second international conference on Computational Life Sciences*, CompLife'06, pages 107–118, Berlin, Heidelberg. Springer-Verlag.

Peter Corbett, Colin Batchelor, and Simone Teufel. 2007. Annotation of chemical named entities. In *Proceedings of the Workshop on BioNLP 2007: Biological, Translational, and Clinical Language Processing*, BioNLP '07, pages 57–64, Stroudsburg, PA, USA. Association for Computational Linguistics.

H Edmundson. 1969. New methods in automatic abstracting. *Journal of ACM*, 16(2):265–284.

Marti Hearst. 1994. Multi-paragraph segmentation of expository text. In *32nd. Annual Meeting of the Association for Computational Linguistics*, pages 9 – 16, New Mexico State University, Las Cruces, New Mexico.

David Jessop, Sam Adams, Egon Willighagen, Lezan Hawizy, and Peter M. Rust. 2011. OSCAR4: a flexible architecture for chemical text-mining. *Journal of Cheminformatics*, 3(1):41+.

Rahul Jha, Amjad Abu-Jbara, and Dragomir Radev. 2013. A system for summarizing scientific topics starting from keywords. In *Proceedings of the 51st Annual Meeting of the Association for Computational Linguistics (Volume 2: Short Papers)*, pages 572–577, Sofia, Bulgaria, August. Association for Computational Linguistics.

Rosie Jones, Benjamin Rey, Omid Madani, and Wiley Greiner. 2006. Generating query substitutions. In *Proceedings of the 15th international conference on World Wide Web*, WWW '06, pages 387–396, New York, NY, USA. ACM.

Christopher D. Manning, Prabhakar Raghavan, and Hinrich Schütze. 2008. *Introduction to Information Retrieval*. Cambridge University Press, New York, NY, USA.

Qiaozhu Mei and ChengXiang Zhai. 2008. Generating impact-based summaries for scientific literature. In *Proceedings of ACL-08: HLT*, pages 816–824, Columbus, Ohio, June. Association for Computational Linguistics.

David Milne and Ian H. Witten. 2008. Learning to link with wikipedia. In *Proceedings of the 17th ACM conference on Information and knowledge management*, CIKM '08, pages 509–518, New York, NY, USA. ACM.

Andrew J. Milsted, Jennifer R. Hale, Jeremy G. Frey, and Cameron Neylon. 2013. Labtrove: A lightweight, web based, laboratory blog as a route towards a marked up record of work in a bioscience research laboratory. *PLoS ONE*, 8(7):e67460, 07.

Saif Mohammad, Bonnie Dorr, Melissa Egan, Ahmed Hassan, Pradeep Muthukrishan, Vahed Qazvinian, Dragomir Radev, and David Zajic. 2009. Using citations to generate surveys of scientific paradigms. In *Proceedings of Human Language Technologies: The 2009 Annual Conference of the North American Chapter of the Association for Computational Linguistics*, NAACL '09, pages 584–592, Stroudsburg, PA, USA. Association for Computational Linguistics.

Denis Parra and Peter Brusilovsky. 2009. Collaborative filtering for social tagging systems: an experiment with citeulike. In *Proceedings of the third ACM conference on Recommender systems*, pages 237–240. ACM.

G. Salton and M. J. McGill. 1983. *Introduction to modern information retrieval*. McGraw-Hill, New York.

Stephen Wan and Cécile Paris. 2008. In-browser summarisation: Generating elaborative summaries biased towards the reading context. In *Proceedings of ACL-08: HLT, Short Papers*, pages 129–132, Columbus, Ohio, June. Association for Computational Linguistics.

Chong Wang and David M. Blei. 2011. Collaborative topic modeling for recommending scientific articles. In *Proceedings of the 17th ACM SIGKDD international conference on Knowledge discovery and data mining*, KDD '11, pages 448–456, New York, NY, USA. ACM.

A Comparative Study of Two Procedures for Calculating Likelihood Ratio in Forensic Text Comparison: Multivariate Kernel Density vs. Gaussian Mixture Model-Universal Background Model

Shunichi Ishihara
Department of Linguistics
Australian National University
shunichi.ishihara@anu.edu.au

Abstract

We compared the performances of two procedures for calculating the likelihood ratio (LR) on the same set of text data. The first procedure was a multivariate kernel density (MVKD) procedure which has been successfully applied to various types of forensic evidence, including glass fragments, handwriting, fingerprint, voice, and texts. The second procedure was a Gaussian mixture model – universal background model (GMM-UBM), which has been commonly used in forensic voice comparison (FVC) with so-called automatic features. Previous studies have applied the MVKD system to electronically-generated texts to estimate LRs, but so far no previous studies seem to have applied the GMM-UBM system to such texts. It has been reported that the latter GMM-UBM system outperforms the MVKD system in FVC. The data used for this study was chatlog messages collected from 115 authors, which were divided into test, background and development databases. Three different sample sizes of 500, 1500 and 2500 words were used to investigate how the performance is susceptible to the sample size. Results show that regardless of sample size, the performance of the GMM-UBM system was better than that of the MVKD system with respect to both validity (= accuracy) (of which the metric is the log-likelihood-ratio cost, C_{llr}) and reliability (= precision) (of which the metric is the 95% credible interval, *CI*).

1 Introduction

There are a large number of authorship analysis studies claiming to be forensic, particularly in the fields of computational linguistics and natural language processing (Iqbal et al. 2008, Iqbal et al. 2010, Lambers & Veenman 2009, Teng et al. 2004). Although they describe highly sophisticated statistical and computational methodologies, many of them consider the problem as a classification problem: for example, whether a system correctly identifies text as having been written by the same author or by different authors, etc. However, it is critical to appreciate that the role of the forensic scientist in this situation is *not* to give a definitive answer to the question of authorship or to give an opinion on the likely authorship (whether the incriminating text was written by the suspect or not). This is the task of the trier-of-fact. (Aitken 1995, Aitken & Stoney 1991, Aitken & Taroni 2004, Robertson & Vignaux 1995). The above point is emphasised in the following quote.

> It is very tempting when assessing evidence to try to determine a value for the probability of guilt of a suspect, or the value for the odds in favour of guilt and perhaps even reach a decision regarding the suspect's guilt. However, this is the role of the jury and/or judge. It is not the role of forensic scientist or statistical expert witness to give an opinion on this (Aitken 1995: 4).

So, what is the role of the forensic scientist? Aitken and Stoney (1991), Aitken and Taroni (2004) and Robertson and Vignaux (1995) state that the role of forensic scientist is to estimate the strength of evidence, technically called the likelihood ratio (LR).

This paper employs the LR framework, which has been advocated in major textbooks (e.g. Robertson & Vignaux 1995) and by forensic statisticians (e.g. Aitken & Stoney 1991, Aitken & Taroni 2004) as a logically and legally correct way of analysing and presenting forensic evidence. The LR framework is also the standard framework in DNA profiling. Emulating DNA forensic science, many fields of forensic sciences, such as fingerprint (Neumann et al. 2007), handwriting (Bozza et al. 2008), voice (Morrison 2009) and so on, have started adopting the LR framework to quantify evidential strength (= LR).

Researchers engaged in forensic authorship analysis are well aware of LR and its importance in forensic comparative science. For example, the word 'LR' appears many times in papers, included in the 2nd issue of volume 21 of *Journal of Law and Policy*, which was published in 2013 as the proceedings of the papers presented at a forensic authorship attribution workshop[1] held in October 2012. However, LR-based studies on forensic authorship analysis are conspicuous in their rarity. To the best of our knowledge, only a handful of studies so far have been based on the LR framework (e.g. Ishihara 2011, 2012a, b, Grant 2007).

There are several different procedures for calculating LRs (e.g. Lindley 1977, Aitken & Lucy 2004, Reynolds et al. 2000, Ishihara & Kinoshita 2010, Ishihara 2011). The Multivariate Kernel Density (MVKD) procedure is a popular one which has been successfully applied to various types of forensic evidence, such as voice (Rose et al. 2004), handwriting (Bozza et al. 2008) and text messages (Ishihara 2012b). Approaches based on Gaussian Mixture Model (GMM) are commonly used in forensic voice comparison (FVC) (Meuwly & Drygajlo 2001) and, in particular, it was reported that the adapted version of the GMM procedure, namely the Gaussian Mixture Model - University Background Model (GMM-UBM) procedure outperformed the MVKD procedure in FVC (Morrison 2011a). However, to the best of our knowledge, the GMM-UBM procedure has not been applied to texts yet.

Thus, the first aim of this study is to test the GMM-UBM procedure for use on electronically-generated texts, more specifically chatlog messages, in order to investigate how the GMM-UBM procedure performs in comparison to the MVKD procedure. The second aim is to investigate how their performance is influenced by sample size.

The performance of these procedures was assessed in terms of the log-likelihood-ratio cost (C_{llr}) (Brümmer & du Preez 2006) and the 95% credible interval (*CI*) (Morrison 2011b) (see §3.5).

[1] http://www.brooklaw.edu/newsandevents/events/2012/10-11-2012a.aspx

We have called our study 'Forensic Text Comparison (FTC)' study, instead of using the term 'forensic authorship analysis', to emphasise that the task of the forensic expert is to estimate and present the strength of evidence (= LR) in order to assist the decision of the trier-of-fact.

2 Likelihood Ratio

The LR is the probability that the evidence would occur if an assertion was true, relative to the probability that the same evidence would occur if the assertion was not true (Robertson & Vignaux 1995). Thus, the LR can be expressed as 1).

$$LR = \frac{p(E|H_p)}{p(E|H_d)} \qquad 1)$$

For FTC, it will be the probability of observing the difference (referred to as the evidence, *E*) between the offender's and the suspect's samples if they had come from the same author (H_p) (i.e. if the prosecution hypothesis is true) relative to the probability of observing the same evidence (*E*) if they had been produced by different authors (H_d) (i.e. if the defence hypothesis is true). The relative strength of the given evidence with respect to the competing hypotheses (H_p vs. H_d) is reflected in the magnitude of the LR. The more the LR deviates from unity (LR = 1; logLR = 0), the greater support for either the prosecution hypothesis (LR > 1; logLR > 0) or the defence hypothesis (LR < 1; logLR < 0).

For example, an LR of 20 means that the evidence (= the difference between the offender and suspect samples) is 20 times more likely to occur if the offender and the suspect had been the same individual than if they had been different individuals. Note that an LR value of 20 does *not* mean that the offender and the suspect are 20 times more likely to be the same person than different people, given the evidence.

3 Testing

Two types of comparisons are necessary to assess the performance of an FTC system: one is so-called same-author comparisons (SA comparisons) and the other is different-author comparisons (DA comparisons). For SA comparisons, two groups of messages produced by the same author will be compared and evaluated with the derived LR. Given that they are written by the same author, it is expected that the derived LR is higher than 1. In DA comparisons, two groups of messages written by different authors will be compared and evaluated. They are expected to receive LR lower than 1, given that they are written by different authors.

3.1 Database

In this study, we used an archive of chatlog messages[2] which is a collection of real pieces of chatlog evidence used to prosecute paedophiles. As of August 2013, the archive contains messages from 550 criminals (= authors). From the archive, we used messages collected from 115 authors (D_{all}), which were reformatted for the present study.

In order to set up SA and DA comparisons, we needed two non-contemporaneous groups of messages from each of the authors. For this, we added messages one by one from the chronologically ordered messages to the groups. For one message group, we started from the top of the chronologically sorted messages, while for the other group of the same author, we started from the bottom, and then the two groups of messages were checked to see if they were truly non-contemporaneous.

The 115 authors of the D_{all} were divided into three mutually-exclusive sub databases of the test database (D_{test} = 39 authors), the background database ($D_{background}$ = 38 authors) and the development database ($D_{development}$ = 38 authors). The D_{test} is for assessing the performance of the FTC system; the $D_{background}$ as the reference database for calculating LRs, and the $D_{development}$ is for calibrating the derived LRs for the SA and DA comparisons of the D_{test}. From the testing database (D_{test}) of 39 authors, we can conduct independent 39 SA and 1482 DA comparisons.

For the actual testing, we differentiate the number of words included in each message group; 500, 1500, and 2500, in order to investigate the second research aim. 500 means that each message group was modelled using a total of approximately 500 words. Since we cannot perfectly control the number of words appearing in one message, it needs to be *approximately* 500 words.

3.2 Text processing and feature extractions

The chatlog messages were tokenised using the *WhitespaceTokenizer* function of the Natural Language Toolkit[3]. As the name indicates, the *WhitespaceTokenizer* provides a simple tokenisation based on whitespaces. Thus, messages were whitespace-tokenised one by one. A message may have contained two or more sentences, but the words of each message were treated as a sequence of words without parsing them into sentences.

We used three different features in this study, of which the effectiveness has been proven in previous studies (Ishihara 2012a, b). They are:

- the number of words appearing in each message;
- the average character number per word in each message; and
- the ratio of punctuation characters (, . ? ! ; : ' ") to the total number of characters in each message.

The results of Ishihara (2012a, b), in which the different permutations of 12 so-called word- and character-based lexical features were investigated in their performances, showed that 1) a vector of four to five features (not as many as 12) yielded the best performing results and 2) the above three features performed consistently well regardless of the sample size. Thus, the above-listed features were chosen.

3.3 Likelihood ratio procedures

As mentioned earlier, two different procedures were used in order to calculate LRs: the Multivariate Kernel Density (MVKD) procedure (Aitken & Lucy 2004) and the Gaussian Mixture Model - Universal Background Model (GMM-UBM) procedure (Reynolds et al. 2000).

Multivariate kernel density (MVKD) procedure

In their paper, Aitken and Lucy (2004) addressed the problem of estimating LRs from correlated variables, and proposed the MVKD procedure for this problem. This procedure allows us to estimate a single LR from correlated variables, discounting the correlation between them. Following the initial application of the procedure to data from glass fragments, it has been successfully applied to various types of forensic evidence, such as voice (Rose et al. 2004), handwriting (Bozza et al. 2008), and text (Ishihara 2012b). The MVKD procedure is described mathematically in (2) and (3) which are the numerator and denominator of the formula respectively.

[2] http://pjfi.org/

[3] http://nltk.org/

numerator of MVLR (H_p= *true*), $p(\bar{y}_1, \bar{y}_2|U,C,h)$ = (2)

$$(2\pi)^{-p}|D_1|^{-1/2}|D_2|^{-1/2}|C|^{-1/2}(mh^p)^{-1}\left|D_1^{-1}+D_2^{-1}+(h^2C)^{-1}\right|^{-1/2}$$
$$\times\, exp\{-\tfrac{1}{2}(\bar{y}_1-\bar{y}_2)^T\,(D_1+D_2)^{-1}(\bar{y}_1-\bar{y}_2)\}$$
$$\times \textstyle\sum_{i=1}^{m} exp[-\tfrac{1}{2}(y^*-\bar{x}_i)^T\left\{\left(D_1^{-1}+D_2^{-1}\right)^{-1}+(h^2C)\right\}^{-1}(y^*-\bar{x}_i)]$$

Denominator of MVLR (H_d= *true*), $p(\bar{y}_1, \bar{y}_2|U,C,h)$= (3)

$$(2\pi)^{-p}|C|^{-1}(mh^p)^{-2}\times \textstyle\prod_{l=1}^{2}[|D_l|^{-1/2}|D_l^{-1}+(h^2C)^{-1}|^{-1/2}$$
$$\times \textstyle\sum_{i=1}^{m} exp\{-\tfrac{1}{2}(\bar{y}_l-\bar{x}_i)^T(D_l+h^2C)^{-1}(\bar{y}_l-\bar{x}_i)\}]$$

where m = number of groups (e.g. authors) in the background data;
p = number of assumed correlated variables measured on each object (e.g. message);
n_i = number of objects in each group in the background data;
x_{ij} = measurements constituting the background data = $(x_{ij1},\ldots,x_{ijp})^T$,
$i = 1,\ldots,m,\ j = 1,\ldots,n_i$;
$\bar{x}_i$ = within-object means of the background data = $\frac{1}{n_i}\sum_{j=1}^{n_i} x_{ij}$;
y_{lj} = measurements constituting offender ($l = 1$) and suspect ($l = 2$) data = $(y_{lj1},\ldots,y_{ljp})^T$,
$l = 1,2,\ j = 1,\ldots,n_l$;
$\bar{y}_l$ = offender ($l = 1$) and suspect ($l = 2$) means = $\frac{1}{n_l}\sum_{j=1}^{n_l} y_{lj}$, $l = 1,2$.
U, C = within-group and between-group variance/covariance matrices;
D_l = offender ($l = 1$) and suspect ($l = 2$) variance/covariance matrices = $n_l^{-1}U$, $l = 1,2$;
h = optimal kernel smoothing parameter = $(4/(2p+1))^{1/(p+4)}m^{-1/(p+4)}$;
$y^* = \left(D_1^{-1}+D_2^{-1}\right)^{-1}(D_1^{-1}\bar{y}_1+D_2^{-1}\bar{y}_2)$.

Although the reader needs to refer to Aitken and Lucy (2004) for the full mathematical exposition of the formula, we would like to point out some important parts of the formula, having its application to this study in mind. The numerator of the MVLR formula (2) calculates the likelihood of evidence, which is the difference between the offender and suspect samples (e.g. the difference between the message group produced by the offender and that by a suspect) when it is assumed that both of them came from the same origin (e.g. both message groups were produced by the same author, or the prosecution hypothesis (H_p) is true). For that, we need the mean vectors of the offender and suspect samples which are denoted as $\bar{y}_1, \bar{y}_2$ respectively in the formula, and the within-group (= within-author) variance, which is given in the form of a variance/covariance matrix (denoted as U in the formula). The same mean vectors of the offender and suspect samples ($\bar{y}_1, \bar{y}_2$) and the between-group (= between-author) variance (denoted as C in the formula) are used in the denominator of the formula (3), to estimate the likelihood of getting the same evidence when it is assumed that they are from different origins (e.g. the defence hypothesis (H_d) is true). These within-group and between-group variances (U and C of the formula) are estimated from the $D_{background}$ consisting of 38 authors (m = 38), from each message group from which the above-mentioned three feature values (a three-dimensional feature vector) (p = 3) were extracted.

The difference of two feature vectors is evaluated using a *Mahalanobis* distance of which the general form is the product $(\bar{X}-\bar{Y})^T(\Sigma)^{-1}(\bar{X}-\bar{Y})$ in the formula (e.g. the difference between offender and suspect means $(\bar{y}_1, \bar{y}_2) = (\bar{y}_1-\bar{y}_2)^T(D_1-D_2)^{-1}(\bar{y}_1-\bar{y}_2)$. The MVKD formula assumes normality for within-group variance while it uses a kernel density model for between-group variance. The remaining complexities of the formula result mainly from modelling a kernel density for the between-group variance.

Gaussian mixture model – universal background mode (GMM-UBM)

A Gaussian mixture model (GMM) is a parametric probability density function represented as a weighted sum of M component Gaussian densities. In FTC, GMM parameters are estimated from the training data (e.g. suspect samples) using the iterative Expectation-Maximisation (EM) algorithm with the maximum likelihood (ML) estimation. The main idea of the GMM-UBM is that the GMM, which was built in the above process for a suspect, is adapted to a universal background model (UBM) which was built based on the $D_{background}$. This way of estimating GMM parameters is called Maximum A Posterior (MAP) estimation. The above process is mathematically represented in terms of GMM parameters: mixture weight (ω), mixture mean (μ) and mixture variance/covariance (ε) in (4), (5) and (6) respectively. The formulae given in (4), (5) and (6) are based on Reynolds et al. (2000), but modified for text data.

$$\hat{\omega}_i^n = \left[\frac{\alpha_i^{\omega}\omega_i^{UBM}}{T} + (1-\alpha_i^{\omega})\omega_i^n\right]\gamma \qquad (4)$$

$$\hat{\mu}_i^n = \alpha_i^{\mu}\mu_i^{UBM} + (1-\alpha_i^{\mu})\mu_i^n \qquad (5)$$

$$\hat{\varepsilon}_i^n = \alpha_i^{\varepsilon}\mu_i^{UBM} + (1-\alpha_i^{\varepsilon})\varepsilon_i^n \qquad (6)$$

where, ω_i^n, μ_i^n and ε_i^n = the weight, mean and variance/covariance of the i-th component of speaker n's GMM;
ω_i^{UBM}, μ_i^{UBM} and ε_i^{UBM} = the weight, mean and variance/covariance of the i-th component of UBM;
$\hat{\omega}_i^n$, $\hat{\mu}_i^n$ and $\hat{\varepsilon}_i^n$ = the adapted weight, mean and variance/covariance of the i-th component of speaker n's GMM;
$\alpha_i^p, p \in \{\omega, \mu, \varepsilon\}$ = a data-dependent adaptation coefficient, which is defined as $\alpha_i^{\omega} = \alpha_i^{\mu} = \alpha_i^{\varepsilon} = \omega_i^n/(\omega_i^n + r)$;
r = a relevance factor which controls the magnitude of the adaptation step in each iteration;
T = the number of background samples used to train UBM
γ is automatically computed over all adapted mixture weights to ensure that they sum to unity.

If a mixture component (i) of the UBM has a low count for the corresponding mixture component of a given author's (n) sample, thus low in ω_i^n, then $\alpha_i^{\{\omega,\mu,\varepsilon\}} \to 0$. This will result in de-emphasising the parameters of this mixture component of the UBM, and emphasising the given author's original GMM parameters.

A score, which was transformed to an LR using a calibration technique (refer to §3.4) in a subsequent process, was calculated as the relative value of the adapted GMM function of the suspect and the UBM function at each of the values extracted from the offender sample.

In this study, we conducted a series of experiments by altering the number of Gaussian components and the relevance factor (r) between 8 and 24. The number of iteration for the EM algorithm was set to 7.

3.4 Calibration

A logistic-regression calibration (Brümmer & du Preez 2006) was applied to the derived LRs (or scores) from the MVKD and GMM-UBM procedures. Given two sets of LRs (or scores) derived from the SS and DS comparisons and a decision boundary, calibration is a normalisation procedure involving linear monotonic shifting and scaling of the LRs relative to the decision boundary in order to minimise a cost function. The FoCal toolkit[4] was used for the logistic-regression calibration in this study (Brümmer & du Preez 2006). The logistic-regression weight was obtained from the $D_{development}$.

3.5 Evaluation of performance: validity and reliability

The performance of the FTC system was assessed using the log-likelihood-ratio cost (C_{llr}) (Brümmer & du Preez 2006) and the 95% credible intervals (CI) (Morrison 2011b) which are the metrics of validity and reliability respectively. Suppose that we have two authors and two sets of message groups for each of author. We denote the sets of messages as A1.1, A1.2, A2.1, and A2.2, where A = author, and 1 & 2 = the first set and the second set of messages (A1.1 refers to the first set of messages collected from (A)uthor1, and A1.2 the second set from that same author). From these sets, two independent DA comparisons are possible; A1.1 vs. A2.1 and A1.2 vs. A2.2. Suppose then that we conducted two separate FTC tests in the same way, but using two different features (Features 1 and 2), and that we obtained the $\log_{10}$LRs given in Table 1 for these two DA comparisons.

DA comparison	Feature 1	Feature 2
A1.1 vs. A2.1	-3.5	-2.1
A1.2 vs. A2.2	-3.3	0.2

Table 1: Example LRs used to explain the concept of validity and reliability.

[4] https://sites.google.com/site/nikobrummer/focal

Since the comparisons given in Table 1 are DA comparisons, the desired $log_{10}LR$ value is lower than 0, and the greater the negative $log_{10}LR$ value is, the better the system is since it more strongly supports the correct hypothesis. For Feature 1, both of the comparisons revealed $log_{10}LR < 0$ while for Feature 2, only one of them showed a $log_{10}LR < 0$. Feature 1 is better not only in that both $log_{10}LR$ values are smaller than 0 (supporting the correct hypothesis) but also in that their magnitude is a lot greater than the $log_{10}LR$ values of Feature 2. As a result it can be said that the validity (= accuracy) of Feature 1 is higher than that of Feature 2. This is the basic concept of validity.

As pointed out in §1, almost all previous studies of forensic authorship analysis treated the problem as a two-way classification problem (correct vs. incorrect). Consequently the validity of the methodology has been assessed in terms of classification accuracy such as precision, recall, equal error rate (*EER*), F-score, etc. However, Morrison (2011b: 93) argues that these metrics based on classification-accuracy/classification-error rates are inappropriate for use within the LR framework because they implicitly refer to posterior probabilities, which is the province of the trier-of-fact, rather than LRs, which is the province of forensic scientists. Furthermore, "they are based on a categorical thresholding, error versus non-error, rather than a gradient strength of evidence." Thus it has been argued that an appropriate metric for the validity of the LR-based forensic comparison system is the log-likelihood-ratio cost (C_{llr}), which is a gradient metric based on LRs. See 7) for calculating C_{llr} (Brümmer & du Preez 2006).

$$C_{llr} = \frac{1}{2}\left(\frac{1}{N_{H_p}} \sum_{i \, for \, H_p = true}^{N_{H_p}} log_2\left(1 + \frac{1}{LR_i}\right) + \frac{1}{N_{H_d}} \sum_{j \, for \, H_d = true}^{N_{H_d}} log_2\left(1 + LR_j\right) \right) \qquad 7)$$

In 7), N_{Hp} and N_{Hd} are the numbers of SA and of DA comparisons, and LR_i and LR_j are the LRs derived from the SA and DA comparisons respectively. If the system is producing desired LRs, all the SA comparisons should produce LRs greater than 1, and the DA comparisons should produce LRs less than 1. In this approach, LRs which support counter-factual hypotheses are given a penalty. The size of this penalty is determined according to how significantly the LRs deviate from the neutral point. That is, an LR supporting a counter-factual hypothesis with greater strength will be penalised more heavily than the ones whose strength is closer to the unity, because it is more misleading. The FoCal toolkit[4] was also used for calculating C_{llr} in this study (Brümmer & du Preez 2006). The lower the C_{llr} value is, the better the performance.

Both of the DA comparisons given in Table 1 are the comparisons between A1 and A2. Thus one can expect that the LR values obtained for these two DA comparisons to be similar since they are comparing the same authors. However, one can see that the $log_{10}LR$ values based on Feature 1 are closer to each other (-3.5 and -3.3) than those $log_{10}LR$ values based on Feature 2. In other words, the reliability (= precision) of Feature 1 is higher than that of Feature 2. This is the basic concept of reliability.

As the metric of reliability (= precision), we used credible intervals which are the Bayesian analogue of frequentist confidence intervals. Following Morrison (Morrison 2011b: 62), we calculated the 95% credible intervals (*CI*) using the parametric method on the DA comparison pairs.

That is, for each member of the pair of LRs from each DA pair of authors (x_a and x_b), the mean value of the pair ($\bar{x}$) was subtracted, as shown in 8).

$$y_a = x_a - \bar{x}, \; y_b = x_b - \bar{x}, \; \bar{x} = (x_a + x_b) \qquad 8)$$

The equations given in 8) convert each absolute value (x_a and x_b) to a deviation-from-mean value (y_a and y_b). Then, the deviation-from-mean value from each DA comparison pair of authors was pooled altogether to calculate *CI*. The smaller the credible intervals, the better the reliability.

Tippett plots were also used in this study to visually present the magnitude of the derived LRs, including both consistent-with-fact and contrary-to-fact LRs. A more detailed explanation of Tippett plots is given in §4, in which some Tippett plots are presented.

4 Experimental Results and Discussions

The results of the experiments are given as Tippett plots in Figure 1, in which the calibrated LRs, which are equal to or greater than the value indicated on the x-axis, are cumulatively plotted separately for the SA comparisons (black) and for the DA comparisons (grey). Please note that the $log_{10}LR$ is used in Figure 1, and so the unity is not 1 but 0. For the GMM-UMB, the best performing results are given for the different sample sizes (500, 1500, 2500 words) with the number of Gaussian mixture (g) and the relevance factor

(r), displayed in Figure 1. Figure 1 also contains *EER* values, but these are only for reference.

We can observe from Figure 1 that regardless of the sample size, the GMM-UBM procedure outperforms the MVKD procedure in terms of both validity and reliability. However, the difference in performance, in particular in validity, becomes less salient as the sample size increases. For example, the difference in C_{llr} between the MVKD and GMM-UBM procedures is as large as 0.142 (= 0.638-0.496) when the sample size is 500, while the difference is only 0.026 (= 0.294-0.268) when the sample size is 2500. That is, when the sample size is small - which is more realistic in real casework - the GMM-UBM procedure can be judged to be more appropriate to employ than the MVKD procedure.

Another clear difference between the two procedures is that the MVKD produced greater LRs (with some extreme ones, e.g. LR > 10^{10}) for the DA comparisons than the GMM-UBM, although the former is less well-calibrated than the latter.

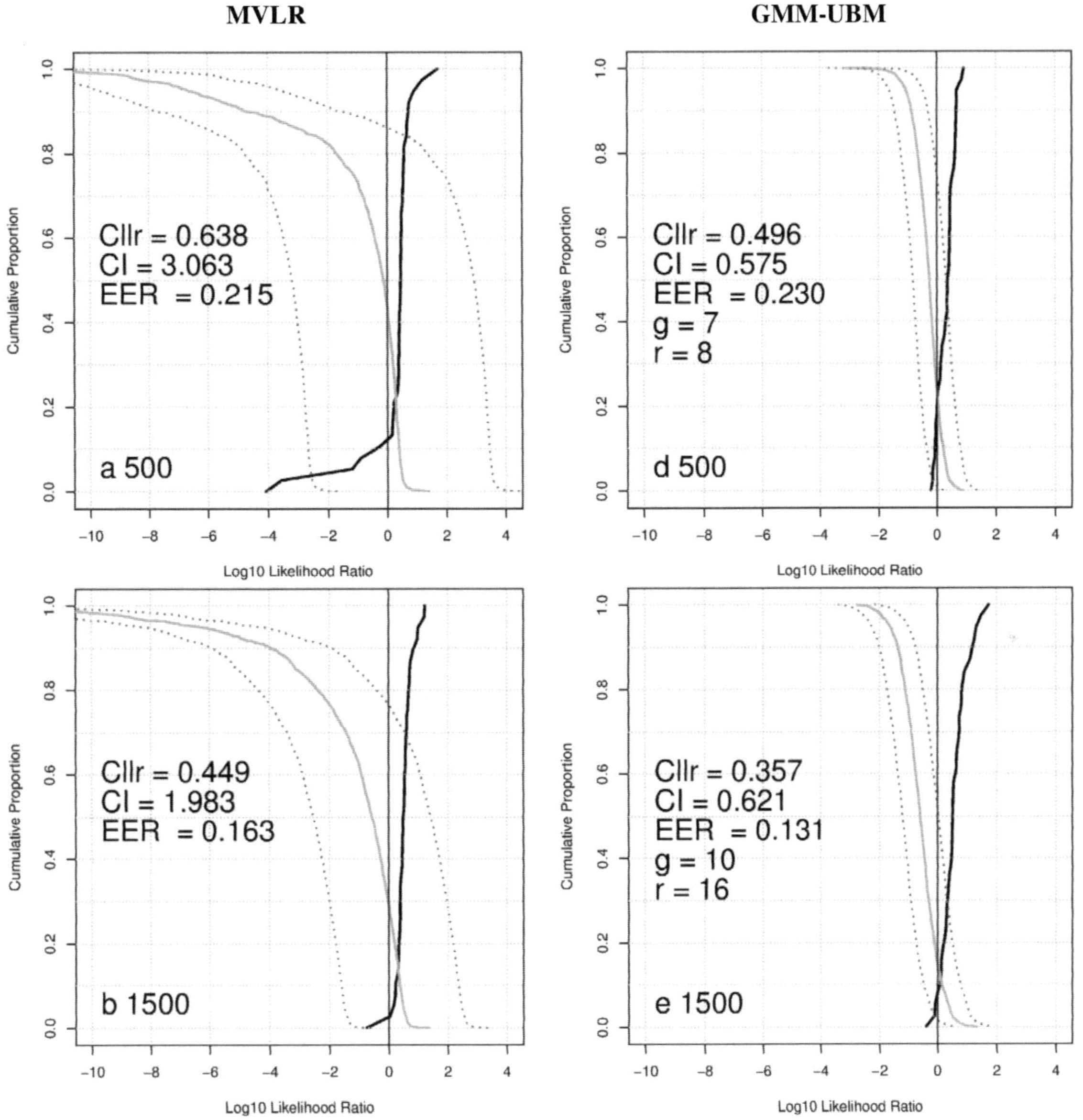

Figure 1: Tippett plots of the MVLR system on the left, and those of the GMM-UBM system (only best-performing ones) on the right. Sample size 500 (a,d); sample size 1500 (b,e). The calibrated SA LRs (solid black line), and the calibrated DA LRs (solid grey line) are plotted separately with the ±95% *CI* band (dotted grey lines) superimposed on the DA LRs. The C_{llr}, *CI* and *EER* values are also given in the plots. x-axis = $\log_{10}$LR; y-axis = cumulative proportion. g = number of Gaussian mixtures; r = the relevance factor. The results of the sample size of 2500 are given on the following page.

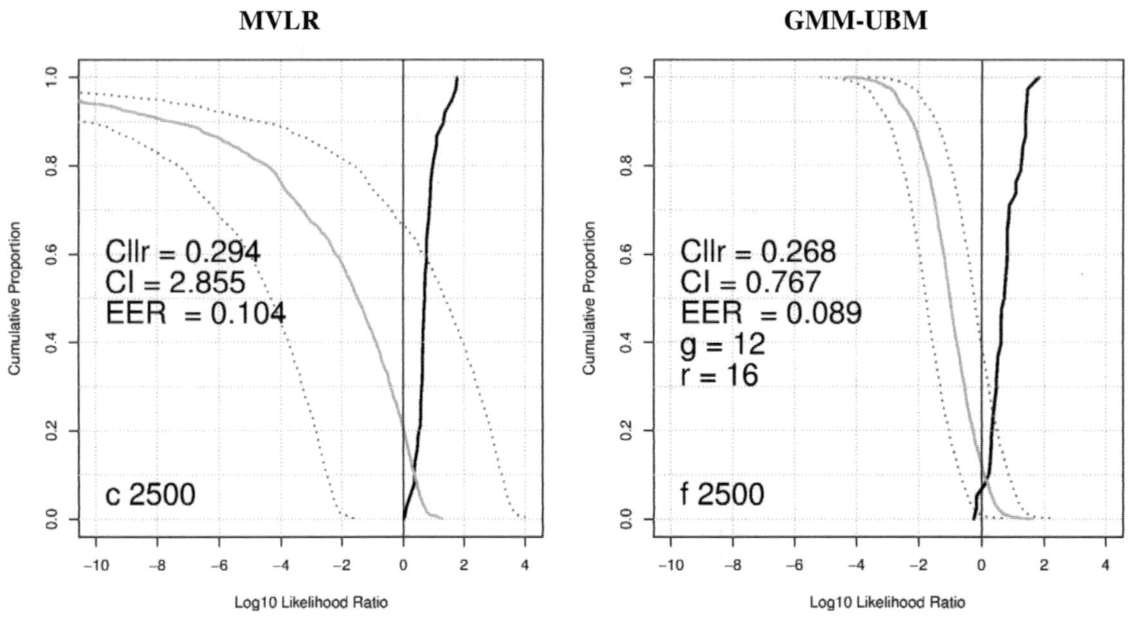

Figure 1 (continued): Sample size 2500 (c.f).

On the other hand, the LRs derived from the GMM-UBM are fairly conservative, in particular for the DA comparisons, but at the same time, their counter-factual LRs are also very weak. This point is particularly evident when the sample size is small (500), in the sense that the DA LRs are overall greater in the MVKD than the GMM-UBM, whereas the former also produced greater contrary-to-fact SA LRs (e.g. LR = ca. -4). This led to heavy penalties in terms of validity, resulting in a higher C_{llr} value (0.638) for the MVKD system. The greater DA LRs for the MVKD procedure in comparison to the GMM-UBM procedure appears to be a general trend as the same trend has been reported in Morrison (2011a), in which these two procedures were compared on speech data.

As for the reliability of the system, the GMM-UBM is far better than the MVKD in that the *CI* is constantly less than 1 in the former whereas it can be higher than 3 in the latter. This higher *CI* value (= lower in reliability) of the MVKD system, being compared to the GMM-UBM, has also been pointed out in Morrison (2011a).

It is worth pointing out that although the GMM-UBM procedure performs better in validity and reliability than the MVKD procedure, the LRs that the GMM-UBM estimated in the current study are fairly weak (this is also true of the MVKD procedure to a certain extent), in particular from the view point that the $\log_{10}$LR between -1 and 1 can only provide limited support for either hypothesis. (Champod & Evett 2000). This is partly because only three features were used in this study, but some previous studies (e.g. Ishihara 2012b) also reported that the LRs obtained from electronically-generated texts are relatively weak.

5 Conclusions and Future Directions

In this study, two procedures for the calculation of LRs: MVKD and GMM-UBM, were tested on the same feature set extracted from chatlog messages, and their performance was compared in terms of validity (= accuracy) and reliability (= precision). The experimental results demonstrated that the GMM-UBM system performed better in both validity and reliability than the MVKD system. Moreover, regardless of the sample size (500, 1500 and 2500 words), the reliability of the GMM-UBM system was consistently better than the MVKD system while the difference in validity between the two procedures decreased as the sample size increased. Results also showed that although the GMM-UBM is generally better in performance than the MVKD, the magnitude of the DA LRs is more conservative in the former than the latter.

As mentioned in §1, there are several different procedures for estimating LRs. It would be worthwhile to test other procedures to see which procedure appears to be suited to text evidence.

Acknowledgments

The author greatly appreciates the very detailed comments of the three anonymous reviewers.

References

Aitken CGG 1995 *Statistics and the Evaluation of Evidence for Forensic Scientists* John Wiley Chichester.

Aitken CGG & D Lucy 2004 'Evaluation of trace evidence in the form of multivariate data' *Journal of the Royal Statistical Society Series C-Applied Statistics* 53: 109-122.

Aitken CGG & DA Stoney 1991 *The Use of Statistics in Forensic Science* Ellis Horwood New York; London.

Aitken CGG & F Taroni 2004 *Statistics and the Evaluation of Evidence for Forensic Scientists* Wiley Chichester.

Bozza S, F Taroni, R Marquis & M Schmittbuhl 2008 'Probabilistic evaluation of handwriting evidence: Likelihood ratio for authorship' *Journal of the Royal Statistical Society: Series C (Applied Statistics)* 57(3): 329-341.

Brümmer N & J du Preez 2006 'Application-independent evaluation of speaker detection' *Computer Speech and Language* 20(2-3): 230-275.

Champod C & IW Evett 2000 'Commentary on A. P. A. Broeders (1999) 'Some observations on the use of probability scales in forensic identification', Forensic Linguistics 6(2): 228-41' *International Journal of Speech Language and the Law* 7(2): 238-243.

Grant T 2007 'Quantifying evidence in forensic authorship analysis' *International Journal of Speech Language and the Law* 14(1): 1-25.

Iqbal F, R Hadjidj, B Fung & M Debbabi 2008 'A novel approach of mining write-prints for authorship attribution in e-mail forensics' *Digital Investigation* 5(Supplement): S42-S51.

Iqbal F, LA Khan, BCM Fung & M Debbabi 2010 'E-mail authorship verification for forensic investigation' *Proceedings of the 2010 ACM Symposium on Applied Computing*: 1591-1598.

Ishihara S 2011 'A forensic authorship classification in SMS messages: A likelihood ratio based approach using N-gram' *Proceedings of the Australasian Language Technology Workshop 2011*: 47-56.

Ishihara S 2012a 'A forensic text comparison in SMS messages: A likelihood ratio approach with lexical features' *Proceedings of the seventh International Workshop on Digital Forensics and Incident Analysis*: 55-65.

Ishihara S 2012b 'Probabilistic evaluation of SMS messages as forensic evidence: Likelihood ration based approach with lexical features' *International Journal of Digital Crime and Forensics* 4(3): 47-57.

Ishihara S & Y Kinoshita 2010 'Filler words as a speaker classification feature' *Proceedings of the 13th Australasian International Conference on Speech Science and Technology*: 34-37.

Lambers M & CJ Veenman 2009 'Forensic authorship attribution using compression distances to prototypes' in Z Geradts, KY Franke & CJ Veenman (eds) *Computational Forensics* Lecture Notes in Computer Science. Springer Link: 13-24.

Lindley DV 1977 'Problem in Forensic-Science' *Biometrika* 64(2): 207-213.

Meuwly D & A Drygajlo 2001 'Forensic speaker recognition based on a Bayesian framework and Gaussian Mixture Modelling (GMM)' *Proceedings of 2001 Odyssey-The Speaker Recognition Workshop.*

Morrison GS 2009 'Forensic voice comparison and the paradigm shift' *Science & Justice* 49(4): 298-308.

Morrison GS 2011a 'A comparison of procedures for the calculation of forensic likelihood ratios from acoustic-phonetic data Multivariate kernel density (MVKD) versus Gaussian mixture model-universal background model (GMM-UBM)' *Speech Communication* 53(2): 242-256.

Morrison GS 2011b 'Measuring the validity and reliability of forensic likelihood-ratio systems' *Science & Justice* 51(3): 91-98.

Neumann C, C Champod, R Puch-Solis, N Egli, A Anthonioz & A Bromage-Griffiths 2007 'Computation of likelihood ratios in fingerprint identification for configurations of any number of minutiae' *Journal of forensic sciences* 52(1): 54-64.

Reynolds DA, TF Quatieri & RB Dunn 2000 'Speaker verification using adapted Gaussian mixture models' *Digital Signal Processing* 10(1-3): 19-41.

Robertson B & GA Vignaux 1995 *Interpreting Evidence: Evaluating Forensic Science in the Courtroom* Wiley Chichester.

Rose P, D Lucy & T Osanai 2004 'Linguistic-acoustic forensic speaker identification with likelihood ratios from a multivariate hierarchical random effects model: A "non-idiot's Bayes" approach' *Proceedings of the 10th Australian International Conference on Speech Science and Technology*: 492-497.

Teng GF, MS Lai, JB Ma & Y Li 2004 'E-mail authorship mining based on SVM for computer forensic' *Proceedings of 2004 International Conference on Machine Learning and Cybernetics* 2: 1204-1207 vol. 1202.

Finding Fires with Twitter

Robert Power robert.power@csiro.au
Bella Robinson bella.robinson@csiro.au
David Ratcliffe david.ratcliffe@csiro.au
CSIRO Computational Informatics
G.P.O. Box 664
Canberra, ACT 2601, Australia

Abstract

This paper presents a notification system to identify in near-real-time Tweets describing fire events in Australia. The system identifies fire related 'alert words' published on Twitter which are further processed by a classifier to determine if they correspond to an actual fire event. We describe how the classifier has been established and report preliminary results.

The original notification system did not include a classifier and could not discriminate between messages unrelated to 'real' fire events. In the first three months of operation, the system generated 42 'fire' email notifications of which 20 related to actual fires and 12 of those contained Tweets that may have been of interest to fire fighting agencies. If the classifier had been used, 21 emails would have been issued: an improvement in accuracy from 48% to 78%. However, the recall score reduced from 1 to 0.8 which is not desirable for this particular task. We propose extensions to address this short coming.

1 Introduction

In Australia bushfire management is a state and territory government responsibility and each jurisdiction has its own agency which takes the lead in coordinating community preparedness and responding to bushfires when they occur. For example, the Rural Fire Services (RFS) in NSW, the Country Fire Authority (CFA) in Victoria and so on, are each responsible for firefighting activities, training to prepare communities to protect themselves, land management hazard reduction as well as situations involving search and rescue.

During the Australian disaster season, early October through to the end of March, these fire agencies continuously monitor weather conditions in preparation for responding to events when they occur. They also inform the community about known incidents, see for example the NSW RFS Current Fires and Incidents page[1].

These agencies publish incident information on social media sites such as Facebook and Twitter. This provides a new channel of communication to interact with the community to both provide information about known events and to receive crowd-sourced content from the general public.

This engagement of social media is yet to be fully utilised. During crisis events, the emergency services effectively use social media to provide information to the community, but their ability to obtain information from the public is limited (Lindsay, 2011). While there are social media success stories, for example the Queensland Police Force during the Brisbane Floods in 2011 (Charlton, 2012), they are not yet widespread.

Our aim is to develop an emergency management tool that sources information from social media in near-real-time. The challenges are many: the most significant being how to reliably extract relevant information about emergency events of interest for crisis coordinators. The test case described in this paper is to extract current information published on Twitter about actual fire events.

The rest of the paper is organised as follows. First (§2) we review the use of social media for situational awareness during emergency events and describe the platform used in our study. An outline of the problem is then presented including a description of our initial notification system based on identifying 'fire' alerts from Twitter (§3). The process of incorporating a text classifier to improve our alerts is then presented (§4) and analysed (§5). We conclude with an outline of further work (§6) and a discussion of our findings (§7).

[1] http://www.rfs.nsw.gov.au/dsp_conent.cfm?cat_id=683

2 Background

2.1 Related Work

In Australia, the Victorian 2009 Black Saturday Bushfires killed 173 people and impacted 78 towns with losses estimated at A$2.9 billion (Stephenson et al., 2012). A recommendation from the subsequent Royal Commission[2] was that there needs to be improved access to information for emergency planning and response. Similarly, it has been recognised that information published by the general public on social media would be relevant to emergency managers and that social media is a useful means of providing information to communities that may be impacted by emergency events (Anderson, 2012; Lindsay, 2011).

More recently, tools are being developed that specifically focus on crowdsourced information to improve the situational awareness of events as they unfold. For example, Twitcident (Abel et al., 2012) performs real-time monitoring of Twitter messages to increase safety and security. They can target large gatherings of people for purposes of crowd management such as illegal parties, riots and organised celebrations. Their tool is adjustable to specific locations and incident types.

Tweet4act (Chowdhury et al., 2013) uses keyword methods to retrieve Tweets related to a crisis situation. Text classification techniques are then applied to automatically assign those Tweets to pre-incident, during-incident and post-incident classes. Other research (Imran et al., 2013) has used machine learning techniques to map Tweets related to a crisis situation into classes defined in a disaster-related ontology to find informative Tweets that contribute to situational awareness.

Another approach (Schulz and Ristoski, 2013; Schulz et al., 2013) for real-time identification of small-scale incidents using microblogs combines information from the social and the semantic web. They define a machine learning algorithm combining text classification and semantic enrichment of microblogs using Linked Open Data. Their approach has been applied to detect three classes of small-scale incident: car, fire and shooting.

Case studies have been reported (Stollberg and de Groeve, 2012; Beneito-Montagut et al., 2013) that demonstrate the importance of placing social media information in the correct context. Emergency managers operate under a command and control structure and while drivers exist to embrace this new technology to improve situational awareness, there are still barriers to adoption based on organisational constraints. It is our belief that these barriers will be overcome with the increasing acceptance of social media, so long as the veracity of this information is suitably characterised.

[2] `http://www.royalcommission.vic.gov.au/`

2.2 Social Media Platform

We started investigating the utility of information published on social media for emergency management in March 2010 (Yin et al., 2012b). When a developing emergency event was known in advance, for example Tropical Cyclone Ului (March 2010), the Twitter search API was used to gather Tweets originating from the impact area.

In late September 2011, we established eight Twitter search API captures to cover Australia and New Zealand and we have been continuously collecting Tweets from these regions since then. By this time we had developed a comprehensive toolset (Cameron et al., 2012) that includes: a statistical language model that characterises the expected discourse on Twitter; an alert detector based on the language model to identify deviations from the expected discourse; a notification system that targets specific alert keywords and generates email messages (examples can be seen in Figure 1); clustering techniques for condensing and summarising information content; and interfaces supporting forensic analysis tasks. To date, over one billion Tweets have been processed and we currently collect Tweets at a rate of approximately 1500 per minute (Robinson et al., 2013a).

3 The Problem

The task is to filter the alerts generated by our Social Media platform that match fire related keywords and refine them using a classifier to identify those that relate to actual fire events.

Fire identification provides a useful test case for our Social Media platform to extend the capabilities of the existing filtering features (by keywords) and refine the results (using classifiers). The benefit is that other use cases can be readily supported by incorporating different purpose built classifiers developed for other emergency management scenarios, for example earthquakes, cyclones, severe storms, tsunami, landslides, volcanic eruptions, floods; or for crisis management incidents, for example terrorist attacks and criminal behaviour.

```
red 'fire' alert generated at: Sun, 9 Jun 2013 17:02:58 +1000

Statistics:
  Number of tweets (including retweets): 20
  Retweets: 50%
  Geographic spread: 0

View in the ESA Alert Monitor: https://esa.csiro.au/nsw/index.html?date=2013-06-09&time=17:02&alert=fire

Location Summary (excluding retweets):
  Newcastle (-32.928089,151.772324) - 2 tweets
  *unknown location - 8 tweets

Cluster Topics:
  Apartment Block in Brisbane City - 7 tweets
  Crews Work to Rescue People Trapped Inside - 3 tweets
  Apartment Building in Cathedral Place - 2 tweets
  Update of fire Services Incident - 2 tweets
  Other Topics - 6 tweets

Tweets (excluding retweets):
  09/06/2013 16:58:41 (Brisbane) Fire in an apartment building in Cathedral Place, The Valley..
Evacuations underway.. Full details @7NewsBrisbane 6pm
  09/06/2013 17:00:06 (Brisbane City, Australia) Large fire at apartments close to Meriton Tower
Brisbane. #Australia #Aus #Travel #SunshineCoast… http://t.co/ajlra36gs0
  09/06/2013 17:00:33 (Brisbane, Australia) Screams can be heard from Fortitude Valley apartment complex
as fire crews work to rescue people trapped inside. http://t.co/ouHmstYWTZ
  09/06/2013 17:01:09 (Newcastle, NSW Australia.) Here's one Ciobo might enjoy "Texas cops fired after
jailhouse beating of black woman caught on tape" http://t.co/cEFx5UmVrl
  09/06/2013 17:01:48 (Brisbane, Australia) DEVELOPING: fire is in an apartment in the Cathedral Palace
building in Fortitude Valley.... Reports person is unconscious. @9NewsBrisbane
  09/06/2013 17:01:50 (Brisbane, Australia) . That Cathedral Place fire photo was scary.
  09/06/2013 17:02:02 (Brisbane, Australia) Update of Fire Services Incident 4th Alarm raised. Crews in
action Gotha Street Fortitude Valley http://t.co/puyMpuOxly #brisbane
  09/06/2013 17:02:03 (Newcastle, NSW Australia) who knows which block the fire is in #Brisbane
  09/06/2013 17:02:35 (Brisbane, Australia) Oh no! Cathedral Place on fire in the valley :(
http://t.co/Ojmy9W8IRI
  09/06/2013 17:02:52 (Brisbane, Australia) Update of Fire Services Incident Multiple units attending
rescues under way Gotha Street Fortitude Valley http://t.co/puyMpuOxly
```

```
red 'fire' alert generated at: Wed, 10 Jul 2013 23:28:35 +1000

Statistics:
  Number of tweets (including retweets): 17
  Retweets: 5.88%
  Geographic spread: 0.01

View in the ESA Alert Monitor: https://esa.csiro.au/nsw/index.html?date=2013-07-10&time=23:28&alert=fire

Location Summary (excluding retweets):
  Sydney (-33.869629,151.206955) - 9 tweets
  Bronte (-33.902931,151.260513) - 1 tweets
  Surry Hills (-33.879051,151.212982) - 1 tweets
  *unknown location - 5 tweets

Cluster Topics:
  Siddle - 11 tweets
  BlackBerry Fires U.S. Sales Chief - 4 tweets
  Trott - 3 tweets
  England 4-124 Ashes - 2 tweets
  Social Media - 2 tweets
  Other Topics - 2 tweets

Tweets (excluding retweets):
  10/07/2013 23:23:50 (Sydney) Social Media News Report: BlackBerry Fires U.S. Sales Chief, More Layoffs
Planned: Lower-than-expected sales w... http://t.co/xnkHWYbjGl
  10/07/2013 23:24:41 (Sydney Australia) Report: BlackBerry Fires U.S. Sales Chief, More Layoffs Planned
http://t.co/e5WTxbb2Eo
  10/07/2013 23:24:42 (Canberra) Siddle on fire! You ripper! #ashes
  10/07/2013 23:24:46 (Surry Hills Sydney) Social Media: Report: BlackBerry Fires U.S. Sales Chief, More
Layoffs Planned http://t.co/vJEt2yncUp
  10/07/2013 23:25:18 (Sydney, Australia) Watching Ellen Degeneres by the fire!! Lovely evening blogging
and on Pinterest in Aus. Loving my Bonds jumper too #onlyinaus
  10/07/2013 23:25:28 (broadbeach) siddle of fire c'mon Aussies
  10/07/2013 23:25:29 (Sydney, Australia) Siddle is on FIRE...Trott bowled 48
  10/07/2013 23:25:30 (sydney) Report: BlackBerry Fires U.S. Sales Chief, More Layoffs Planned
http://t.co/FtgL8mTjf2
  10/07/2013 23:25:32 (Bronte NSW) Peter Siddle is on absolute  fire! #Ashes #CmonAussie
  10/07/2013 23:25:43 (Canberra, Australia) Siddle is on fire! Sends Trott's middle stump out flying out
of the ground and the Aussies are on top. England 4-124 #ashes
```

Figure 1: Examples of positive (left) and negative (right) emails.

3.1 Preliminary Work

Our Social Media platform collects Tweets from Australia and New Zealand and processes them to identify unusually frequent words that may be of interest. This processing involves extracting the individual words in the text; removing punctuation; stemming them into their common 'root' words (Porter, 1980), for example *firing*, *fires* and *fired* all have the same stem word of *fire*; calculating the observed frequency of real-time stems; and comparing this observed frequency against the historical value previously calculated and recorded in a background language model. When a stem frequency is statistically much greater than the expected value, an alert is identified.

Alerts are generated in colour from highest to lowest as: *red*, *orange*, *yellow*, *purple*, *blue* and *green*. 'Higher' alerts have a greater statistical deviation from the background language model.

In June 2013, the notification system was configured to target 17 fire related keywords, including 'fire', 'bushfire', 'grassfire', 'grass', 'bush' and 'smoke'. Each of these target keywords are associated with a different alerting colour threshold to manage the quantity of notifications generated. For example, 'smoke' and 'fire' require a high alert level (*red*) whereas 'bushfire' and 'grassfire' have a low threshold since alerts triggered from these words are considered more likely to be of interest. The notification system is currently configured to monitor alerts generated from Tweets originating from a geographic region roughly equivalent to the state of New South Wales.

The notification is delivered to registered users as an email message. Two example emails can be seen in Figure 1; both have been triggered by an alert for the keyword 'fire' and were categorised as *red* alerts. This can be seen at the top of the email which also notes the time of the alert. Currently only *red* alerts trigger an email and there must be at least two Tweets contributing to the alert; these settings are configurable. The remainder of the email is structured to help the reader decide if the alert is based on useful information sourced from Twitter describing an actual fire event. This information includes: summary statistics; a link to the web interface to explore the Tweets (the link is only accessible to authorised users) a summary of the probable locations of the Twitter users; the result of processing the Tweets into clusters; and a list of the source Tweets. Note that both examples in Figure 1 have the list of Tweets edited to save space and that expletives have been blurred.

3.2 Example Fire Alerts

The process described above, filtering 'trends' or 'bursts' from Twitter to identify words of interest, has previously been investigated for earthquake events (Robinson et al., 2013a; Robinson et al., 2013b). Specifically, they target the word 'earthquake' and its derivatives as well as the hash tag '#eqnz' and apply heuristics based on the number of retweets and tweet locations to identify first hand reports of earthquakes from Twitter. A similar process has not to our knowledge been attempted for bushfires, particularly in Australia.

For the first three months of operation the notification system described above generated 42 emails triggered by *red* 'fire' alerts, but only 20 related to real fires and of these only 12 contained Tweets that may have been of interest to fire fighting agencies. These results highlight that the word 'fire' is also used on Twitter for other purposes, as demonstrated by the example Tweets in Table 1.

It is our expectation that using a classifier will improve the accuracy of our fire detector. Note that for this work we will attempt to use a classifier to identify Tweets related to real fires only.

4 Building the Classifiers

We have used the Support Vector Machine (SVM) (Joachims, 1998) method for text classification to identify Tweets about actual fire events. In this section, we describe the method used to develop an SVM for this purpose. We begin by identifying a test and training dataset (§4.1), and consider the features used in representing Tweets as feature vectors (§4.2). To assess whether a small labelled dataset would suffice to train an SVM with acceptable classification performance, we investigated the use of a Transductive SVM which takes a small labelled dataset and a collection of unlabelled examples, and also tested which fractions of the full dataset were required to train the standard (inductive) SVM to achieve maximum performance (§4.3). We conclude with a selection of the best available classifier to use in our goal to improve fire reporting (§4.4).

4.1 Gathering Training Data

Tweets mentioning 'fire' were identified from alerts generated by our Social Media platform during January and February 2013. This period in Australian was colloquially known as the 'Angry Summer'[3], where record high temperatures were recorded across most of the continent. Most notably, a series of devastating bushfires occurred around Coonabarabran in NSW and throughout South-Eastern Tasmania[4].

An impression of the number of candidate Tweets available for this process can be seen in Figure 2 which shows the daily count of Tweets that include the word 'fire'. Also shown are the results of processing these Tweets with the final classifier (to be described in Section 5) indicating the number of Tweets that were determined to be positive or negative. Note the gap around April. This was due to an issue with Twitter not correctly geo-locating Australian Tweets for approximately a two week period.

[3] http://climatecommission.gov.au/report/the-angry-summer/

[4] http://en.wikipedia.org/wiki/2012-13_Australian_bushfire_season

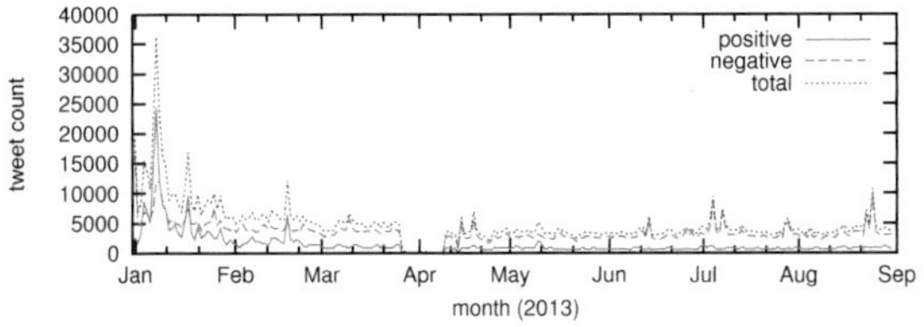

Figure 2: Daily 'fire' Tweet counts.

A selection of candidate Tweets which contributed to alerts during January and February were examined and manually labelled as positive or negative. Positive examples were first-hand witness and second-hand reports of actual fire events, as well as Tweets about fires from official sources (fire services) and news agencies. All other Tweets were considered negative examples. Our positive Tweets relate to a variety of fire events, including bushfires in Tasmania, Victoria, New South Wales and Western Australia, as well as local house and vehicle fire incidents. Negative examples were selected from 'fire' alerts that weren't to do with an actual fire. These included Tweets about fireworks, people getting fired, wood fired pizzas, fireplaces, people or sporting teams being 'on fire' and books, computer games, movies and songs with titles containing the word fire. Note that only original Tweets were labelled; retweets were excluded from this process.

A final dataset was identified consisting of 794 labelled Tweets containing the word 'fire'. This dataset consisted of an even split of positive/negative examples. Table 1 shows a sample of positive and negative Tweets from this dataset. Note that user mentions and hyperlinks that may identify user accounts have been redacted.

4.2 Feature Selection

The features selected for transforming Tweet text into feature vectors suitable for training an SVM were chosen from the following characteristics: (1) number of words; (2) user mention count; (3) hashtag count; (4) hyperlink count; (5) uni-gram occurrences; (6) bi-gram occurrences.

To determine the best combination of features to train an SVM for our problem, we performed an exhaustive search of all combinations of features ($2^6 - 1 = 63$) to train an SVM with a linear kernel. We then ranked the relative performance of each SVM by average accuracy with a 10-fold cross-validation procedure (Hastie et al., 2009), which divides the dataset into ten 90%–10% splits as training and test data (respectively). The best

(+)	Went with the other friend to the lake cause there was a HUGE fire. 2 fires actually. This photo was taken 1 km away http://t.co/...
(+)	Can see the smoke from the fire burning near craigieburn from long way. Stay safe everyone. #melbweather #hot
(+)	Fire! There's a bushfire down the road. :/
(+)	EMERGENCY WARNING issued by #TFS for uncontrolled fire at Middle Tea Tree Rd, Richmond #TAS under Extreme fire... http://t.co/...
(+)	Fires raging near ski fields in the alpine region, threatening lives and homes. Locals being told it's too late to leave #newsfeed #mthotham
(-)	the fire works are amazing this year
(-)	7 head coaches and 5 gm's got fired in the NFL and it's not 1:30 pm yet. Wow!!!
(-)	Shots fired during Auckland robberies http://t.co/...
(-)	@... @... you'll love it!! Mariah was on fire in GC.
(-)	Finally forced myself to stop reading Catching Fire. #bedtime

Table 1: Example positive (+) and negative (-) 'fire' Tweets.

result of this test is shown in Table 2, which was a combination of both (5) uni-gram occurrences and (2) user mention count as indicated by †. Subsequent rows in Table 2 show how the accuracy and F_1 scores were reduced when each of the features were excluded.

Features	Accuracy	F_1 Score
$\{2, 5\}^\dagger$	$84.54\% \pm 3.2\%$	0.831
$\{5\}$	$81.96\% \pm 4.65\%$	0.797
$\{2\}$	$54.31\% \pm 3.31\%$	0.658

Table 2: Feature combination results.

4.3 Semi-Supervised Learning

Labelling Tweets to generate training and test datasets is a labour-intensive process. To address this issue, we sought to test whether a small number of labelled positive/negative examples together with a relatively large set of unlabelled example Tweets could be used to train a Transductive SVM (TSVM) with acceptable classification performance. TSVMs have been shown to perform well for text classification problems (Joachims, 1999b), and are particularly effective over Twitter-based data (Zhang et al., 2012).

To test the performance of the TSVM relative to the standard (inductive) SVM, we used the full labelled dataset ($n = 794$) with the best determined feature combination (uni-gram occurrences and user mention count). Using this set, we aimed to test if an SVM trained on a small fraction k of the labelled examples was outperformed by a TSVM which was trained on the same set of labelled examples together with the remaining fraction $1 - k$ of the examples with their labels removed. We tested for various $k \in \{0.05, 0.10, 0.15, 0.20\}$.

For each choice of k, we created a set of experiments E where $|E| = \lceil \frac{1}{k} \rceil$. Each $e \in E$ consisted of two sets $e = \langle L, U \rangle$, where L is a randomly sampled set of $n \times k$ labelled examples (maintaining the same positive to negative example ratio as in the original dataset) which were different for each e with minimal overlap, and where U contained the remaining $n \times (1 - k)$ examples which had their labels removed, relative to each L.

For each experiment e, a two-fold cross-validation method was then used to train an SVM over set L_{train} and test over set L_{test} (where $L = L_{train} \cup L_{test}$). In each fold, a TSVM was also trained over $L_{train} \cup U$ and tested over L_{test}. The average accuracies and standard deviations for these experiments for each choice of k is shown in Table 3.

k	l/u	Type	Avg. Accuracy
0.05	40/754	SVM	61.58 ± 5.95
		TSVM	64.08 ± 8.00
0.10	80/714	SVM	69.112 ± 6.02
		TSVM	73.711 ± 4.08
0.15	120/674	SVM	68.61 ± 3.93
		TSVM	72.36 ± 3.73
0.20	159/635	SVM	69.13 ± 4.07
		TSVM	74.00 ± 5.30

Table 3: SVM versus TSVM: best features.

Experiments for both the SVM and TSVM were performed using SVM^{light} (Joachims, 1999a). As the authors of SVM^{light} have noted, aggressive feature selection has the potential to reduce the performance of a TSVM because there are often few irrelevant features in a text classification problem. For this reason, we also ran the same test for feature vectors consisting of all available features as described in §4.2, for which performance using the standard (inductive) SVM was nearly as high as the best combination of features determined by the selection process (with $n = 794$, the accuracy was $82.89\% \pm 2.84\%$ and F_1 score 80.94). The results of this test, Table 4, show that classification accuracy was not significantly different from results using the SVM and TSVM trained with feature vectors based on the best determined combination.

k	l/u	Type	Avg. Accuracy
0.05	40/754	SVM	57.89 ± 7.45
		TSVM	61.84 ± 5.21
0.10	80/714	SVM	66.60 ± 7.79
		TSVM	71.57 ± 4.99
0.15	120/674	SVM	69.72 ± 2.35
		TSVM	74.72 ± 2.37
0.20	159/635	SVM	69.00 ± 1.77
		TSVM	73.88 ± 4.42

Table 4: SVM versus TSVM: all features.

While the TSVM consistently outperformed the SVM for all cases, the improvement in accuracy was not comparable to the performance of the SVM trained on more labelled examples. It is worth noting that if we were to train a TSVM on unlabelled examples for which the proportion of positive to negative examples was unknown (which was otherwise the case in our experiment), much more experimental training and testing may be needed to determine the best assumed proportion for best performance. We did not perform such an analysis, but leave this for future work. Instead, we continued testing various proportions k in 5% increments for the SVM case to determine how the average classification accuracy changed with varying training set sizes. The results of this test are shown in Figure 3, showing that the maximum accuracy is achieved by training with around half or more ($n > 400$) of the full dataset.

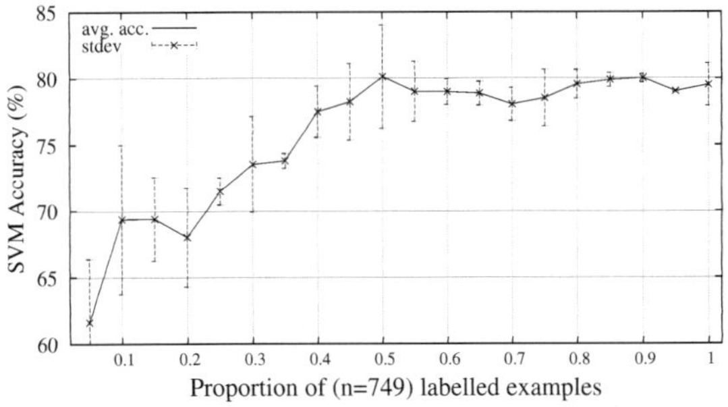

Figure 3: Learning curve for SVM^{light}.

Running the comparison experiment again for $k = 0.5$ yielded a TSVM with negligible difference in classification accuracy when compared to the SVM.

4.4 Results

As the TSVM did not outperform the standard inductive SVM in terms of classification accuracy, we opted to use the SVM trained on the best feature combination selected in §4.2 (uni-gram occurrences and user mention count) over all labelled data ($n = 794$) with a linear kernel function.

5 Improved Fire Alerting

The current email notification system has been configured to generate an email when a *new red* 'fire' alert is detected. A sequence of alerts where the gap between them is no more than 30 minutes is defined as an alert *event*. An email is generated when the first alert within an *event* that passes the notification criteria is detected; in the case of 'fire' this was configured to be a minimum alert colour of *red*. A maximum of one email is generated for each alert *event*. Figure 4 shows distribution of alerts per event for 'fire' events over an eight month period (January to August 2013). There were a lot of short events that consisted of few alerts (335 events consisted of a single alert) and on the other end of the scale there were a few long running events that consisted of a large number of alerts (the longest event had 250 alerts).

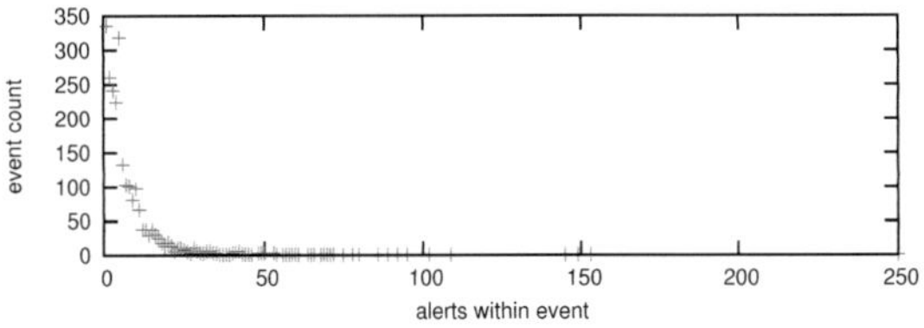

Figure 4: Alerts per event.

5.1 Analysis of Notification Emails

The 42 email notifications corresponding to *red* 'fire' alerts for June to September 2013 were examined to determine how many related to Tweets about actual fires. 20 were found to have at least one Tweet about a fire; these were labelled as true positives. The rest were labelled as false positives.

The email notification system was then configured to make use of the best performing classifier as defined in the previous section and all 'fire' alerts for the three month period were replayed to observe the effect. Various minimum positive percentage cutoff rates where also trialled to see how this affected the accuracy of the notifications.

It should be noted that as our Social Media platform is Java based, a Java implementation of LIBSVM (Chang and Lin, 2011) was used for these experiments. This was configured and trained in the same manner as the SVM^{light} software used in the classifier experiments detailed above. To verify that both SVM software packages produced equivalent results, we ran the same feature selection 10-fold cross validation experiment using LIBSVM and this produced accuracy measures that were within 5% of those achieved with

SVM^{light}. The results, Table 5, show the precision, recall, F_1 score, accuracy (percentage correct) and number of notification emails that would have been produced for each configuration.

Config	Prec	Rec	F_1	Acc	Emails
no class	0.48	1.00	0.65	47.6	42
10% pos	0.76	0.80	0.78	78.6	21
20% pos	0.81	0.65	0.72	76.2	16
30% pos	0.83	0.50	0.63	71.4	12
40% pos	0.82	0.45	0.58	69.0	11
50% pos	0.80	0.40	0.53	66.7	10

Table 5: Analysis of emails: Jun to Sep 2013.

These results show that the introduction of a classifier would have improved the overall accuracy of the email notification system, with the best result being achieved with a rule that at least 10% of Tweets contributing to the *red* 'fire' alert must be classified as positive. This improved the accuracy from 47.5% to 78.6% and the F_1 score from 0.65 to 0.78. While the number of false positives was greatly reduced (from 22 to 5) a number of false negatives were also introduced (4) which indicates that some actual fire events were missed. This is not a desirable outcome. It should also be noted that in some cases when using the classifier the generation of the notification email was delayed because the initial *red* 'fire' alerts did not pass the classification test. The notification system will keep checking follow up alerts until one passes the test and an email notification is sent.

5.2 Expected Fire Season Performance

To explore the performance of the notification system over the previous fire season, this experiment was re-run over the alerts that were generated by our Social Media platform over the months January to May 2013. During periods when there are many active bushfires it appears that the use of a classifier will not provide much benefit: for the 22 *red* 'fire' email notifications that would have been generated if our system has been running during January 2013, all of them would have been true positives without the use of a classifier. The results of this experiment are shown in Table 6 which shows the gain in accuracy by introducing a classifier is minimal and the number of emails produced is not reduced significantly.

Config	Prec	Rec	F_1	Acc	Emails
no class	0.79	1.00	0.88	79.2	48
10% pos	0.84	0.97	0.90	83.3	44
20% pos	0.91	0.84	0.88	81.3	35
30% pos	0.94	0.79	0.86	79.2	32
40% pos	0.94	0.79	0.86	79.2	32
50% pos	0.94	0.76	0.84	77.1	31

Table 6: Analysis of emails: Jan to May 2013.

6 Further Work

The notification system based on fire alerts has so far only been operating in the winter season. The results that would have been achieved if the system had been operating last summer have also been explored. The real test will be the upcoming disaster season: how well will the classifier perform? We will actively review the emails as they are generated to check they describe real fire events (true positives), while also checking the alerts that don't generate an email notification (true negatives) to verify they do not correspond to real fire events.

Our original hypothesis was that a classifier would be useful to identify real fire events from the keyword filtering of alerts generated by our Social Media platform. This was found to be true during the winter season but less so for the summer months. We will explore bypassing the alert filtering by keyword and instead focus on classification of Tweets directly. This will have performance implications, especially if there are many classifiers in operation looking for different event types.

Another avenue to explore is to analyse 'fire' alerts at a lower level than *red*. It may be possible to detect new fire events earlier, based on a smaller set of Tweets. The use of a classifier to filter out the non-fire related alerts will become more important here as the system currently generates a large number of alerts that are not at the *red* level.

There are a number of other questions to explore. The classifier developed has been trained on example Tweets from the last fire season. Will this classifier be applicable for the next fire season? Are there regional differences? For example, can the classifier trained on Australian Tweets identify fire events in New Zealand? Should Tweets from the different regions in Australia be used to train individual region specific classifiers?

To improve classification performance, we aim to try ensemble learning to combine different classifiers using a boosting strategy such as AdaBoost (Freund and Schapire, 1997; Li et al., 2008). Furthermore, the strategy we used of under-sampling the negative Tweet class to train SVMs with balanced datasets is not without drawbacks. Therefore, we aim to test learning strategies which take the underlying example imbalance directly into account (Akbani et al., 2004). We are also interested in using the confidence or probability of individual classification determinations per Tweet to rank them in order of importance.

There are also other areas to explore with our Social Media platform. Twitter specific Natural Language Processing (NLP), Information Extraction, Word Sense Disambiguation (WSD), Part of Speech (POS) and Named Entity Recognition (NER) techniques will be investigated. For example, POS taggers (Gimpel et al., 2011; Owoputi et al., 2013; Derczynski et al., 2013) could be used to improve the identification and categorisation of fire related words. Similarly, the background language model can be extended to look at n-gram features to extend the uni-grams currently used and the existing clustering techniques can be extended to identify when alerting words are related or to make use of a WSD dictionary. NER tools can be used to better approximate the location of a Tweeter as demonstrated by Lingad et al. (2013). Also, the notification features will be extended to include other emergency use cases such as earthquakes, cyclone tracking, flood events and crisis management incidents, for example terrorist attacks and criminal behaviour.

Another area of consideration is to explore using an online incremental learning SVM similar to that described by Cauwenberghs and Poggio (2000) and Zheng et al. (2010). The aim is to dynamically refine the classifier using feedback obtained from domain specialists: incorrectly labelled Tweets can be corrected at run-time and used to re-train the classifier dynamically as an event unfolds to customize the classifier for specific events.

7 Conclusions

Our Social Media platform identifies 'alerts' based on stemmed words extracted from Tweets (Cameron et al., 2012; Yin et al., 2012a; Yin et al., 2012b). When a stem frequency is statistically much greater than the expected value, an alert is generated. These unusual events (alerts) can be filtered for keywords of interest and used as the basis for a notification system.

We have used our platform to identify occurrences of current events involving fire, such as those referring to a current *bushfire* or *grassfire*. Our system works well for words that have unambiguous and specific meanings such as these, however not for other words, such as *fire*. To improve the accuracy of the system when generating email notifications based on alerts for actual fire events, we explored the use of an SVM to discern only the relevant Tweets mentioning *fire*.

We generated a dataset of 794 Tweets with an even proportion of Tweets mentioning actual fire events to those which did not from a period during which Australia endured a particularly bad bushfire season. With this dataset, we performed an exhaustive feature selection process to train an SVM for our task. As the creation of the dataset was laborious, we also explored if a Transductive SVM (TSVM) could be used to train a model with acceptable performance with many less labelled examples in combination with more unlabelled examples, which did not prove to be the case.

Using the best trained SVM (with an accuracy of 84.54% and an F_1 score of 0.831) as a post alert filter, we found that it significantly improved the quality of the generated event notifications. In the first three months of operation, the system generated 42 'fire' email notifications where only 20 corresponded to real fire events. Filtering these alerts using the classifier resulted in 21 notifications: an improvement in accuracy from 48% to 78%, albeit with a reduction in recall from 1 to 0.8. As mentioned above however, these accuracy improvements were not obtained during the high fire danger period during the summer months.

Future work will include deploying and analysing our system in operation during the next bushfire season; exploring the use of different training datasets; improving classification accuracy using ensemble methods; ranking Tweets based on a classifier's prediction of confidence or probability to improve how notifications are interpreted; applying standard NLP techniques; and testing our system for use in other emergency management scenarios, such as earthquakes, cyclone, flood and terrorism events.

Acknowledgments

Thanks go to our colleagues Allan Yin, Sarvnaz Karimi and Jie Yin for developing some of the classification software used for our experiments. Mark Cameron was responsible for the alerting component of our Social Media platform and contributed some of the ideas for future work. Thanks also to the anonymous reviewers for their helpful comments and suggestions.

References

Fabian Abel, Claudia Hauff, Geert-Jan Houben, Richard Stronkman, and Ke Tao. 2012. Twitcident: fighting fire with information from social web streams. In Alain Mille, Fabien L. Gandon, Jacques Misselis, Michael Rabinovich, and Steffen Staab, editors, *WWW (Companion Volume)*, pages 305–308. ACM.

Rehan Akbani, Stephen Kwek, and Nathalie Japkowicz. 2004. Applying support vector machines to imbalanced datasets. In Jean-Franois Boulicaut, Floriana Esposito, Fosca Giannotti, and Dino Pedreschi, editors, *Machine Learning: ECML 2004*, volume 3201 of *Lecture Notes in Computer Science*, pages 39–50. Springer Berlin Heidelberg.

Martin Anderson. 2012. Integrating social media into traditional management command and control structures: the square peg into the round hole. In Peter Sugg, editor, *Australian and New Zealand Disaster and Emergency Management Conference*, pages 18–34, Brisbane Exhibition and Convention Centre, Brisbane, QLD. AST Management Pty Ltd.

Roser Beneito-Montagut, Susan Anson, Duncan Shaw, and Christopher Brewster. 2013. Resilience: Two case studies on governmental social media use for emergency communication. In *Proceedings of the Information Systems for Crisis Response and Management conference (ISCRAM 2013 12-15 May, 2013)*.

Mark A. Cameron, Robert Power, Bella Robinson, and Jie Yin. 2012. Emergency situation awareness from twitter for crisis management. In *Proceedings of the 21st international conference companion on World Wide Web*, WWW '12 Companion, pages 695–698, New York, NY, USA. ACM.

Gert Cauwenberghs and Tomaso Poggio. 2000. Incremental and Decremental Support Vector Machine Learning. In *NIPS*, pages 409–415.

Chih-Chung Chang and Chih-Jen Lin. 2011. LIBSVM: A library for support vector machines. *ACM Transactions on Intelligent Systems and Technology*, 2:27:1–27:27. Software available at `http://www.csie.ntu.edu.tw/~cjlin/libsvm`.

Kym Charlton. 2012. Disaster management and social media - a case study. Technical report, Media and Public Affairs Branch, Queensland Police Service, GPO Box 4356 Melbourne VIC 3001. [Accessed: 26 April 2013].

Soudip Roy Chowdhury, Muhammad Imran, Muhammad Rizwan Asghar, Sihem Amer-Yahia, and Carlos Castillo. 2013. Tweet4act: Using incident-specific profiles for classifying crisis-related messages. In *The 10th International Conference on Information Systems for Crisis Response and Management (ISCRAM)*, May.

Leon Derczynski, Alan Ritter, Sam Clark, and Kalina Bontcheva. 2013. Twitter part-of-speech tagging for all: Overcoming sparse and noisy data. In *Proceedings of the International Conference on Recent Advances in Natural Language Processing*. Association for Computational Linguistics.

Yoav Freund and Robert E Schapire. 1997. A decision-theoretic generalization of on-line learning and an application to boosting. *Journal of Computer and System Sciences*, 55(1):119 – 139.

Kevin Gimpel, Nathan Schneider, Brendan O'Connor, Dipanjan Das, Daniel Mills, Jacob Eisenstein, Michael Heilman, Dani Yogatama, Jeffrey Flanigan, and Noah A. Smith. 2011. Part-of-speech tagging for twitter: annotation, features, and experiments. In *Proceedings of the 49th Annual Meeting of the Association for Computational Linguistics: Human Language Technologies: short papers - Volume 2*, HLT '11, pages 42–47, Stroudsburg, PA, USA. Association for Computational Linguistics.

Trevor Hastie, Robert Tibshirani, and Jerome Friedman. 2009. *The elements of statistical learning: data mining, inference and prediction*. Springer, 2nd edition.

Muhammad Imran, Shady Mamoon Elbassuoni, Carlos Castillo, Fernando Diaz, and Patrick Meier. 2013. Extracting information nuggets from disaster-related messages in social media. In *The 10th International Conference on Information Systems for Crisis Response and Management (ISCRAM)*, May.

Thorsten Joachims. 1998. Text categorization with suport vector machines: Learning with many relevant features. In *Proceedings of the 10th European Conference on Machine Learning*, ECML '98, pages 137–142, London, UK, UK. Springer-Verlag.

Thorsten Joachims. 1999a. Advances in kernel methods. chapter Making Large-Scale SVM Learning Practical, pages 169–184. MIT Press, Cambridge, MA, USA.

Thorsten Joachims. 1999b. Transductive inference for text classification using support vector machines. In *Proceedings of the Sixteenth International Conference on Machine Learning*, ICML '99, pages 200–209, San Francisco, CA, USA. Morgan Kaufmann Publishers Inc.

Xuchun Li, Lei Wang, and Eric Sung. 2008. Adaboost with svm-based component classifiers. *Engineering Applications of Artificial Intelligence*, 21(5):785 – 795.

Bruce R. Lindsay. 2011. Social media and disasters: Current uses, future options, and policy considerations. Technical report, Analyst in American National Government, GPO Box 4356 Melbourne VIC 3001, September. `http://www.fas.org/sgp/crs/homesec/R41987.pdf`.

John Lingad, Sarvnaz Karimi, and Jie Yin. 2013. Location extraction from disaster-related microblogs. In Leslie Carr, Alberto H. F. Laender, Bernadette Farias Lóscio, Irwin King, Marcus Fontoura, Denny Vrandecic, Lora Aroyo, José Palazzo M. de Oliveira, Fernanda Lima, and Erik Wilde, editors, *WWW (Companion Volume)*, pages 1017–1020. International World Wide Web Conferences Steering Committee / ACM.

Olutobi Owoputi, Brendan OConnor, Chris Dyer, Kevin Gimpel, Nathan Schneider, and Noah A Smith. 2013. Improved part-of-speech tagging for online conversational text with word clusters. In *Proceedings of NAACL-HLT*, pages 380–390.

Martin F. Porter. 1980. An Algorithm for Suffix Stripping. *Program*, 14(3):130–137. `http://www.tartarus.org/~martin/PorterStemmer`.

Bella Robinson, Robert Power, and Mark Cameron. 2013a. An evidence based earthquake detector using twitter. In *Proceedings of the Workshop on Language Processing and Crisis Information 2013*, pages 1–9, Nagoya, Japan, October. Asian Federation of Natural Language Processing.

Bella Robinson, Robert Power, and Mark Cameron. 2013b. A sensitive twitter earthquake detector. In *Proceedings of the 22nd international conference on World Wide Web companion*, WWW '13 Companion, pages 999–1002, Republic and Canton of Geneva, Switzerland, May. International World Wide Web Conferences Steering Committee.

Axel Schulz and Petar Ristoski. 2013. The car that hit the burning house: Understanding small scale incident related information in microblogs. In *Seventh International AAAI Conference on Weblogs and Social Media*.

Axel Schulz, Petar Ristoski, and Heiko Paulheim. 2013. I see a car crash: Real-time detection of small scale incidents in microblogs. In Philipp Cimiano, Miriam Fernàndez, Vanessa Lopez, Stefan Schlobach, and Johanna Völker, editors, *The Semantic Web: ESWC 2013 Satellite Events*, number 7955 in Lecture Notes in Computer Science, pages 22–33. Springer Berlin Heidelberg.

Catherine Stephenson, John Handmer, and Aimee Haywood. 2012. Estimating the net cost of the 2009 black saturday fires to the affected regions. Technical report, RMIT, Bushfire CRC, Victorian DSE, Feb.

Beate Stollberg and Tom de Groeve. 2012. The use of social media within the global disaster alert and coordination system (gdacs). In *Proceedings of the 21st international conference companion on World Wide Web*, WWW '12 Companion, pages 703–706, New York, NY, USA. ACM.

Jie Yin, Sarvnaz Karimi, Bella Robinson, and Mark A. Cameron. 2012a. Esa: emergency situation awareness via microbloggers. In Xue wen Chen, Guy Lebanon, Haixun Wang, and Mohammed J. Zaki, editors, *CIKM*, pages 2701–2703. ACM.

Jie Yin, Andrew Lampert, Mark Cameron, Bella Robinson, and Robert Power. 2012b. Using social media to enhance emergency situation awareness. *IEEE Intelligent Systems*, 27(6):52–59.

Renxian Zhang, Dehong Gao, and Wenjie Li. 2012. Towards scalable speech act recognition in twitter: tackling insufficient training data. In *Proceedings of the Workshop on Semantic Analysis in Social Media*, pages 18–27, Stroudsburg, PA, USA. Association for Computational Linguistics.

Jun Zheng, Hui Yu, Furao Shen, and Jinxi Zhao. 2010. An online incremental learning support vector machine for large-scale data. In Konstantinos I. Diamantaras, Wlodek Duch, and Lazaros S. Iliadis, editors, *ICANN (2)*, volume 6353 of *Lecture Notes in Computer Science*, pages 76–81. Springer.

Short papers

Impact of Corpus Diversity and Complexity on NER Performance

Tatyana Shmanina[1,2], **Ingrid Zukerman**[1,2], **Antonio Jimeno Yepes**[1,3], **Lawrence Cavedon**[1,3], **Karin Verspoor**[1,3]
[1]NICTA Victoria Research Laboratory, Melbourne, Australia
[2]Clayton School of Information Technology, Monash University, Australia
[3]Department of Computing and Information Systems, University of Melbourne, Australia
Tatyana.Shmanina@nicta.com.au, Ingrid.Zukerman@monash.edu, Antonio.Jimeno@gmail.com, {Lawrence.Cavedon, Karin.Verspoor}@nicta.com.au

Abstract

We describe a cross-corpora evaluation of disease mention recognition for two annotated biomedical corpora: the *Human Variome Project Corpus* and the *Arizona Disease Corpus*. Our analysis of the performance of a state-of-the-art NER tool in terms of the characteristics and annotation schema of these corpora shows that these factors significantly affect performance.

1 Introduction

The recent growth of on-line biomedical literature has spawned an increasing number of NLP tools for content analysis that help researchers and practitioners access the latest developments in their fields. Examples of these tools include: *BANNER* – a *Named Entity Recognizer* (*NER*) for the biomedical domain (Leaman and Gonzalez, 2008); *ABNER* – a NER for molecular biology (Settles, 2004); and *Whatizit* – a Web service which provides functionality to perform text-mining tasks (Rebholz-Schuhmann et al., 2008). These tools in turn require the development of annotated training corpora, e.g., (Kim et al., 2003; Rosario and Hearst, 2004; Kulick et al., 2004; Pestian et al., 2007; Jimeno-Yepes et al., 2008; Bada et al., 2012).

Studies have been conducted to examine the performance of different NLP tools on a single corpus, e.g., (Jacob et al., 2013; Verspoor et al., 2012). However, experience shows that the characteristics of a corpus influence performance, e.g., (Cao and Zukerman, 2012) for sentiment analysis and (Pyysalo et al., 2008) in the biomedical space. In this paper, we analyze how the characteristics and annotation schemas of two corpora influence *BANNER*'s performance on the recognition of diseases (note that *BANNER* outperforms *ABNER* in the recognition of diseases (Leaman and Gonzalez, 2008)). The corpora in question are the *Human Variome Project Corpus* (*HVPC*) developed at NICTA (Verspoor et al., 2013), and the *Arizona Disease Corpus* (*AZDC*) – a popular medical resource developed at the University of Arizona (Leaman et al., 2009).[1]

Our results show that *BANNER*'s performance on *HVPC* significantly exceeds its performance on *AZDC*. This is (at least partly) explained by differences in corpus characteristics, such as reduced disease mention diversity resulting from *HVPC*'s specific focus, and by some requirements of *HVPC*'s annotation schema. These observations suggest that corpus analysis should be conducted along with performance evaluation in order to appropriately assess the obtained results and the suitability of a corpus for training general NER tools.

2 Biomedical Corpora

AZDC is a biomedical textual resource focusing on disease annotation (Leaman et al., 2009). It was extracted from a corpus created by Craven and Kumlien (1999), which consists of sentences selected from MEDLINE® abstracts via queries for six proteins. All disease mentions in *AZDC* are annotated, with each disease annotation containing a *Unified Medical Language System®* (*UMLS®*) concept unique identifier (where possible).

HVPC is an annotated biomedical textual resource pertaining to human genetic variation and its relation to diseases (Verspoor et al., 2013). At present, the corpus comprises ten double-annotated plain-text full journal publications on inherited colorectal cancer, which were selected on the basis of their relevance to the genetics of the Lynch Syndrome. The annotation schema, which is tailored to the focus of the corpus, covers thirteen *relations*, such as "gene-has-mutation", "mutation-has-size" and "disease-related-to-body-part"; and eleven *entity types*, such as genomic categories (e.g., "gene", "mutation"), phenotypic categories (e.g., "disease", "body-part"), categories

[1]Of the above corpora, only Kulick *et al.*'s focuses on diseases at the same level of detail as the corpora considered in this paper, and may be investigated in the future.

related to the occurrence of mutations in a disease (e.g., "age", "ethnicity"), and a "characteristic" category as a catch-all for information of interest that is otherwise uncategorized.

2.1 Comparison of Annotation Schemas

Both *HVPC* and *AZDC* annotate duplicate disease mentions in the same sentence, and abbreviations specific to the analyzed article (e.g., "Huntington disease (HD)"). In addition, they do not annotate stand-alone generic words (e.g., "disease", "syndrome"), and disease names embedded into entities of other types (e.g., "Peter MacCallum *Cancer* Centre"). However, there are significant differences between these annotation schemas:

- *HVPC*'s annotation guidelines define the "disease" entity type as "an abnormal condition affecting the body of an organism", and annotates modifiers such "healthy", "unaffected" and "normal" as diseases of healthy individuals. In contrast, *AZDC* requires that disease mentions correspond to one of the several semantic types of the UMLS® Semantic Group "disorders" (e.g., "disease or syndrome", "injury or poisoning", "mental dysfunction", "sign or symptom"). As a result, disease effects are annotated as diseases in *AZDC*, but not in *HVPC*.
- *AZDC* requires mention boundaries to be set to a minimum span of text necessary to describe the most specific form of a disease. In contrast, *HVPC* seems to be more restrictive with respect to disease mention boundaries. Specifically, many of the modifiers describing the type of a disease (which are included in disease mentions in *AZDC*) are attributed to the "characteristic" entity type (Section 1). For example, "classical galactosemia" and "unilateral retinoblastoma" are disease mentions according to *AZDC*, while only the head noun is a disease mention according to *HVPC*.
- *HVPC* annotates only the last and most complete part of a disease coordination[2] (e.g., in "breast and *ovarian cancer*", "breast" is annotated as a body part[3]), while *AZDC* annotates a coordination as separate but overlapping mentions of a disease (e.g., "*breast and ovarian cancer*" and "*ovarian cancer*").

[2]This was originally done in response to the BRAT annotation tool (Stenetorp et al., 2012) not allowing annotation of discontinuous entities (since rectified).

[3]A refinement is to consider *(body-part, disease)* related pairs as multi-word disease names, which would boost the mention-length counts for *HVPC* in Figure 2.

These aspects account for the simplicity, brevity and higher structural regularity of *HVPC* disease mentions compared to those in *AZDC* (Section 2.2).

2.2 Comparison of Corpora Parameters

We have analyzed *HVPC* and *AZDC* with respect to the following parameters: size of the corpora in terms of number of sentences and tokens; number of disease mentions and unique disease mentions; and distribution of sentence length, disease mention length and disease mention frequency. The results, which appear in Tables 1 and 2, and Figures 1 and 2, reveal the following differences between *HVPC* and *AZDC*, which explain why *AZDC* is more difficult to analyze automatically than *HVPC*:

- **Unique disease mentions –** The ratio of *unique* disease mentions to *total* disease mentions in *HVPC* (8.4%) is much lower than in *AZDC* (37.2%) (Table 1). In addition, in *HVPC* a small set of unique mentions has very high frequency compared to *AZDC* (Table 2). These properties of *HVPC* may be attributed to its narrow focus on the Lynch Syndrome.
- **Sentence length and complexity –** In general, sentence length is significantly higher in *AZDC* (Figure 1). This may be attributed in part to the way in which *HVPC* and *AZDC* were constructed: *AZDC* contains only sentences extracted from biomedical paper abstracts, while *HVPC* consists of full papers, which in addition to sentences, contain section headings and table and figure captions.
- **Disease mention length –** Most disease mentions in *HVPC* consist of 1 or 2 terms, while *AZDC* contains a large number of multi-word complex disease mentions (Figure 2).

3 NER Performance

In this section, we describe the experiments we performed to evaluate the performance achieved for *HVPC* and *AZDC* by a state-of-the-art NER tool, viz *BANNER* (Leaman and Gonzalez, 2008) (Section 1). We also analyze the types of errors made by *BANNER* on each corpus, and discuss their connection to the annotation guidelines.

BANNER is a NER system developed for use in the biomedical domain. It uses a mechanism based on Conditional Random Fields (CRF) (Lafferty et al., 2001) to assign labels to input tokens, and considers the following features: (1) lemma for a token; (2) part of speech; (3) orthographic features, such as capitalization, presence of digits, prefixes and suffixes, and 2 and 3-character n-grams.

Parameter	*HVPC*	*AZDC*
# of sentences	2116	2783
# of tokens	52454	79950
Total # of disease mentions	1552	3228
# of unique disease mentions	130	1202

Table 1: Various quantitative parameters of *HVPC* and *AZDC*. Unique mentions refer to all (case-sensitive) textually identical disease mentions.

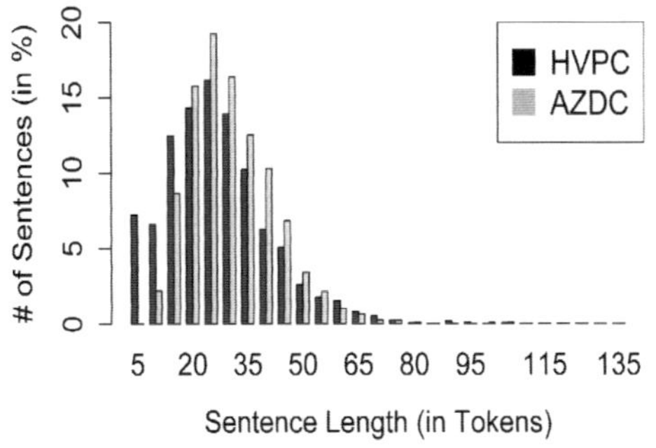

Figure 1: Distribution of sentence lengths (binned with step 5) in *HVPC* and *AZDC*.

Parameter	*HVPC*	*AZDC*
Frequency mean	11.94	2.73
Frequency standard deviation	22.39	5.65
Ratio of top N frequent mentions to all mentions		
$N = 10$	0.51	0.14
$N = 20$	0.73	0.22
$N = 30$	0.85	0.28

Table 2: Frequencies of disease mentions.

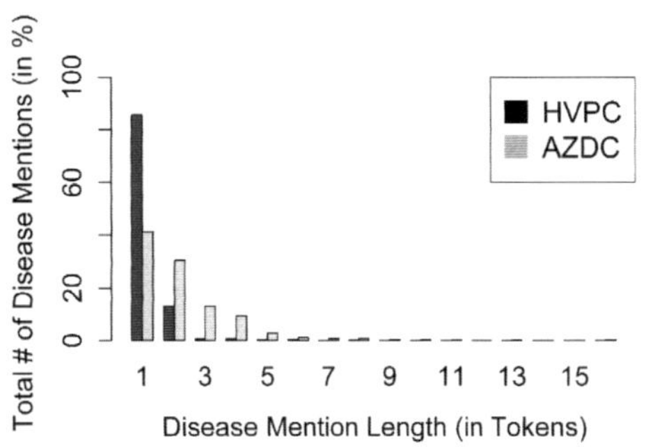

Figure 2: Distribution of disease mention lengths in *HVPC* and *AZDC*.

3.1 Experimental Set-Up

***BANNER* configuration:** We used the 19th SVN revision of *BANNER* (`sourceforge.net/p/banner/code/HEAD/tree/`) with the following parameters: (1) parenthesis post-processing, post processing of abbreviations specific to an article, and numeric normalization switched "on"; (2) IOB (Inside, Outside, Begin) label model with second order CRF model; and (3) no dictionary.

Matching schemes: *BANNER*'s performance was assessed using the following matching schemes: (1) exact, (2) left border, (3) right border, (4) left or right border, (5) entity inclusion (one entity is a subset of another), and (6) entity overlap. The first scheme provides the most stringent measure of performance, while the other schemes provide different types of fuzzy matches.

Dataset preparation: *BANNER* contains a dataset loader specifically created for *AZDC*, while *HVPC* had to be segmented into sentences. This was done by training the OpenNLP sentence splitter (`opennlp.apache.org/`) on 70% of *HVPC*, and manually fixing the nine errors that remained after automatic sentence splitting.

3.2 Performance Evaluation

We performed 10-fold cross validation over both corpora, and employed the standard performance metrics of *Precision*, *Recall* and *F-score*.

The results in Table 3 show that *BANNER* achieves excellent performance (*F-score*=0.9164) for *HVPC* on exact matches, which cannot be substantially improved by relaxing the matching scheme. In contrast, *AZDC*'s *F-score*=0.7365 for the exact matching scheme increases by up to 15% with matching-scheme relaxation.[4]

The good performance of *BANNER* on *HVPC* may be attributed to the single-disease focus of the corpus, its sentence brevity, and its disease-mention properties, which in turn are influenced by the annotation schema (Section 2). The latter may also explain the relative insensitivity of *BANNER* to the matching scheme relaxation: *BANNER* tends to have NE boundary detection problems mostly for long disease mentions, which are under-represented in *HVPC*.

With regard to *AZDC*, the results in Table 3 indicate that the main cause of the relatively low performance of *BANNER* is its inaccurate left boundary detection, which affects performance for both the exact and left-border schemes.

[4] In another set of experiments, *BANNER* trained on *AZDC* and tested on *HVPC* exhibited inferior performance (*F-score*=0.4453 for the exact matching scheme and *F-score*=0.6166 for overlap matching), thus confirming the large difference and non-interchangeability of these two datasets and their annotation schemas.

Scheme	Corpus	*Precision*	*Recall*	*F-score*
Exact	*AZDC*	0.7772	0.7003	0.7365
	HVPC	0.9322	0.9026	0.9164
Left Border	*AZDC*	0.8009	0.7217	0.7590
	HVPC	0.9372	0.9076	0.9214
Right Border	*AZDC*	0.8706	0.7844	0.8250
	HVPC	0.9512	0.9215	0.9353
Left or Right Border	*AZDC*	0.8870	0.7992	0.8406
	HVPC	0.9555	0.9258	0.9396
Inclusion	*AZDC*	0.8897	0.8016	0.8431
	HVPC	0.9593	0.9293	0.9433
Overlap	*AZDC*	0.8931	0.8046	0.8463
	HVPC	0.9599	0.9299	0.9439

Table 3: 10-fold X-validation for *AZDC* and *HVPC*.

3.3 NER Errors

Below we consider the errors identified in (Leaman et al., 2009) for *AZDC* (items 1-3), and add another type of error (item 4):

1. Improper handling of coordinations (*AZDC*), which occurs quite often, despite the addition of a coordination-handling post-processing step. *BANNER* tends to combine separate mentions of the form "disease1 and disease2" (false positives), while sometimes missing annotated coordinations (false negatives).
2. Inability to correctly detect boundaries of disease mentions (*AZDC* and *HVPC*). This problem is exacerbated in *AZDC* when diseases are referred to by their effects rather than their names (e.g., "premature periodontal destruction"), or disease names contain attributes (e.g., "high myopia").
3. Incorrect identification of acronyms and abbreviations specific to the analyzed article (*AZDC* and *HVPC*).
4. Overlooking (false negatives) or mistaken annotation (false positives) of disease names (*AZDC* and *HVPC*). In particular, this happens for words characterizing a health condition, e.g., "affected", "normal" or "healthy" (*HVPC* only), and diseases referred to by their effects (*AZDC* only).

This analysis confirms that the difference in *BANNER*'s performance on *HVPC* and *AZDC* is partly caused by differences in the annotation guidelines for these two corpora:

- *AZDC* contains many coordinations, while *HVPC*'s annotation guidelines circumvent the "coordination problem" (Section 2).
- Disease effects and characteristics are not annotated as disease names in *HVPC*. In contrast, the number of such mentions in *AZDC* is high, and its disease mentions in general are usually longer and more diverse than disease mentions in *HVPC*.

These factors explain the increased difficulty of disease-mention identification and mention-boundary detection in *AZDC* compared to *HVPC*.

3.4 Baseline Performance on *HVPC*

The simplicity of *HVPC* is further demonstrated by evaluating the performance of a very simple baseline algorithm that extracts disease mentions from *HVPC*. This algorithm applies the Unix string-matching utility *grep* to each word in a small (42 word) dictionary that was quickly constructed. The dictionary was created by collecting all the disease mentions and their morphological variations from the Wikipedia article about the Lynch Syndrome, and adding six terms ("healthy", "normal", "unaffected", "polyp", "polyps" and "polyposis"). The results obtained by this baseline for the exact matching scheme (*Precision* = 0.8777, *Recall* = 0.7352 and *F-score*=0.8001) are significantly better than the *BANNER* scores for *AZDC*.

4 Conclusion

In this paper, we presented a case study of two corpora with disease annotations. Our results show that the domain and construction method of a corpus, the restrictions imposed on disease definitions, and other annotation schema requirements are likely to have a high impact on NER performance. In particular, *HVPC* is an easy corpus for NER in comparison with *AZDC* due to its low lexical variability, the brevity and high regularity of its disease names, and the requirements of the *HVPC* annotation schema.

We conclude that corpus features identified in this paper are predictive of NER performance, and possibly of performance in other tasks, and should be taken into account during corpus selection. In particular, we note that *HVPC* is not very suitable for the development of NER tools for disease name recognition in general. However, this corpus may be useful for the development and assessment of (disease) relation extraction (RE) tools, as it minimizes the noise introduced by incorrect NER. In addition, it may be suitable for training NER and RE tools for applications focused on particular diseases.

Future research directions include studying other biomedical corpora and specializing high-diversity corpora (e.g., *AZDC*) to determine characteristics that most affect NER performance.

Acknowledgements

NICTA is funded by the Australian Government through the Department of Communications and by the Australian Research Council through the ICT Centre of Excellence Program.

References

M. Bada, M. Eckert, D. Evans, K. Garcia, K. Shipley, D. Sitnikov, W.A. Baumgartner, K. Bretonnel Cohen, K.M. Verspoor, J.A. Blake, and L.E. Hunter. 2012. Concept annotation in the CRAFT corpus. *BMC Bioinformatics*, 13(161).

M.D. Cao and I. Zukerman. 2012. Experimental evaluation of a lexicon- and corpus-based ensemble for multi-way sentiment analysis. In *ALTA-2012 – Proceedings of the Australasian Language Technology Workshop*, pages 52–60, Dunedin, New Zealand.

M. Craven and J. Kumlien. 1999. Constructing biological knowledge bases by extracting information from text sources. In *ISMB 1999 – Proceedings of the International Conference on Intelligent Systems in Molecular Biology*, pages 77–86, Heidelberg, Germany.

C. Jacob, P. Thomas, and U. Leser. 2013. Comprehensive benchmark of Gene Ontology concept recognition tools. In *Proceedings of BioLINK SIG 2013*, pages 20–26, Berlin, Germany.

A. Jimeno-Yepes, E. Jimenez-Ruiz, V. Lee, S. Gaudan, R. Berlanga, and D. Rebholz-Schuhmann. 2008. Assessment of disease named entity recognition on a corpus of annotated sentences. *BMC Bioinformatics*, 9(S-3).

J.-D. Kim, T. Ohta, Y. Tateisi, and J. Tsujii. 2003. Genia corpus – a semantically annotated corpus for bio-textmining. *Bioinformatics*, 19(suppl. 1):i180–i182.

S. Kulick, A. Bies, M. Liberman, M. Mandel, R. McDonald, M. Palmer, A. Schein, L. Ungar, S. Winters, and P. White. 2004. Integrated annotation for biomedical information extraction. In *HLT/NAACL-2004 – Proceedings of the Human Language Technology Conference and the Annual Meeting of the North American Chapter of the Association for Computational Linguistics*, pages 61–68, Boston, Massachusetts.

J.D. Lafferty, A. McCallum, and F.C.N. Pereira. 2001. Conditional Random Fields: Probabilistic models for segmenting and labeling sequence data. In *ICML'2001 – Proceedings of the 18th International Conference on Machine Learning*, pages 282–289, Williamstown, Massachusetts.

R. Leaman and G. Gonzalez. 2008. BANNER: an executable survey of advances in biomedical named entity recognition. In R.B. Altman, A.K. Dunker, L. Hunter, T. Murray, and T.E. Klein, editors, *Pacific Symposium on Biocomputing*, pages 652–663. World Scientific.

R. Leaman, C. Miller, and G. Gonzalez. 2009. Enabling recognition of diseases in biomedical text with machine learning: corpus and benchmark. In *LBM2009 – Proceedings of the 3rd International Symposium on Languages in Biology and Medicine*, pages 82–89, Jeju Island, South Korea.

J.P. Pestian, C. Brew, P. Matykiewicz, D.J. Hovermale, N. Johnson, K. Bretonnel Cohen, and W. Duch. 2007. A shared task involving multi-label classification of clinical free text. In *BioNLP'07 – Proceedings of the Workshop on Biological, Translational, and Clinical Language Processing*, pages 97–104, Prague, Czech Republic.

S. Pyysalo, A. Airola, J. Heimonen, J. Björne, F. Ginter, and T. Salakoski. 2008. Comparative analysis of five protein-protein interaction corpora. *BMC Bioinformatics*, 9(Suppl. 3):S6.

D. Rebholz-Schuhmann, M. Arregui, S. Gaudan, H. Kirsch, and A. Jimeno-Yepes. 2008. Text processing through Web services: calling Whatizit. *Bioinformatics*, 24(2):296–298.

B. Rosario and M.A. Hearst. 2004. Classifying semantic relations in bioscience texts. In *ACL'2004 – Proceedings of the 42nd Annual Meeting of the Association for Computational Linguistics*, pages 431–438, Barcelona, Spain.

B. Settles. 2004. Biomedical named entity recognition using Conditional Random Fields and rich feature sets. In *Proceedings of the International Joint Workshop on Natural Language Processing in Biomedicine and its Applications*, pages 104–107, Geneva, Switzerland.

P. Stenetorp, S. Pyysalo, G. Topic, T. Ohta, S. Ananiadou, and J Tsujii. 2012. BRAT: A Web-based tool for NLP-assisted text annotation. In *EACL'2012 – Proceedings of the 13th Conference of the European Chapter of the Association for Computational Linguistics*, pages 102–107, Avignon, France.

K.M. Verspoor, K.B. Cohen, A. Lanfranchi, C. Warner, H.L. Johnson, C. Roeder, J.D. Choi, C. Funk, Y. Malenkiy, M. Eckert, N. Xue, W.A. Baumgartner, M. Bada, M. Palmer, and L.E. Hunter. 2012. A corpus of full-text journal articles is a robust evaluation tool for revealing differences in performance of biomedical natural language processing tools. *BMC Bioinformatics*, 13(107).

K.M. Verspoor, A. Jimeno-Yepes, L. Cavedon, T. McIntosh, A. Herten-Crabb, Z. Thomas, and J.P. Plazzer. 2013. Annotating the biomedical literature for the human variome. *Database: the journal of biological databases and curation*, 2013.

Cumulative Progress in Language Models for Information Retrieval

Antti Puurula
The University of Waikato
Private Bag 3105
Hamilton 3240, New Zealand
asp12@students.waikato.ac.nz

Abstract

The improvements to ad-hoc IR systems over the last decades have been recently criticized as illusionary and based on incorrect baseline comparisons. In this paper several improvements to the LM approach to IR are combined and evaluated: Pitman-Yor Process smoothing, TF-IDF feature weighting and model-based feedback. The increases in ranking quality are significant and cumulative over the standard baselines of Dirichlet Prior and 2-stage Smoothing, when evaluated across 13 standard ad-hoc retrieval datasets. The combination of the improvements is shown to improve the Mean Average Precision over the datasets by 17.1% relative. Furthermore, the considered improvements can be easily implemented with little additional computation to existing LM retrieval systems. On the basis of the results it is suggested that LM research for IR should move towards using stronger baseline models.

1 Introduction

Research on ad-hoc Information Retrieval (IR) has been recently criticized for being based on incorrect baseline comparisons. According to extensive evaluation of IR systems from over a decade, no progress has been demonstrated on standard datasets (Armstrong et al., 2009a; Armstrong et al., 2009b).

In this paper we propose that although much of this criticism is valid, much of the more recent progress in Language Model-based (LM) IR has not been evaluated or received the attention that it deserved. We evaluate on 13 standard IR datasets some of the improvements that have been suggested to LMs over the years. It is shown that the combination of Pitman-Yor Process smoothing, TF-IDF feature weighting and Model-based Feedback produces a substantial and cumulative improvement over the common baseline LM smoothing methods.

2 Improvements to LMs for IR

2.1 LM Approach to IR

The LM approach to ad-hoc IR considers documents and queries to be generated by underlying n-gram LMs. The Query Likelihood (QL) framework for LM retrieval (Hiemstra, 1998) treats queries as being generated by document models, reducing the retrieval of the most relevant documents into ranking documents by the posterior probability of each document given the query. Unigram LMs and a uniform distribution over document priors is commonly assumed, so that the QL-score for each document correspond to the conditional log-probability of the query given the document:

$$\log p_m(\boldsymbol{w}) = \log Z(\boldsymbol{w}) + \sum_n w_n \log p_m(n), \quad (1)$$

where $Z(\boldsymbol{w})$ is a Multinomial normalizer, $\boldsymbol{w}$ is the query word count vector, and $p_m(n)$ is given by a Multinomial estimated from the document word count vector $\boldsymbol{d}_m$:

$$p_m(n) = \frac{d_{mn}}{||\boldsymbol{d}_m||_1} \quad (2)$$

The QL framework is the standard application of LMs to IR. It is equivalent to using a Multinomial Naive Bayes model for ranking, with classes corresponding to documents, and a uniform prior over the document models.

2.2 Pitman-Yor Process Smoothing

The standard choices for LM model smoothing in IR have been Dirichlet Prior (DP) and 2-stage Smoothing (2SS) (Zhai and Lafferty, 2004; Smucker and Allan, 2007; Zhai, 2008). A recent improvement has been Pitman-Yor Process (PYP) smoothing, derived as approximate inference on a Hierarchical Pitman-Yor Process (Momtazi and Klakow, 2010; Huang and Renals, 2010). All methods interpolate document model parameter estimates linearly with a background model, differing in how the interpolation weight is determined. PYP applies additionally power-law discounting of the document counts. For all methods the smoothed parameter estimates can be expressed in the form:

$$p_m(n) = (1 - \alpha_m)\frac{d'_{mn}}{||\boldsymbol{d}'_m||_1} + \alpha_m p^c(n), \quad (3)$$

where $\boldsymbol{d}'_m$ is the discounted count vector, $p^c(n)$ is the background model and α_m is the smoothing weight.

DP chooses the smoothing weight as $\alpha_m = 1 - \frac{||\boldsymbol{d}_m||_1}{||\boldsymbol{d}_m||_1+\mu}$, where μ is a parameter. 2SS combines DP with Jelinek-Mercer smoothing, using $\alpha_m = 1 - \frac{||\boldsymbol{d}_m||_1 - \beta||\boldsymbol{d}_m||_1}{||\boldsymbol{d}_m||_1+\mu}$, where β is a linear interpolation parameter. PYP uses $\alpha_m = 1 - \frac{||\boldsymbol{d}'_m||_1}{||\boldsymbol{d}_m||_1+\mu}$, with the discounted counts $d'_{mn} = \max(d_{mn} - \Delta_{mn}, 0)$, where $\Delta_{mn} = \delta d^{\delta}_{mn}$ is produced by Power-law Discounting (Huang and Renals, 2010) with the discounting parameter δ. Replacing the discounting in PYP with the linear Jelinek-Mercer smoothing reproduces the 2SS estimates: $||\boldsymbol{d}'_m||_1 = ||\boldsymbol{d}_m||_1 - \beta||\boldsymbol{d}_m||_1$. PYP is therefore a non-linear discounting version of 2SS.

The background model $p^c(n)$ is commonly a collection model estimated by treating all available documents as a single large document: $p^c(n) = \sum_m \frac{d_{mn}}{\sum_{n'}\sum_{m'} d_{m'n'}}$. A uniform distribution is less commonly used: $p^c(n) = \frac{1}{|N|}$.

2.3 TF-IDF Feature Weighting

Unigram LMs make several incorrect modeling assumptions about natural language, such as considering all words equally informative. Feature weighting has shown to be useful in improving the effectiveness of Multinomial models in both IR (Smucker and Allan, 2006; Momtazi et al., 2010) and other uses (Rennie et al., 2003; Frank and Bouckaert, 2006). This is in contrast to earlier theory in IR that considered smoothing with collection model as non-complementary to feature weighting (Zhai and Lafferty, 2004).

TF-IDF word weighting for dataset documents can be done by:

$$d_n = \log(1 + \frac{d''_n}{||\boldsymbol{d}''||_0}) \log \frac{M}{M_n}, \quad (4)$$

where $\boldsymbol{d}''$ is the unweighted count vector, $||\boldsymbol{d}''||_0$ the number of unique words in the document, M the number of documents and M_n the number of documents where the word n occurs.

The first factor in Equation 4 is a TF log transform, using unique length normalization (Singhal et al., 1996). The second factor is Robertson-Walker IDF (Robertson and Zaragoza, 2009). Weighting query word vectors works identically. Collection model smoothing has an overlapping function to IDF weighting (Hiemstra and Kraaij, 1998). Here this interaction is taken into account by changing the background smoothing distribution into a uniform distribution.

2.4 Feedback Models

Pseudo-feedback is a traditional method used in IR that can have a large impact on retrieval performance. The top ranked documents can be used to construct a query model for a second pass of retrieval. With LMs there are two different ways to formalize this: KL-divergence Retrieval (Zhai and Lafferty, 2001) and Relevance Models (Lavrenko and Croft, 2001). Both methods enable replacing the query vector with a model (Zhai, 2008).

A number of variants exist for LM feedback modeling. Practical modeling choices are using only the top K retrieved documents, and truncating the query model to the words present in the original query (Zhai, 2008). The documents can be weighted according to the posterior probability of the document given the query, $p(\boldsymbol{d}_m|\boldsymbol{w}) \propto p_m(\boldsymbol{w})$ (Lavrenko and Croft, 2001).

The query model can also be interpolated linearly with the original query (Zhai and Lafferty, 2001). These modeling choices are combined here, resulting in a robust feedback model that has the same complexity for inference as the original query.

Using the top $K = 50$ retrieved documents, the query words $w_n > 0$ can be interpolated with the top document models $p_k(n)$:

$$w_n = (1-\lambda)\frac{w'_n}{||\boldsymbol{w}'||_1}\lambda\sum_k \frac{p_k(\boldsymbol{w}')\,p_k(n)}{Z}, \quad (5)$$

where $\boldsymbol{w}'$ is the original query, λ is the interpolation weight, and Z is a normalizer for the feedback counts: $Z = \sum_{n:w'_n>0}\sum_k p_k(\boldsymbol{w}')p_k(n)$.

Table 1: Dataset documents, test queries

Data	Development		Evaluation	
	Docs	Test	Docs	Test
fire_en	21919	90	16075	60
ohsu_trec	36890	63	196555	63
trec_ap	47172	118	33474	80
trec_cr	5063	38	4006	29
trec_doe	10053	28	7717	10
trec_fbis	23207	68	17315	48
trec_fr	25185	112	20581	75
trec_ft	41452	113	30549	75
trec_la	25944	87	17834	56
trec_pt	1635	9	1792	5
trec_sjmn	9160	29	6469	19
trec_wsj	21847	60	15839	41
trec_zf	19901	60	13763	39

2.5 Experiments

Combining the LM improvements was evaluated on standard ad-hoc IR datasets. These are the TREC 1-5[1] datasets split according to data sources, OHSU-TREC[2] and FIRE 2008-2011[3]. Each dataset was filtered by stopwording, short word removal and Porter-stemming. The datasets were each split into a development set for calibrating parameters and a held-out evaluation set. The OHSU-TREC dataset was split according to documents, using ohsumed.87 for development and ohsumed.88-91 for evaluation. The TREC and FIRE datasets were split according to queries, using the first $3/5$ of queries for each year as development data and the remaining $2/5$ as the evaluation data. For OHSU-TREC the queries consisted of the title and description sections of queries 1-63. For TREC and FIRE the description sections were used from queries 1-450 and 26-175, respectively. Table 1 summarizes the dataset split sizes.

The software used for the experiments was SGMWeka version 1.44, an open source toolkit for generative modeling[4]. Ranking effectiveness for the experiments was evaluated using Mean Average Precision from the top 50 documents (MAP@50). Smoothing parameters were optimized for MAP@50 using a parallelized Gaussian random search algorithm (Luke, 2009) on the development sets. The significance of experiment results was tested on the evaluation set MAP@50 scores of each dataset, using paired one-sided t-tests, with significance level $p < 0.05$.

The experiment results are shown in Table 2. Comparing PYP to DP and 2SS, PYP improves significantly on DP smoothing. The difference to 2SS is considerable as well, but not statistically significant due to variance. Adding TF-IDF (+TI) weighting to PYP, the improvement becomes significant over the 2SS baseline. Adding feedback (+FB) results in an improvement that is significant compared to both other improvements. The overall mean improvement over 2SS is 4.07 MAP@50, a 17.1% relative improvement.

2.6 Discussion

This paper presented an empirical evaluation of combining improvements to information retrieval language models. Experiments on standard ad-hoc IR datasets show that several improvements significantly and cumulatively improve on the baseline methods of LM retrieval using 2SS and DP smoothing methods. This contrasts with the reported illusionary improvements in IR literature (Armstrong et al., 2009a; Armstrong et al., 2009b). The considered improvements require very little additional computation and can be implemented with small modifications to existing IR search engines.

[1] http://trec.nist.gov/data/test_coll.html
[2] http://trec.nist.gov/data/t9_filtering.html
[3] http://www.isical.ac.in/~clia/
[4] http://sourceforge.net/projects/sgmweka/

Table 2: Ranking effectiveness as % MAP@50.

Dataset	DP	2SS	PYP	PYP +TI	PYP +TI +FB
fire_en	44.44	44.46	45.16	44.68	48.04
ohsu_trec	29.73	29.72	28.77	31.24	32.33
trec_ap	22.76	23.05	24.41	24.91	28.55
trec_cr	17.03	17.17	18.02	17.88	19.47
trec_doe	26.49	24.97	30.58	30.98	34.66
trec_fbis	23.51	23.57	24.66	26.14	28.81
trec_fr	18.42	18.53	18.72	18.86	19.68
trec_ft	23.26	23.55	24.65	23.73	24.80
trec_la	18.05	19.27	19.06	20.43	20.78
trec_pt	13.23	11.57	11.64	22.45	27.53
trec_sjmn	20.84	21.47	20.27	16.83	17.12
trec_wsj	32.00	32.44	33.77	34.53	38.41
trec_zf	17.92	18.48	17.54	19.52	20.97
mean	23.67	23.71	24.40	25.55	27.78

Several LM improvements have also been developed that require considerable additional computation. Methods such as document neighborhood smoothing, passage-based language models, word correlation models and bigram language models have all been shown to substantially improve LM performance (Miller et al., 1999; Song and Croft, 1999; Clinchant et al., 2006; Krikon and Kurland, 2011). Unfortunately, like the improvements discussed in this paper, many of these methods lack publicly available implementations, have been pursued by few researchers, and have been evaluated on a limited number of datasets. Evaluation of methods such as these could yield practical tools for IR and other applications of LMs.

The criticism of progress in ad-hoc IR (Armstrong et al., 2009a; Armstrong et al., 2009a; Trotman and Keeler, 2011) has missed valuable developments in LM-based IR. A second matter neglected in this criticism is the shift towards the learning-to-rank framework of IR (Joachims, 2002; Li, 2011), where individual retrieval models have reduced roles as base rankers and features. In this context it is not necessary for models to improve on a single measure or replace older ones; rather, it is sufficient that new models provide complementary information for combination of results.

The work reported here is preliminary and further experiments are required to understand possible interaction effects between the combined improvements. Given the performance and simplicity of the evaluated improvements, the commonly used DP and 2SS baselines for LMs should not generally be used as primary baselines for IR experiments. The combination of improvements shown in this paper is one potential baseline.

References

Timothy G. Armstrong, Alistair Moffat, William Webber, and Justin Zobel. 2009a. Has adhoc retrieval improved since 1994? In *Proceedings of the 32nd international ACM SIGIR conference on Research and development in information retrieval*, SIGIR '09, pages 692–693, New York, NY, USA. ACM.

Timothy G. Armstrong, Alistair Moffat, William Webber, and Justin Zobel. 2009b. Improvements that don't add up: ad-hoc retrieval results since 1998. In *Proceedings of the 18th ACM conference on Information and knowledge management*, CIKM '09, pages 601–610, New York, NY, USA. ACM.

Stéphane Clinchant, Cyril Goutte, and Eric Gaussier. 2006. Lexical entailment for information retrieval. In *Proceedings of the 28th European conference on Advances in Information Retrieval*, ECIR'06, pages 217–228, Berlin, Heidelberg. Springer-Verlag.

Eibe Frank and Remco R. Bouckaert. 2006. Naive bayes for text classification with unbalanced classes. In *Proceedings of the 10th European conference on Principle and Practice of Knowledge Discovery in Databases*, PKDD'06, pages 503–510, Berlin, Heidelberg. Springer-Verlag.

Djoerd Hiemstra and Wessel Kraaij. 1998. Twenty-one at trec-7: Ad-hoc and cross-language track. In *In Proc. of Seventh Text REtrieval Conference (TREC-7*, pages 227–238.

Djoerd Hiemstra. 1998. A linguistically motivated probabilistic model of information retrieval. In *Research and Advanced Technology for Digital Libraries*, volume 1513 of *Lecture Notes in Computer Science*, pages 569–584, Berlin, Germany. Springer Verlag.

Songfang Huang and Steve Renals. 2010. Power law discounting for n-gram language models. In *ICASSP*, pages 5178–5181. IEEE.

Thorsten Joachims. 2002. Optimizing search engines using clickthrough data. In *Proceedings of the eighth ACM SIGKDD international conference on Knowledge discovery and data mining*, KDD '02, pages 133–142, New York, NY, USA. ACM.

Eyal Krikon and Oren Kurland. 2011. A study of the integration of passage-, document-, and cluster-based information for re-ranking search results. *Inf. Retr.*, 14(6):593–616, December.

Victor Lavrenko and W. Bruce Croft. 2001. Relevance based language models. In *Proceedings of the 24th annual international ACM SIGIR conference on Research and development in information retrieval*, SIGIR '01, pages 120–127, New York, NY, USA. ACM.

Hang Li. 2011. A short introduction to learning to rank. *IEICE Transactions*, 94-D(10):1854–1862.

Sean Luke. 2009. *Essentials of Metaheuristics*. Lulu, version 1.2 edition. Available for free at http://cs.gmu.edu/~sean/book/metaheuristics/.

David R. H. Miller, Tim Leek, and Richard M. Schwartz. 1999. A hidden markov model information retrieval system. In *Proceedings of the 22nd annual international ACM SIGIR conference on Research and development in information retrieval*, SIGIR '99, pages 214–221, New York, NY, USA. ACM.

Saeedeh Momtazi and Dietrich Klakow. 2010. Hierarchical Pitman-Yor language model for information retrieval. In *Proceedings of the 33rd international ACM SIGIR conference on Research and development in information retrieval*, SIGIR '10, pages 793–794, New York, NY, USA. ACM.

Saeedeh Momtazi, Matthew Lease, and Dietrich Klakow. 2010. Effective term weighting for sentence retrieval. In *Proceedings of the 14th European conference on Research and advanced technology for digital libraries*, ECDL'10, pages 482–485, Berlin, Heidelberg. Springer-Verlag.

Jason D. Rennie, Lawrence Shih, Jaime Teevan, and David R. Karger. 2003. Tackling the poor assumptions of naive bayes text classifiers. In *ICML'03*, pages 616–623.

Stephen Robertson and Hugo Zaragoza. 2009. The probabilistic relevance framework: Bm25 and beyond. *Found. Trends Inf. Retr.*, 3:333–389, April.

Amit Singhal, Chris Buckley, and Mandar Mitra. 1996. Pivoted document length normalization. In *Proceedings of the 19th annual international ACM SIGIR conference on Research and development in information retrieval*, SIGIR '96, pages 21–29, New York, NY, USA. ACM.

Mark D. Smucker and James Allan. 2006. Lightening the load of document smoothing for better language modeling retrieval. In *Proceedings of the 29th annual international ACM SIGIR conference on Research and development in information retrieval*, SIGIR '06, pages 699–700, New York, NY, USA. ACM.

Mark D. Smucker and James Allan. 2007. An Investigation of Dirichlet Prior Smoothings Performance Advantage. Technical report, Department of Computer Science, University of Massachusetts, Amherst.

Fei Song and W. Bruce Croft. 1999. A general language model for information retrieval. In *Proceedings of the eighth international conference on Information and knowledge management*, CIKM '99, pages 316–321, New York, NY, USA. ACM.

Andrew Trotman and David Keeler. 2011. Ad hoc ir: not much room for improvement. In *Proceedings of the 34th international ACM SIGIR conference on Research and development in Information Retrieval*, SIGIR '11, pages 1095–1096, New York, NY, USA. ACM.

Chengxiang Zhai and John Lafferty. 2001. Model-based feedback in the language modeling approach to information retrieval. In *Proceedings of the tenth international conference on Information and knowledge management*, CIKM '01, pages 403–410, New York, NY, USA. ACM.

Chengxiang Zhai and John Lafferty. 2004. A study of smoothing methods for language models applied to information retrieval. *ACM Trans. Inf. Syst.*, 22(2):179–214, April.

ChengXiang Zhai. 2008. Statistical language models for information retrieval a critical review. *Found. Trends Inf. Retr.*, 2(3):137–213, March.

Error Detection in Automatic Speech Recognition

Farshid Zavareh, Ingrid Zukerman, Su Nam Kim and Thomas Kleinbauer
Faculty of Information Technology, Monash University
Clayton, VICTORIA 3800, Australia
sfhos2@student.monash.edu,
{Ingrid.Zukerman,Su.Kim,Thomas.Kleinbauer}@monash.edu

Abstract

We offer a supervised machine learning approach for recognizing erroneous words in the output of a speech recognizer. We have investigated several sets of features combined with two word configurations, and compared the performance of two classifiers: Decision Trees and Naïve Bayes. Evaluation was performed on a corpus of 400 spoken referring expressions, with Decision Trees yielding a high recognition accuracy.

1 Introduction

One of the main stumbling blocks for spoken Natural Language Understanding (NLU) systems is the lack of reliability of Automatic Speech Recognizers (ASRs) (Pellegrini and Trancoso, 2010). Recent research prototypes of ASRs yield Word Error Rates (WERs) between 15.6% (Pellegrini and Trancoso, 2010) and 18.7% (Sainath et al., 2011) for broadcast news. However, the WER of the ASR we employed (Microsoft Speech SDK 6.1) is 34% when trained on an open vocabulary plus a small language model for our corpus. This WER is consistent with that obtained in the 2010 Spoken Dialogue Challenge (Black et al., 2011).

In this paper, we offer a supervised machine learning approach to detect erroneous words in ASR output (this step will be followed by automatic error correction). Our approach was evaluated on a corpus of 400 spoken referring expressions, with the best-performing option yielding an average accuracy of 89% (Section 5).

The rest of this paper is organized as follows. In the next section, we discuss related work. In Section 4, we describe our experimental design, focusing on the features considered for our machine-learning approach. In Section 5, we discuss our results, followed by concluding remarks.

2 Related Research

Approaches for improving the performance of spoken NLU systems may be classified into *prevention* and *recovery*.

Prevention avoids errors by constraining the vocabulary (Gorniak and Roy, 2005; Sugiura et al., 2009) and grammatical constructs (Brooks and Breazeal, 2006) understood by an ASR. ASRs that employ this approach can process expected utterances efficiently, and work well in restricted domains. However, these ASRs have trouble processing unexpected utterances.

Recovery involves *error detection* followed by *correction*. During detection, an NLU system posits that a word in an utterance was incorrectly recognized. Three approaches to error recovery are described in (López-Cózar and Griol, 2010; Ringger and Allen, 1996; Zhou et al., 2006).

López-Cózar and Griol (2010) consider statistical information, and lexical, syntactic, semantic and dialogue-related information to correct ASR errors (i.e., replace, insert or delete words in a textual ASR output), and syntactic approaches to modify tenses of verbs and grammatical numbers to better match grammatical expectations.

Ringger and Allen (1996) use statistical information to construct a language model that quantifies the likelihood of word sequences, and a noisy channel model that predicts errors made by an ASR. They perform error detection and correction at the same time based on these models, which are trained using the words expected in the domain.

Zhou *et al.* (2006) perform error detection and correction of utterances, words and characters in Mandarin. They experiment with the *Generalized Word Posterior Probability* (*GWPP*) of an utterance, computed from word hypotheses, utterance length, language model, and acoustic observations; and features based on the N-best hypotheses, obtained from acoustic, language model and purity scores. When an erroneous word is de-

(a) Projective relations and "end, edge, corner" and "center" of a table

(b) Colour, size, positional relation and intervening object in a room

Figure 1: Two of the scenarios used to construct our corpus.

tected, all the characters in it are deemed to be wrong. Correction is then performed using a list of candidate alternatives for each erroneous character to generate a list of word hypotheses, and a linguistic model based on mutual information and trigrams to select the best word hypothesis.

Like these researchers, we offer corpus-based techniques to detect ASR errors. However, we employ features of the ASR output, rather than actual words or expectations from the context. By doing this, we hope to avoid over-fitting to domain-specific words and expectations.

3 The Corpus

Error detection performance was evaluated using the corpus constructed by Kleinbauer *et al.* (2013). The corpus originally comprised 432 free-form descriptions spoken by 26 trial subjects to refer to 12 designated objects in four scenarios (three objects per scenario, where a scenario contains between 8 and 16 objects; two scenarios appear in Figure 1). Half of the participants were native English speakers, and half were non-native. All the speakers were proficient in English, but the non-native speakers had a foreign accent, and some had idiosyncratic turns of phrase.

We manually filtered out 32 descriptions that were broken up by the ASR due to pauses made by the speakers, leaving 400 descriptions, which comprise 3,128 words in total, and 118 unique words. The descriptions, which varied in length and complexity, had an average length of 10 words and a median length of 8 words, with the longest description containing 21 words. Sample descriptions are: "the green plate next to the screwdriver at the top of the table", "the large pink ball in the middle of the room", "the plate in the corner of the table", and "the picture on the wall".

The ASR produced up to 50 alternative textual interpretations for each spoken description, ranked in descending order of probability. In total, 4,249 texts, with 33,927 words (706 unique) were generated. It is worth noting that more alternatives, with a higher average WER for the top-ranked options, were generated for non-native speakers than for native speakers.

We used the Levenshtein distance to align each alternative produced by the ASR with the reference (correct) description. The words in the alternative were then labeled as follows: **C**orrect, **I**nserted – absent from the reference interpretation, **R**eplaced – an incorrect word instead of the reference word, and **D**eleted – a placeholder for a reference word that is not in the alternative. The Inserted and Replaced words comprise the *Wrong* class (Deleted words cannot be modeled).

4 Experimental Design

In this section, we discuss the classifiers we considered, our feature sets, and evaluation methods.

Classifiers. We investigated two classifiers to decide whether a word in a text produced by the ASR is correct: Decision Trees (DT) (Quinlan, 1993) and Naïve Bayes classifiers (NB) (Domingos and Pazzani, 1997) (`cs.waikato.ac.nz/ml/weka/`).[1] For NB, we used equal-width binning to discretize continuous features (Catlett, 1991; Kerber, 1992).

Features. The target classes are *Correct* or *Wrong*, and three types of features were computed for each word w in a text: word based (5), sentence based (6), and phoneme based (2).

Word-based features. (1) *Part of Speech (PoS)* as determined by the Stanford PoS Tagger

[1]Initially we also considered linear chain Conditional Random Fields (CRF) (Lafferty et al., 2001) (`mallet.cs.umass.edu`), but they exhibited inferior performance.

(nlp.stanford.edu/software/tagger.shtml); (2) *Stop Word* as determined by the list in webconfs.com/stop-words.php; (3) *Position* of w in the text, defined as a nominal feature taking one of the values **B**eginning, **M**iddle or **E**nd; (4) *Time* taken by the speaker to pronounce word w (in fraction of a second); and (5) *Confidence Score* given to word w by the ASR.

Sentence-based features. (6) *Repetition Count* – number of alternatives where w is repeated; (7) *Repetition Ratio* (equivalent to purity score (Zhou et al., 2006)) – *Repetition Count* divided by the total number of alternatives; (8) *Replacement Ratio* – number of alternatives which, when aligned with the current alternative, label w with "R", divided by the total number of alternatives; (9) *Insertion Ratio* – number of alternatives which, when aligned with the current one, label w with "I", divided by the total number of alternatives; (10) *Rank* of the alternative containing w in the ASR output; and (11) *Sentence Length* – number of words in the current alternative.

Phoneme-based features (according to the CMU Pronunciation Dictionary, speech.cs.cmu.edu/cgi-bin/cmudict). (12) *Broad Sound Groups (BSGs)* – a vector of length 8 that represents the number of times each BSG occurs in word w, e.g., the word "problem" has 2 vowels, 2 stops, 2 liquids, and 1 nasal; and (13) *Phonemes* – a vector of length 39 that represents the number of times a phonetic symbol appears in w's phonetic transcription.

We experimented with the following sets of features: (1) *Word + Sentence* features, (2) *BSGs*, and (3) *Phonemes*. These features were computed for the current word (C), which is being classified, and for the previous, current and next word (*PCN*). For example, the following vector is produced when all 58 features are used for the current word (the first and last word in an alternative have missing features for P and N respectively):

$$\underbrace{f_1, \ldots, f_5}_{Word}, \underbrace{f_6, \ldots, f_{11}}_{Sentence}, \underbrace{f_{12}, \ldots, f_{19}}_{BSGs}, \underbrace{f_{20}, \ldots, f_{58}}_{Phonemes}.$$

Sets of features that included actual words produced accuracies of over 95%, but were unlikely to generalize. This was evident by inspecting the generated decision tree, which was shallow and wide. In fact, when w was used, most other features were ignored. Consequently, we decided not to include the actual words in our feature sets.

Table 1: Accuracy of DT versus NB: Different feature combinations.

Classifier	Features	Micro-average	Macro-average
NB	*Word+Sentence, C*	0.8156	0.8146
NB	*Word+Sentence, PCN*	0.8060	0.8066
NB	*BSGs, C*	0.6479	0.6446
NB	*BSGs, PCN*	0.6476	0.6479
NB	*Phonemes, C*	0.6610	0.6605
NB	*Phonemes, PCN*	0.6722	0.6731
DT	*Word+Sentence, C*	0.8110	0.8110
DT	*Word+Sentence, PCN*	0.8082	0.8121
DT	*BSGs, C*	0.7959	0.7974
DT	*BSGs, PCN*	0.8308	0.8324
DT	*Phonemes, C*	0.8614	0.8591
DT	***Phonemes, PCN***	**0.8771**	**0.8770**

Evaluation method. We employed 13-fold cross validation to train and test our corpus, where each fold comprises descriptions spoken by one native English speaker and one non-native speaker (Section 3). The per-speaker split ensures that sentences spoken by one trial subject do not appear in both training and test sets; and the native/non-native pairing balances the test sets, in the sense that they are of similar size, and ASR performance is similar for all sets (Section 3).

5 Results

Table 1 shows the results of our initial tests, which compare the performance of DT with that of NB in terms of micro- and macro-averaged accuracy (recall that the majority class of *Correct* words is 66%, Section 1). The odd-numbered rows contain the results for the three sets of features computed only for C, and the even-numbered rows contain the results for *PCN*. The statistically significant best result is boldfaced (statistical significance was calculated using the Paired Student's t-test).

As seen in Table 1, compared to C, *PCN* has a mixed effect on NB's performance, depending on the base features: *PCN* yields a statistically significant drop in accuracy for *Word+Sentence* (*p-value*=0.03), no statistically significant change for *BSGs*, and an improvement for *Phonemes* (*p-value*=0.015). The results are more consistent for DT: there is no significant difference in performance between C and *PCN* for *Word + Sentence*, but *PCN* yields statistically significant improvements for the other feature sets (*p-value* ≤ 0.05).

There were no statistically significant differences in accuracy between DT and NB for *Word+Sentence* with C and *PCN*. However, DT significantly outperformed NB in the remaining tests (*p-values* $<< 0.01$). In addition, *PCN*

Table 2: Accuracy comparison for DT with *Phonemes* plus different feature combinations.

Features *Phonemes, PCN +*	Micro-average	Macro-average
	0.8771	0.8770
Word+Sentence	0.8775	0.8787
BSGs	0.8776	0.8783
Word+Sentence and BSGs	0.8741	0.8754
PoS	**0.8902**	**0.8906**
PoS and BSGs	**0.8972**	**0.8971**

yielded a better performance than C for DT. Hence, our next tests are carried out using DT with *PCN* only.

Table 2 shows the results of combining *Phonemes*, which give the best accuracy (Table 1), with three feature sets: *Word+Sentence*, *BSGs* and *PoS*. The last two rows in Table 2 (boldfaced) show the feature sets that yield the highest (statistically equivalent) accuracies. These results, which were obtained with *PoS*, with and without *BSGs*, are significantly better than those achieved when *Word + Sentence* features or *BSGs* were used (*p-value* $\leq$ 0.05). Also, combining *Phonemes* with *Word+Sentence*, *BSGs* and both *Word+Sentence* and *BSGs* does not yield significant performance changes.

The most significant features in the best-performing decision trees are (in descending order): presence of the phonemes TH and Z, number of occurrences of N ($\leq$1 versus 1<), whether *PoS*=JJ (adjective), and whether the next word contains a stop *BSG* (at level 5 in the tree). This indicates that certain phonemes are prone to ASR mis-interpretation — an insight that has significant implications for the next stage of the ASR process, which consists of proposing replacements for words that are classified as *Wrong*. For example, we could create a confusion matrix between error-prone phonemes produced by the ASR and likely replacement phonemes, and suggest replacement words that include these hypothesized phonemes (Thomas et al., 1997; Zhou et al., 2006). It is worth noting that the ASR's *Confidence Score* was not used in the best-performing DTs. In fact, we observed that this score is often inconsistent with the *Correct/Wrong* class of a word.

As mentioned in Section 4, using the actual words as a classification feature yielded decision trees that over-fitted the data. Thus, it is possible that a similar effect takes place when *Phonemes* are used. Additional tests on different datasets should be conducted to rule out this possibility. Notice, however, that *BSGs* with *PCN* yield a creditable performance (third last row in Table 1), which improves statistically significantly (*p-value* << 0.01) when *BSGs* are combined with *PoS* and *Word+Sentence* (Table 3). This is noteworthy because *BSGs* are abstractions of *Phonemes*, and hence are less likely than *Phonemes* to fit a small number of words. Further, a correction procedure similar to that suggested for *Phonemes* would be applicable for *BSGs*.

Table 3: Accuracy comparison for DT with *BSGs* plus different feature combinations.

Features *BSGs, PCN +*	Micro-average	Macro-average
	0.8308	0.8324
Word+Sentence	**0.8640**	**0.8626**
PoS	**0.8639**	**0.8632**

6 Conclusions and Future Work

We have proposed a supervised learning method to predict the correctness of words in an ASR output. Our best classifier yields 89% accuracy. However, these results were obtained on a relatively small corpus with a limited vocabulary (Section 3). Hence, further tests with larger, more diverse corpora are needed to verify our results.

As mentioned in Section 3, we aligned the alternatives returned by the ASR with the reference text in order to label the words in each alternative. In addition, we aligned the alternatives with each other to compute multi-alternative features, such as *Repetition count* and *Replacement ratio*. In doing so, we implicitly assumed that there is a one-to-one mapping between the words in an alternative and those in the reference text, and also between the words in alternatives generated for the same spoken description. However this assumption is not always valid: we have observed cases where one word has been split into two words by the ASR, or a few words have been merged into one. Ringger and Allen (1996) have proposed a statistical solution to this problem, but unfortunately their method relies heavily on the vocabulary on which the system was trained. This problem will be addressed in the future.

The methods offered in this paper do not distinguish between a *Wrong* word and *Noise* (sighs or hesitations that are often mis-heard by the ASR as "and", "on" or "in"). In the future, we propose to retrain our system to deal with three classes, viz *Correct*, *Wrong* and *Noise*.

Acknowledgments

This research was supported in part by grants DP110100500 and DP120100103 from the Australian Research Council. The authors thank Masud Moshtaghi for his help with statistical issues.

References

A. Black, S. Burger, A. Conkie, H. Hastie, S. Keizer, O. Lemon, N. Merigaud, G. Parent, G. Schubiner, B. Thomson, J.D. Williams, K. Yu, S. Young, and M. Eskenazi. 2011. Spoken dialog challenge 2010: Comparison of live and control test results. In *Proceedings of the 11th SIGdial Conference on Discourse and Dialogue*, pages 2–7, Portland, Oregon.

A.G. Brooks and C. Breazeal. 2006. Working with robots and objects: Revisiting deictic reference for achieving spatial common ground. In *Proceedings of the 1st ACM SIGCHI/SIGART Conference on Human-robot Interaction*, pages 297–304, Salt Lake City, Utah.

J. Catlett. 1991. On changing continuous attributes into ordered discrete attributes. In *EWSL-91 – Proceedings of the European Working Session on Learning*, pages 164–178, Porto, Portugal.

P. Domingos and M. Pazzani. 1997. On the optimality of the simple Bayesian classifier under zero-one loss. *Machine Learning*, 29:103–130.

P. Gorniak and D. Roy. 2005. Probabilistic grounding of situated speech using plan recognition and reference resolution. In *ICMI'05 – Proceedings of the 7th International Conference on Multimodal Interfaces*, pages 138–143, Trento, Italy.

R. Kerber. 1992. ChiMerge: Discretization of numeric attributes. In *AAAI92 – Proceedings of the 10th National Conference on Artificial Intelligence*, pages 123–128, San Jose, California.

Th. Kleinbauer, I. Zukerman, and S.N. Kim. 2013. Evaluation of the *Scusi?* spoken language interpretation system – A case study. In *IJCNLP2013 – Proceedings of the 6th International Joint Conference on Natural Language Processing*, pages 225–233, Nagoya, Japan.

J.D. Lafferty, A. McCallum, and F.C.N. Pereira. 2001. Conditional Random Fields: Probabilistic models for segmenting and labeling sequence data. In *ICML'2001 – Proceedings of the 18th International Conference on Machine Learning*, pages 282–289, Williamstown, Massachusetts.

R. López-Cózar and D. Griol. 2010. New technique to enhance the performance of spoken dialogue systems based on dialogue states-dependent language models and grammatical rules. In *Proceedings of Interspeech 2010*, pages 2998–3001, Makuhari, Japan.

T. Pellegrini and I. Trancoso. 2010. Improving ASR error detection with non-decoder based features. In *Proceedings of Interspeech 2010*, pages 1950–1953, Makuhari, Japan.

J. R. Quinlan. 1993. *C4.5: Programs for Machine Learning*. Morgan Kaufmann Publishers, San Mateo, California.

E. Ringger and J.F. Allen. 1996. A fertility channel model for post-correction of continuous speech recognition. In *ICSLP-96 – Proceedings of the 4th International Conference on Spoken Language Processing*, pages 897–900, Philadelphia, Pennsylvania.

T.N. Sainath, B. Ramabhadran, M. Picheny, D. Nahamoo, and D. Kanevsky. 2011. Exemplar-based sparse representation features: From TIMIT to LVCSR. *IEEE Transactions on Audio, Speech and Language Processing*, 19(8):2598–2613.

K. Sugiura, N. Iwahashi, H. Kashioka, and S. Nakamura. 2009. Bayesian learning of confidence measure function for generation of utterances and motions in object manipulation dialogue task. In *Proceedings of Interspeech 2009*, pages 2483–2486, Brighton, United Kingdom.

I.E. Thomas, I. Zukerman, I. Oliver, D. Albrecht, and B. Raskutti. 1997. Lexical access for speech understanding using Minimum Message Length encoding. In *UAI'97 – Proceedings of the 13th Annual Conference on Uncertainty in Artificial Intelligence*, pages 464–471, Providence, Rhode Island.

Z. Zhou, H.M. Meng, and W.K. Lo. 2006. A multi-pass error detection and correction framework for Mandarin LVCSR. In *Proceedings of Interspeech 2006*, pages 17–21, Pittsburgh, Pennsylvania.

Working with Defaults in a Controlled Natural Language

Rolf Schwitter
Department of Computing
Macquarie University
Sydney NSW 2109, Australia
Rolf.Schwitter@mq.edu.au

Abstract

In this paper, we discuss how statements about defaults and various forms of exceptions to them can be incorporated into an existing controlled natural language. We show how these defaults and exceptions are translated and represented in the answer set programming paradigm in order to support automated reasoning.

1 Introduction

Defaults are statements in natural language that contain words such as *generally*, *normally*, or *typically* and generalise over what a particular kind of objects does. These kinds of statements are very useful in human communication, since we often do not have complete information about the world, but must be able to draw conclusions based on incomplete information. These conclusions are preliminary, and we may be forced to withdraw them later when new information becomes available. In this paper, we investigate how statements about defaults and exceptions to them can be incorporated into an existing controlled natural language (White and Schwitter, 2009) and what kind of formal machinery is required to process these defaults and to reason with them in the answer set programming paradigm (Gelfond and Lifschitz, 1988; Lifschitz, 2008; Gebser et al., 2012). Answer set programming (ASP) has its roots in logic programming and non-monotonic reasoning and is well suited for solving problems which involve commonsense reasoning (Eiter et al., 2009).

It is important to note that we are working here with a controlled natural language (for a survey see (Kuhn, 2013)). Our controlled natural language (CNL) consists of a well defined subset of English and has been designed to serve as a knowledge representation language with automated reasoning support (White and Schwitter, 2009). The CNL allows domain specialists to write a textual specification using the vocabulary of the application domain. The writing process of the CNL is guided by an intelligent authoring tool, and there is no need for the human author to formally encode the knowledge since the language processor takes care of this process.

2 CNL and Answer Set Programming

Our CNL processor translates a specification written in CNL with the help of a discourse representation structure (DRS) (Schwitter, 2012) in the spirit of (Kamp and Reyle, 1993; van Eijck and Kamp, 2011) into an executable ASP program.

An ASP program looks similar to a Prolog program but relies on a completely different computational mechanism. Instead of deriving a solution from a program specification using resolution like Prolog does, finding a solution in the ASP paradigm corresponds to computing one or more stable models (Gelfond and Lifschitz, 1988) that in principle always terminate. Stable models are also known as answer sets (Lifschitz, 2008).

The building blocks of an ASP program are atomic formulas (atoms), literals and rules. A rule is an expression of the following form:

$$L_0 \; or \; ... \; or \; L_k \leftarrow L_{k+1}, ..., L_m, \; not \; L_{m+1}, ..., \; not \; L_n.$$

where L_i's are literals. A literal is either an atom a or its classical negation $\neg a$. The symbol *not* stands for negation as failure; *not* L_i means that L_i is not known. The symbol $\leftarrow$ stands for an implication. The expression on the left-hand side of this symbol is called the *head* of the rule and may consist of a disjunction (*or*) of literals. The expression on the right-hand side is called the *body* of the rule. If the body of a rule is empty, then the rule is called a *fact*, and if the head of a rule is empty, then the rule is called a *constraint*. Constraints are not important in the following discussion, but they can be expressed in our CNL (Schwitter, 2012).

Our CNL processor takes, for example, the following text as input:

1. Sam is a child.
2. John is the father of Sam and Alice is the mother of Sam.
3. Every father of a child is a parent of the child.
4. Every mother of a child is a parent of the child.
5. Every parent of a child cares about the child.

and translates it via a DRS into an ASP program. In our case, the resulting ASP program is a positive logic program (without any form of negation or disjunction) and consists of a set of facts and rules:

```
child(sam).
father(john,sam).
mother(alice,sam).
parent(X,Y) :- father(X,Y), child(Y).
parent(X,Y) :- mother(X,Y), child(Y).
care(X,Y)   :- parent(X,Y), child(Y).
```

This program derives the following unique answer set with the help of an answer set solver:

```
{ child(sam) father(john,sam)
  mother(alice,sam) parent(john,sam)
  parent(alice,sam) care(alice,sam)
  care(john,sam) }
```

It contains – among other literals – the two literals `care(alice,sam)` and `care(john,sam)`.

3 Extending the CNL with Defaults

Now, let's assume that we learn the subsequent new information via the CNL sentence (6) and (7):

6. John does not care about Sam.
7. Alice is absent.

In everyday human reasoning this new information does in general not cause problems, since humans seem to able to revise their beliefs with ease. However, the addition of the formal representation `-care(john,sam)` derived from sentence (6) to the above-mentioned ASP program results in an inconsistent answer set. And the addition of the formal representation `absent(alice)` derived from sentence (7) does not have any impact on the conclusion `care(alice,sam)` (humans might have a least some doubts here).

In order to deal with this situation, we have to replace sentence (5) that results in a strict rule by a sentence such as (5') that expresses a default using the keyword *normally*[1] and builds the starting point for non-monotonic reasoning:

5'. Parents of a child normally care about the child.

As we will see, defaults can have two types of exceptions: strong exceptions and weak exceptions (Gelfond and Kahl, 2014). Strong exceptions refute a default's conclusion and derive the opposite of the default as sentence (6) should do. Weak exceptions render a default inapplicable and do not support certain conclusions as sentence (7) should do (the reasoner should not conclude that Alice cares about Sam).

In order to achieve this form of non-monotonic reasoning, we need to translate sentence (5') via a DRS into a suitable rule in ASP. Before we show how this can be done, we discuss in the next section what the target representation for defaults looks like in the ASP paradigm.

4 Representing Defaults in ASP

ASP is well suited for representing defaults since it distinguishes between two kinds of negation: classical negation and negation as failure. Combining both forms of negation allows us to express, for example, the closed world assumption, i.e., the assumption that a literal that is currently not known to be true is false. The closed world assumption is an example of a default (Reiter, 1978). For instance, the following ASP program includes a closed world assumption rule that combines classical negation (`-`) and negation as failure (`not`):

```
r(1). r(2). s(3). s(4). q(1,3). q(2,3).
-q(X,Y) :- r(X), s(Y), not q(X,Y).
```

This ASP program has a unique answer set that includes the two negative literals `-q(2,4)` and `-q(1,4)`:

```
{ r(1) r(2) s(3) s(4) q(1,3) q(2,3)
  -q(2,4) -q(1,4) }
```

It is interesting to note that an ASP program that combines strong negation and weak negation can apply the closed world assumption rule to some of its literals and leave other literals in the scope of the open world assumption. The same technique of combining classical negation and negation as failure can be used in our context.

[1](Pelletier and Asher, 1997) convincingly argue that there exists no univocal (probabilistic-oriented) quantifier (like **most** *parents*) that characterises all defaults.

A default that states that most elements *X* of a class *c* have property *p* can be represented by the following rule in ASP (Gelfond and Kahl, 2014).

```
p(X) :- c(X), not ab(d(X)), not -p(X).
```

That means `p(X)` holds if `c(X)` holds and it cannot be shown (`not`) that `X` is abnormal (`ab`) with respect to a default `d` and that it cannot be shown (`not`) that `-p(X)` does hold. Note that `X` might be abnormal and that `-p(X)` might hold but we currently cannot find any evidence that this is the case.

We can use the same technique to represent sentence (5') that results in a default (`d(care(X,Y))`) with the help of the following rule:

```
care(X,Y) :-
  parent(X,Y), child(Y),
  not ab(d(care(X,Y))),
  not -care(X,Y).
```

The subsequent ASP program that uses this default rule and represents the information derived from sentence (6) and (7) finally leads to a consistent answer set:

```
child(sam).
father(john,sam).
mother(alice,sam).
parent(X,Y) :- father(X,Y), child(Y).
parent(X,Y) :- mother(X,Y), child(Y).

-care(john,sam).
absent(alice).
care(X,Y) :-
  parent(X,Y), child(Y),
  not ab(d(care(X,Y))),
  not -care(X,Y).
```

Note that sentence (6) is a strong exception to the default rule and refutes the conclusion of the default. So far, there is no information in the ASP program that states that the default `d` is not applicable to `care(X,Y)`. In order to ensure that the weak exception `absent(alice)` derived from sentence (7) is correctly processed and can render the default `d` inapplicable, we need to add a so-called cancellation axiom to the ASP program:

```
ab(d(care(X,Y))) :-
  parent(X,Y), child(Y),
  not -absent(X).
```

This cancellation axiom makes sure that an absent parent of a child can be viewed as a weak exception to the default. Adding this cancellation axiom to our ASP program results in a unique answer set where the conclusion `care(alice,sam)` is abnormal (`ab`) with respect to the default `d` and the literal `care(alice,sam)` is unknown to the answer set:

```
{ child(sam) father(john,sam)
  mother(alice,sam) absent(alice)
  -care(john,sam) parent(john,sam)
  parent(alice,sam)
  ab(d(care(alice,sam)))
  ab(d(care(john,sam))) }
```

Note that if our ASP program would contain the information `-absent(alice)` instead of `absent(alice)`, then the default rule would succeed and the answer set would contain the information that Alice cares about Sam. If none of these two literals is available in the ASP, then the default rule does not apply.

5 Translating the CNL with Defaults

Our existing CNL processor consists of a chart parser, a unification-based grammar and a domain-specific lexicon (White and Schwitter, 2009). The language processor takes a CNL text as input and generates an extended DRS (Schwitter, 2012) for that text. This DRS is then translated into an ASP program (Schwitter, 2013) that is executed by *clingo* (Gebser et al., 2011), an ASP tool.

In our case, a DRS is a term of the form `drs(U,C)`. The first argument `U` is a list of discourse referents (i.e. quantified variables), and the second argument `C` is a list of simple and complex conditions for these discourse referents. Simple conditions are logical atoms and complex conditions are built from other DRSs with the help of logical connectors. Our extended DRS uses a reified notation for logical atoms together with a small number of predefined predicates.

Since our existing CNL already distinguishes between classical negation and negation as failure, it is possible to express rules that enforce the closed world assumption (as introduced in the last section). For example, the conditional sentence:

8. If there is no evidence that a mother of a child is absent then the mother is not absent.

is translated during the parsing process into the following DRS:

```
[]
  [A,B]
    relation(mother,A,B)
    object(B,child)
    NAF
      []
      property(absent,A)
  ==>
  []
    NEG
      []
      property(absent,A)
```

This DRS consists of a complex implicative condition (==>). Note that the CNL expression *there is no evidence that* results in a negation as failure operator (NAF) in the antecedent of this DRS and the translation of the expression *does not* leads to a classical negation (NEG) in the consequent. This extended DRS is then further translated into a strict rule in ASP:

```
-absent(X) :-
  mother(X,Y), child(Y),
  not absent(X).
```

This works fine; however, we also have to guarantee that sentences such as (5') are correctly translated into a default rule in an ASP program.

In order to achieve this, this sentence is first translated into the following DRS that uses a new operator ~~> to mark this kind of default:

```
[]
  [A,B]
    relation(parent,A,B)
    object(B,child)
  ~~>
  []
    predicate(care,A,B)
```

This operator helps us to distinguish between a strict rule and a default rule. The subsequent translation process into an ASP program identifies the type of operator in the DRS and translates the DRS into the following ASP rule:

```
care(X,Y) :-
  parent(X,Y), child(Y),
  not ab(d(care(X,Y))),
  not -care(X,Y).
```

This translation is achieved with the help of a Prolog program that takes a DRS as input and applies templates of the following form to generate the default rule:

```
[ Predicate, ':-',
  Term,
  not ab(d(Predicate)),
  not -Predicate ]
```

It is interesting to see that our existing CNL has already all the ingredients that are necessary in order to paraphrase this default rule. But in contrast to sentence (5') that uses the keyword *normally*, we end up with a rather lengthy circumscription:

9. If there is no evidence that a parent abnormally cares about a child and there is no evidence that the parent does not care about the child then the parent cares about the child.

But note that the translation of sentence (5') and sentence (9) result in the same default rule. In the case of sentence (9), the expression *abnormally cares about* translates into the literal ab(d(care(X,Y))).

Finally, we want to make sure that also cancellation axioms that implement a weak exception can be expressed in CNL and be translated into ASP rules. For example, the conditional sentence:

10. If there is no evidence that a parent of a child is not absent then the parent abnormally cares about the child.

represents a cancellation axiom and results in the following ASP rule:

```
ab(d(care(X,Y))) :-
  parent(X,Y), child(Y),
  not -absent(X).
```

Note that we could completely replace the expression *not absent* in our CNL specification by the positive expression *present* and we would end up with the same kind of inferences. That means strong negation is actually only a modelling convenience in ASP (Brewka et al., 2011) but does not increase the expressive power of the language.

6 Conclusion

Most of what we know about the world is normally true, with a few exceptions. Defaults allow us to draw conclusions based on knowledge that is common and normally the case. These defaults are sensitive to strong and weak exceptions and are important to non-monotonic reasoning that plays an important role in everyday human communication.

In this paper, we showed how an existing controlled natural language can be extended to accommodate statements about defaults and exceptions, how these statements can be translated via discourse representation structures into an answer set program, and how this answer set program can be used for automated reasoning. The general strategy for representing these defaults and exceptions to them in answer set programming is based on the work of (Gelfond and Kahl, 2014) and provides a clean and computationally elegant way to deal with these constructions.

To the best of our knowledge, our controlled natural language is the first one that supports the specification of defaults and exceptions in a well-defined subset of natural language and provides access to this form of non-monotonic reasoning via answer set programming.

References

Gerhard Brewka, Thomas Eiter, Miroslaw Truszczyński. 2011. Answer Set Programming at a Glance. In: *Communications of the ACM*, Vol. 54, No. 12, December.

Jan van Eijck and Hans Kamp. 2011. Discourse Representation in Context. In: J. van Benthem and A. ter Meulen (eds.), *Handbook of Logic and Language*, Second Edition, Elsevier, pp. 181–252.

Thomas Eiter, Giovambattista Ianni, Thomas Krennwallner. 2009. Answer Set Programming: A Primer. In: *Reasoning Web. Semantic Technologies for Information Systems*, LNCS, Vol. 5689, pp. 40–110.

Martin Gebser, Roland Kaminski, Benjamin Kaufmann, Max Ostrowski, Torsten Schaub, and Marius Schneider. 2011. Potassco: The Potsdam Answer Set Solving Collection. In: *AI Communications*, Vol. 24, No. 2, pp. 105–124.

Martin Gebser, Roland Kaminski, Benjamin Kaufmann, Torsten Schaub. 2012. *Answer Set Solving in Practice*. Synthesis Lectures on Artificial Intelligence and Machine Learning, Morgan and Claypool Publishers.

Michael Gelfond and Vladimir Lifschitz. 1988. The stable model semantics for logic programming. In: R. Kowalski and K. Bowen (eds.), *Proceedings of International Logic Programming Conference and Symposium*, pp. 1070–1080.

Michael Gelfond and Yulia Kahl. 2014. *Knowledge Representation, Reasoning, and the Design of Intelligent Agents.* The Answer-Set Programming Approach, Cambridge University Press.

Hans Kamp and Uwe Reyle. 1993. *From Discourse to Logic: Introduction to Modeltheoretic Semantics of Natural Language, Formal Logic and Discourse Representation Theory.* Kluwer, Dordrecht.

Tobias Kuhn. 2013. A Survey and Classification of Controlled Natural Languages. In: *Computational Linguistics*, MIT Press.

Vladimir Lifschitz. 2008. What Is Answer Set Programming? In: *Proceedings of AAAI'08*, Vol. 3, pp. 1594–1597.

Francis Jeffry Pelletier and Nicolas Asher. 1997. Generics and Defaults. In: J. van Benthem and A. ter Meulen (eds.), *Handbook of Logic and Language*, Elsevier Science, Chapter 20, pp. 1125–1177.

Raymond Reiter. 1978. On closed world data bases. In: H. Gaillaire and J. Minker (eds.), *Logic and Data Bases*, Plenum Press, New York, pp. 55–76.

Rolf Schwitter. 2012. Answer Set Programming via Controlled Natural Language Processing. In: T. Kuhn and N. E. Fuchs (eds.), *CNL 2012*, LNCS 7427, Springer, pp. 26–43.

Rolf Schwitter. 2013. The Jobs Puzzle: Taking on the Challenge via Controlled Natural Language Processing. In: *Journal of Theory and Practice of Logic Programming*, Vol. 13, Special Issue 4-5, pp. 487–501.

Coline White and Rolf Schwitter. 2009. An Update on PENG Light. In: L. Pizzato and R. Schwitter (eds.), *Proceedings of ALTA 2009*, Sydney, Australia, pp. 80–88.

Poster papers

Rhythm, Metrics, and the Link to Phonology

Jason Brown
Dept. of Applied Language Studies & Linguistics
University of Auckland
jason.brown@auckland.ac.nz

Sam Mandal
University of Western Sydney
and
MARCS Auditory Laboratories
s.mandal@uws.edu.au

Abstract

Since Ramus et al. (1999) a number of statistical *metrics* have been routinely employed by researchers (Ramus 2003, Grabe & Low 2002 etc.) in an effort to rhythmically classify languages. However, recent studies by Arvaniti (2009), Tilsen & Arvaniti (2013), Arvaniti & Rodriquez (2013) etc., have challenged both the validity of these metrics in reflecting speech rhythm, and the physical measurability of rhythm itself. The present study takes a comparative evaluative approach, and explores the applicability of the proposed metrics to a Papuan language (Urama) with a phonology quite different than traditional Western European (W.E.) languages. It is argued here that the statistical underpinning of the existing rhythm metrics is a direct outcome of an overt effort to capture the temporal durational characteristics of the phonotactics of W.E. languages. As such, these metrics are only capable of providing a crude measure of *timing*.

1 Introduction

Approaches to rhythm in language have traditionally viewed languages as falling into either strict or less precisely-defined categories that were based primarily on the notion of *timing* (Abercrombie 1967, Port et al. 1987). *Timing,* as used in these contexts, is more or less a blanket-term referring to all aspects of durational variation in speech. Originally linked to the notion of *isochrony* (Abercrombie 1967), the term has since been increasingly used to refer to the relative temporal durational variability of consonantal and vocalic intervals in running speech (Ramus et al. 1999). The cornerstone of subsequent studies (Grabe & Low 2002, Ramus et al. 2003, Dellwo 2006 etc.) have been a consistent focus on the relative variability of consonantal and vocalic durations across languages, with an effort to establish generalizations in patterns of durational variability to help classify languages into different *rhythm classes.* Metrics were developed as tools of statistical measurement of said durational variability in speech. The efficacy of such efforts, and the phonological basis of the rationale offered for their methodological choices, have been vigorously disputed in recent works. Arvaniti (2009, 2012), Tilsen & Arvaniti (2013), Arvaniti & Rodriquez (2013) present empirical evidence to illustrate that the aforementioned statistical metrics can neither classify non-prototypical languages, nor provide correlates of perceptual discrimination. These authors offer perceptual experimental data to prove that not only is *timing* affected by a multitude of factors (speaking rate, voice quality, stimuli type etc.), but perceptual discrimination is often achieved through attunement to duration-independent acoustic factors such as fundamental frequency (f_0).

This being the case, the present paper aims to investigate the phonological basis for these acoustic metrics, the interrelation between the mathematical formulae they employ and the acoustic correlates of rhythm they are supposed to measure. Our primary hypothesis is that these metrics are simply different statistical measures of how consonant or vowel-heavy a language (or a token) is, and while there might possibly be some correlation between perceptual discrimination abilities of listeners and metric scores, the metrics are rarely complete indicators of the causation of such perceptual abilities. We further argue that 'rhythm' is more of a psychological reality than an acoustic factor, an abstract realization that lacks a single physical/acoustic correlate. It is, rather, the perceptual effect produced in the mind by the internal interactions of the different phonological abstractions that constitute a language. The components that make up the phonology and interact with each other to induce the perceptual effect in the mind of the listener that is *rhythm in speech,* and being a psychological reality rather than an acoustic entity *rhythm* is likely to elude any physical/acoustic probing. Thus, there is not much of a basis for *rhythmic classes* in these metrics (cf. Arvaniti 2009); however, they do reflect the gross phonological properties of a given language. To the extent that these phonological properties are specific properties of individual rhythm classes remains rather unsubstantiated in terms of empirical evidence.

This paper presents an instrumental study of a unique (and under-documented) language, and an elaboration of both whether the traditional methodologies and metrics that have yielded dubious results even for most Western European (W.E.) languages can capture the dynamics of a phonotactically 'strict' language, and what methodological changes may be required in order to accommodate under-studied phonological types.

2 Rhythm Metrics

The search for the proper acoustic metrics to capture the durational variability patterns thought to be indicators of rhythmic typology, Ramus et al. (1999) claim, was based on the observations regarding certain phonotactic regularities in syllable structure within Romance and Germanic languages, as elucidated in Dauer (1983). However, Arvaniti (2009) finds that these metrics are only partially based on the eight parametric criteria elaborated by Dauer (1983), and further that Dauer's (1983) own study contradicts the predictions one would make based on her criteria for languages such as Greek and Spanish (Dauer 1983:58). As Arvaniti points out, the main source of complication is two-fold; (a) Dauer's (1983) criteria have not been rigorously tested with a wide enough cross-linguistic focus, and (b) while Dauer's criteria combine factors that directly reflect phonetic timing as well as ones with no direct link to timing (e.g. function of f_0 in language), the design philosophy employed for the metrics only takes into account *those specific criteria that relate directly to timing* while excluding others. This is inherently problematic given that duration of segments, the main target of these statistical metrics, is affected by a multitude of factors like consonant gemination, phrase-final lengthening, syllable-position, focus-oriented lengthening, etc., all of which fail to be accounted for in the these metrics. As such, it becomes logically evident that these metrical measurements are very loosely based on a small subset of Dauer's (1983) criteria and can, at best, provide a very crude measurement of durational variability in speech.

Despite such obvious shortcomings, Ramus et al. (1999), for example, claims that a combination of %V and ΔC provide the best correlates for acoustic rhythm. Their study was limited to mostly W.E. languages, and Grabe and Low (2002) rightly point out that using different metrics on a large sub-set of languages yield confusing results with the effect of classifying the same language into different rhythmic types. For example, a PVI-based measure classifies Thai as stress-timed and Luxembourgish as syllable-timed, while a combination of %V and ΔC classify the same languages as being syllable-timed and stress-timed, respectively. Similarly, White and Mattys (2007a, 2007b) compared the efficacy of different metrical measurements using different varieties of English, and concluded that a combination of %V and VarcoV yields the most effective results. Other such attempts at arriving at the *perfect metric* abound in the literature, however one significant contribution made by Grabe and Low (2002) is the revelation that none of these metrical measurements fares very well when applied to (prosodically) non-prototypical, non-W.E. languages. One might wonder whether these metrics, and by extension Dauer's (1983) criteria, were a result of a focus on the phonology of these well-documented W.E. languages.

Arvaniti and Rodriquez (2013) point out that not only have rhythm discrimination experiments been conducted on a very small sub-set of languages, but the languages typically used for such experiments differ in other perceptual factors than timing, such as inherent speaking rate. While Germanic languages are typically spoken with a lower speaking rate, Romance languages employ a much faster rate (cf. Arvaniti & Rodriquez 2013). These *non*-rhythmic factors potentially lead to perceptual discrimination, thus rendering the conclusion that discrimination is due to rhythmic differences moot. In fact, Ramus et al. (2003) report that in their experiments Polish was discriminated from both English (stress timed) and Spanish (syllable timed), even though in that study it is classified as a stress-timed language. Clearly, rhythm (as captured by these metrics) cannot be the sole perceptual cue to inter-language discrimination.

The metrics under discussion here are:

%V: Proportion of vocalic intervals within an utterance, an indicator of overall syllable complexity, obtained by calculating the total duration of the utterance that is taken up by the vowels, i.e. [(sum total of all the vocalic intervals in the utterance) / (duration of the utterance)] x 100. The basic problem with this approach is that it was developed with languages like English and German in mind, where Vs and Cs are either present in approximately equal amounts, or Cs slightly outnumber Vs, but where this is balanced out by the fact that vowels get lengthened or shortened regularly due to phonotactics, while consonants remain relatively unaffected. Speaking rate, likewise, affects vowel duration much more than consonant durations.

PVI: The pairwise variability index is calculated by taking into account the durational difference between pairs of successive intervals, then taking the absolute value |x| of the difference and dividing it by the mean duration of the pair. For rPVI, the division step is omitted. The division is done to normalize for speaking rates, and is applied to vowels only. Stress-timed languages like English tend to display high scores for nPVI, as they use full vowels as well as reduced vowels.

Varco: Coefficient of variation (of C and V), i.e. [(the standard deviation of vocalic/consonantal interval durations) / (mean of vocalic/consonantal duration)] x 100.

ΔC & ΔV: Standard deviation of the consonantal and vocalic duration of the utterances.

3 Methods

The present study seeks to apply the various methodologies discussed in the preceding sections to an under-documented language, and test whether they are capable of providing a stable account of durational variability. The language considered for this study is Urama, a Papuan language of New Guinea. Urama is ideal as a test case, as its phonotactics are more 'strict' than W.E. languages: all syllables are open, no consonant clusters are allowed, there exists no vowel reduction, and there is no vowel length contrast. Thus, Urama tolerates long strings of vowels, but not of consonants.

Grabe and Low (2002) have pointed out that the proposed metrics are incapable of handling non-prototypical languages, and fail to classify these languages into any fixed rhythmic category (hence *non-prototypical)*. However, to the best of our knowledge, no one has tested how the durational contrasts of more exotic languages are captured by a system built almost entirely upon data from W.E. languages. Arvaniti (2012) suggests that in order to tap into the true timing pattern of a language, metric scores must be derived for controlled and uncontrolled data. She suggests two types of control-data: type-1 designed to emulate syllable-timing by eliminating consonant clustering, vowel reductions etc. as much as permissible within the language's phonology, and type-2, designed to do just the opposite and emulate stress-timing. Such methodologies, however, fail to account for languages like Urama, which employs a strict (C)V template for its syllable-structure, while lacking any contrastive lengthening of vowels.

In this study, we employ the three most popular metric-combinations (%V-ΔC, CrPVI-VnPVI and %V-VarcoV) and test their effectiveness in capturing the timing patterns of Urama. We compare the scores to other languages in order to establish a cross-linguistic contrast with an effort to test the extent to which these metrics can reflect the differences in the phonological and phonetic properties of these languages.

3.1 Participants and Stimuli

The participant is a female native speaker of Urama. There were two contexts in which speech data was collected: controlled speech contexts, where the participant was instructed to read and/or repeat sentences, spoken at a moderate rate, and spontaneous speech contexts.

For the controlled speech data, the participant was instructed to read/repeat a declarative sentence that was between 12-19 syllables long, and on average approximately 4-5 seconds in duration. In traditional metric-based rhythm studies the standard practice is to use declarative utterances because they are expected to most accurately approximate running speech (Ramus 1999, Grabe & Low 2002). However, in order to test whether clause type has an impact on the metrics, both interrogative and exclamative versions of the declarative sentence were also recorded for this study. There were 5 sentences constructed in this fashion, yielding 15 (3 conditions x 5 base sentences) sentences total. For the spontaneous contexts, a short (approximately 1.5 minute) narrative was collected, spoken at a rate appropriate for this kind of speech style. It is important to note here that if the metrics indeed capture *rhythm in speech*, a property of the inherent prosody of the language, the scores should be independent of both the type and the duration of the utterances used for analyses.

4 Results

The comparisons of each of the metrics for Urama, including interrogatives (Q) and exclamatives (!) vs. English, Dutch, French, and Spanish (from Arvaniti 2012) are presented below for controlled sentences.

	English	Dutch	French	Spanish	Urama	Urama Q	Urama !
%V	40.1	42.3	43.6	43.8	51.45	54.68	57.1
ΔC	0.054	0.053	0.044	0.047	0.016	0.027	0.031
ΔV	0.046	0.042	0.038	0.033	0.025	0.023	0.035
CrPVI	5.6	6.2	4.8	5.25	0.017	0.019	0.021
VnPVI	67	59.8	44.8	42.5	26.711	26.64	23.68

Table 1: Controlled speech metric scores

The scores for spontaneous speech are compared with English, Spanish, and Italian in Table 2.

	English	Spanish	Italian	Urama
varcoV	61.5	67.6	63.1	67.102
VarcoC	58.1	50.9	52.3	35.299
%V	51.9	53.2	54.7	54.16
ΔC (x100)	63.4	47.3	43.1	3.3
VnPVI	62.9	57.2	51.8	60.547
CrPVI	73.8	51.6	46.1	0.039

Table 2: Spontaneous speech metric scores

What can be seen here are extremely low C-scores, especially CrPVI in spontaneous speech.

With respect to %V, it is predicted that it is languages like Urama where this measure would be most likely to fail. Urama vowels, in any given utterance, outnumber consonants significantly. Hence, the longer the utterance, the more vowels there will be; with an increase in total data, the increase in the amount of Cs and Vs is far from equal. Given the controlled data above, the value ranges from 51.4 (for declaratives) to 57.1 (for exclamatives), which is a larger difference than is present between stress-timed English (40.1) and syllable-timed French (43.6).

There are similar problems with PVI values. In Urama vowel reduction is not a factor, not unlike French. The scores however are far greater than French, which is most likely due to the fact that a very low presence of consonants eliminates durational variability in vowels. Similarly, complete absence of consonant clusters contributes to significantly lower CrPVI scores. With respect to Varco, once again, the syllable structure employed by Urama explains the scores. While Spanish and Urama receive similar Varco V scores, the Varco C scores for Urama are substantially lower than any other language. This is again due to an imbalance in Vs vs. Cs.

Considering the mathematical rationale behind the different metrics employed in rhythm studies, it can be readily observed that Δ-values being simply *standard deviation* of vocalic/consonantal intervals remain unaffected by the *sequential patterning* of durational variability of segments- a key element underlying the perceptual effects of *speech rhythm*. The PVI, however, captures this *sequential patterning* by averaging the durational difference between successive vocalic or consonantal intervals:

$$r\,PVI = \left[\sum_{k=1}^{m-1} |d_k - d_{k+1}| / (m-1) \right];$$

However, there are a couple of discrepancies present in the way in which PVI measures are usually applied. First, for vocalic intervals a *normalized* version of the PVI measure is used in order to *supposedly* correct for speaking rate and *tempo fluctuations*. This is achieved by relating the difference between two consecutive intervals to the mean of the two durations.

$$n\,PVI = 100 \times \left[\sum_{k=1}^{m-1} \left| \frac{d_k - d_{k+1}}{(d_k + d_{k+1})/2} \right| / (m-1) \right];$$

The effect, however, is a very *local normalization* that actually ends up reducing length differences caused in running speech due to stress, accent and other phonotactic factors. Second, while it may still be argued that the PVI does indeed capture *some of the sequential patterning effects of duration* it still calculates vocalic and consonantal variations separately, and thus fail to capture any perceptual effects of vocalic and consonantal structure on the auditory rhythmic patterns of languages.

A third surprising result is the higher consonantal variability for all languages in spontaneous speech measures. Such results have been reported elsewhere (Barry & Russo 2003), with spontaneous speech from Italian reportedly exhibiting higher CrPVI values. In rhythmic terms, then, such results would suggest that spontaneous speech from the tested languages is *more* stress-timed than controlled utterances. Such differences between controlled and spontaneous speech data is presumably a direct result of segmental lengthening of vowels and sonorants in running speech, and is likely to exhibit variation as a function of syntactic-lexical structure of phrases, focus, speech style, tempo, etc., all of which occur with greater variability and lesser predictability in *undersigned* and *uncontrolled* speech.

Otherwise, Urama follows the pattern of changes in scores exhibited by other stress vs. syllable-timed languages in the tables, such as higher %V scores than stress-timed languages, lower PVI scores for vowels, etc. It tends to follow the syllable-timed languages in its scores when compared to English, with the only difference being that the difference in scores for Urama is substantial, an effect of the extremely V-heavy nature of the syllable-structure.

5 Conclusion

W.E. languages tend to get grouped according to rhythm classes in metrical analysis, because these metrics were *specifically designed with their syllable structure and phonotactics* in mind. They do not reflect rhythm, only co-incidentally their scores for W.E. languages tend to correlate with rhythmic typology because the mathematic underpinnings of the metrics reflect phonotactic properties. The results reported for Urama illustrate how the variation in metric scores correlates with variation in phonotactics. Thus, these metrics only provide a *very crude* measure of timing, illustrated by the confusing inter-language scores. This has obvious implications for speech technology incorporating rhythmic properties, including automatic recognition of emotion (Ringeval et al. 2012), spoken language identification (Timoshenko & Höge 2007), Zhang & Glass 2009), and clinical applications (Selouani et al. 2012).

References

Abercrombie, D. 1967. *Elements of general phonetics* (Edinburgh University Press, Edinburgh).

Arvaniti, A. 2009. Rhythm, timing and the timing of rhythm. *Phonetica* 66:46-63.

Arvaniti, A. 2012. "The usefulness of metrics in the quantification of speech rhythm. *Journal of Phonetics* 40, 351–373.

Arvaniti, A. & Rodriguez, T. 2013. The role of rhythm class, speaking rate and *F0* in language discrimination. *Laboratory Phonology* 4: 7-38.

Barry, W.J. and Russo, M. 2003. "Measuring rhythm. Is it separable from speech rate?", Proceedings of the International AAI Workshop "Prosodic Interfaces", Nantes 27-29 mars, 2003

Dauer, R. M. 1983. Stress-timing and syllable-timing reanalyzed. *Journal of Phonetics* 11:51-62.

Dellwo, V. 2006. Rhythm and speech rate: A variation coefficient for deltaC. In P. Karnowski & I. Szigeti (Eds.), *Language and Language-Processing: Proceedings of the 38th Linguistics Colloquium*, Piliscsaba 2003 (pp. 231-241). Frankfurt am Main, Germany: Peter Lang.

Grabe, E., & Low, E. L. 2002. Durational variability in speech and the rhythm class hypothesis. In C.Gussenhoven & N. Warner (Eds.), *Laboratory Phonology 7* (pp. 515-546). Berlin: Mouton de Gruyter.

Port, R.R., J. Dalby & M. O'Dell. 1987. Evidence for mora-timing in Japanese. *Journal of the Acoustical Society of America* 81:1574-1585.

Ramus, F., Nespor, M., & Mehler, J. 1999. Correlates of linguistic rhythm in the speech signal. *Cognition* 73:265-292.

Ramus, F. 2002. Acoustic correlates of linguistic rhythm: Perspectives. Proc. Speech Prosody, Aix-en-Provence 2002:115–120.

Ringeval, F., Chetouani, M., & Schuller, B. 2012. Novel metrics of speech rhythm for the assessment of emotion. *Interspeech 2012*, pp. 2763-2766.

Selouani, S.A., Dahmani, H., Amami, R. & Hamam, H. 2012. Using speech rhythm knowledge to improve dysarthric speech recognition. *International Journal of Speech Technology* 15:57-64.

Tilsen, S. & Arvaniti, A. 2013. Speech rhythm analysis with decomposition of the amplitude envelope: Characterizing rhythmic patterns within and across languages. *Journal of the Acoustical Society of America* 134: 628-639.

Timoshenko, E. & Höge, H. 2007. Using speech rhythm for acoustic language identification. *Interspeech 2007*, pp. 182-185.

White, L. & Mattys, S. L. 2007a. Calibrating

rhythm: First language and second language studies. *Journal of Phonetics* 35: 501–522.

White, L. & Mattys, S. L. 2007b. Rhythmic typology and variation in first and second languages., in *Segmental and Prosodic Issues in Romance Phonology,* P. Prieto, J. Mascaró and M. J. Solé (John Benjamins, Amstredam), pp. 237-257.

Zhang, Y. & Glass, J.R. 2009. Speech rhythm guided syllable nuclei detection. *International Conference on Acoustics, Speech and Signal Processing*, pp. 3797-3800.

Differences in Speaker Individualising Information between Case Particles and Fillers in Spoken Japanese

Shunichi Ishihara
Department of Linguistics
Australian National University

shunichi.ishihara@anu.edu.au

Abstract

This study investigates idiosyncrasy manifested in language use in spoken Japanese. For this purpose, we use speaker classification techniques as analytical tools. More precisely, focusing on Japanese case particles and fillers, of which the linguistic functions differ significantly, we aim to investigate 1) the extent of speaker idiosyncrasy in the selection of certain case particles/fillers over others in Japanese monologues, and 2) the differences, if any, between case particles and fillers in the degree of speaker-individualising information. We discuss what contributes to the identified differences between case particles and fillers. This study will contribute to the further development of automatic speaker recognition systems and authorship analysis studies.

1 Introduction

We intuitively know that different people speak/write differently, even when they try to convey the same message. We also know that people tend to use their individually-selected, preferred words despite the fact that, in principle, they can use any word at any time from the vocabulary built up over the course of their lives. Every speaker of a given language has their own distinctive and individual version of the language – which is often referred to as their idiolect (Halliday et al. 1964).

Linguistic idiosyncrasy has been studied in both spoken and written languages (yet, more extensively on written languages) (Baayen et al. 1996, Burrows 1987, Doddington 2001, Ishihara and Kinoshita 2010, Weber et al. 2002). Many of these studies were based on the unique lexical usage of authors (Holmes et al. 2001, Juola and Baayen 2005), assuming that word selection is unique to the individual author, and that their preferred selection is consistent over time (Holmes 1992). In particular, function words are often used as a feature to quantify the unique lexical usage of individual authors, and it has been attested that function words carry author-individualising information (Binongo 2003, Holmes, et al. 2001). In addition to function words, fillers (such as English "um", "you know", and "like"), which are unique to spoken languages, have also been reported to carry speaker idiosyncratic information (Ishihara and Kinoshita 2010, Weber, et al. 2002).

Although the above studies demonstrated that function words and fillers carry speaker/writer idiosyncratic information, the degree/characteristics of the individualising information that they carry may be different as the type of linguistic information they provide is significantly different. We will investigate this in this study. For that purpose, we use case-particles and fillers appearing in Japanese monologues. Case particles are representative function words in Japanese. We use Japanese monologues because many of the previous studies used English as the target language, and research on idiosyncrasy in spoken languages are relatively fewer than those on written languages.

That being said, the current study will investigate 1) the extent of speaker idiosyncrasy in the selection of certain case particles/fillers over others in Japanese monologues, and 2) the differences, if any, between case particles and fillers in the degree of idiosyncrasy.

In order to answer the above questions, we will conduct a series of speaker classification tests. The hypothesis is that the more consistent the individual speaker's selection of words (e.g. particles) is, and the more significantly words selected by one speaker differ from those selected by another, then the more accurate the speaker classification results will be.

1.1 Case Particles and Fillers

Case particles (kaku-joshi), which are function words, provide the grammatical relationship between the predicate of a sentence and the noun phrases appearing in the sentence. In Example 1), the case particles, **-ga**, **-de** and **–o**, are the subjective (SUBJ), instrumental (INS), and accusative (ACC) markers, respectively.

ani-**ga** boo-**de** watashi-**o** tataita Ex 1)
elder.brother-**SUBJ** stick-**INS** I-**ACC** hit.past
My elder brother hit me with a stick.

Fillers function as placeholders when fluency fails and one is searching for a desired expression (Martin 2004:1041). In the database we used for this study, a filler tag is assigned to the preselected words which have the function of 'filling up gaps in utterances'. Fillers are unique to spoken languages.

2 Methodology

Two kinds of comparisons are involved in speaker classification tests. The first is *Same Speaker Comparison* (SS comparison) in which two speech samples produced by the same speaker need to be correctly identified as being from the same speaker. The second is, *mutatis mutandis*, *Different Speaker Comparison* (DS comparison). These comparisons were conducted separately for case particles and fillers. Since the comparisons are yes-no basis, the baseline for these comparisons is 50%.

2.1 Database and Speakers

For this study, we used the monologues from the Corpus of Spontaneous Japanese (CSJ) (Maekawa et al. 2000), which are categorised as *Academic Presentation Speech* (APS) or *Simulated Public Speech* (SPS). APS was mainly recorded live at academic presentations, most of which were 12-25 minutes long. For SPS, 10-12 minute mock speeches on everyday topics were recorded. We selected our speakers from this corpus based on three criteria: availability of multiple and non-contemporaneous recordings, spontaneity (e.g. not reading) of the speech, and speaking in standard modern Japanese. Spontaneity and standardness of the language were assessed on the basis of the rating the CSJ provides. Thus, only those speech samples which are high in spontaneity and uttered entirely in Standard Japanese were selected for this study. This resulted in 416 speech samples (208 speakers: 132 male and 76 female speakers x 2 sessions). From the 416 speech samples, 208 SS and 86112 DS comparisons are possible. From these selected speakers, 64 case particles and 49 fillers were identified.

2.2 Vector Space Model

First of all, the identified words were sorted by their occurrences in descending order. Then, using the sorted order and the occurrences of the identified words, each speech was modelled as a real-valued vector in this study. If n different words are used to represent a given speech S, the dimensionality of the vector is n. That is, S is represented as a vector of n dimensions ($S = (F_1, F_2 \ldots F_n)$, where Fn represents the nth component of S and Fn is the frequency of the nth word). For example, if 5 words (e.g. *ah*, *like*, *OK*, *yes*, *all right*) are used to represent a speech sample (x), and the frequency counts of these words in the speech sample are 3, 10, 4, 18 and 1, respectively, the speech sample x is represented as given in 1).

$$\vec{x} = (3,10,4,18,1) \qquad 1)$$

In this study, the speech samples are modelled using different vector dimensions. This is to see how the performance of the speaker classification system is influenced by the number of dimensions.

2.3 Term Frequency Inverse Document Frequency Weighting

The usefulness of particular words is determined by their uniqueness as well as by how frequently they occur. The *tf·idf* (term frequency inverse document frequency) weight, of which formula is given in 2), was used to evaluate how unique a given word is in the population, and weight was given to that word to reflect its importance to speaker classification (Manning and Schütze 2000)

$$w_{i,j} = tf_{i,j} * log(\frac{N}{df_i}) \qquad 2)$$

In 2), term frequency ($tf_{i,j}$) is the number of occurrences of word i (w_i) in the document (or speech sample) j (d_j). Document frequency (df_i) is the number of documents (or speech samples) in the collection in which that word i (w_i) occurs. N is the total number of documents (or speech samples).

2.4 Cosine Similarity Measure

The similarity (=difference) between two speech samples, which are represented as vectors ($\vec{x}, \vec{y}$), was calculated based on the cosine similarity measure (Manning and Schütze 2000). This particular method (e.g. instead of measuring the distance between two vectors) was selected because the durations of the speech samples are all different. Note that for the experiments of this study, the length of the vectors were standardised by only considering the *X* most frequent case particles and fillers across the speakers.

$$cos(\vec{x},\vec{y}) = \frac{\sum_{i=1}^{n} x_i * y_i}{\sqrt{\sum_{i=1}^{n} x_i^2 * \sum_{i=1}^{n} y_i^2}} \quad 3)$$

The range of difference between the two vectors (similarity($\vec{x},\vec{y}$)) is between 1.0 (=$cos(0°)$) for two vectors pointing in the same direction – e.g. speech samples which are identical – and 0.0 (=$cos(90°)$) for two orthogonal vectors – two speech samples which are completely different, because weights are by their definition not negative.

3 Speaker Classification Tests

The performance of speaker classification was assessed on the basis of the *probability distribution functions* (PDFs) of the difference (E) of the paired speech samples between two contrastive hypotheses. One is the hypothesis that two speech samples were uttered by the same speaker (SS hypothesis) and the other is that two speech samples were uttered by different speakers (DS hypothesis). These probabilities can be formulated as $P(E|H_{ss})$ and $P(E|H_{ds})$ respectively, where E is the difference between two speech samples in comparison, H_{ss} is the SS hypothesis and H_{ds} is the DS hypothesis. In this study, the PDF of the difference assuming the SS hypothesis is true is called the SS PDF (PDF_{ss}), and the PDF of the difference assuming the DS hypothesis is true the DS PDF (PDF_{ds}). Each PDF was modelled using the kernel density function (KernSmooth library of R statistical package), which is a non-parametric way of estimating PDF. Examples of PDF_{ss} and PDF_{ds} are given in Figure 1.

The PDF_{ss} and PDF_{ds} of Figure 1 do not conform to a normal distribution. This is the motivation for the use of the kernel density function. PDF_{ss} and PDF_{ds} are not always monotonic, and may result in more than a single crossing point, particularly when the dimension of a vector is less than 5. Thus, the performance of the system with a vector length less than 5 is not given. These two PDFs also show the accuracy of this particular speaker classification system. If the crossing point (θ) of the PDF_{ss} and the PDF_{ds} is set as the threshold, we can estimate the performance of this particular speaker classification system from these PDFs. Area 1 in Figure 1 – the area bound by the grey line (PDF_{ss}), the vertical dotted line of $x = \theta$ and the line of $y = 0$ – is the predicted error for the SS comparisons. Area 2 of Figure 1 – the area bound by the black line (PDF_{ds}), the vertical dotted line of $x = \theta$, and the line of $y = 0$ – is the predicted error for the DS comparisons. The accuracy/error rate of a speaker classification system (both in SS and DS comparisons) was estimated by calculating Areas 1 and 2.

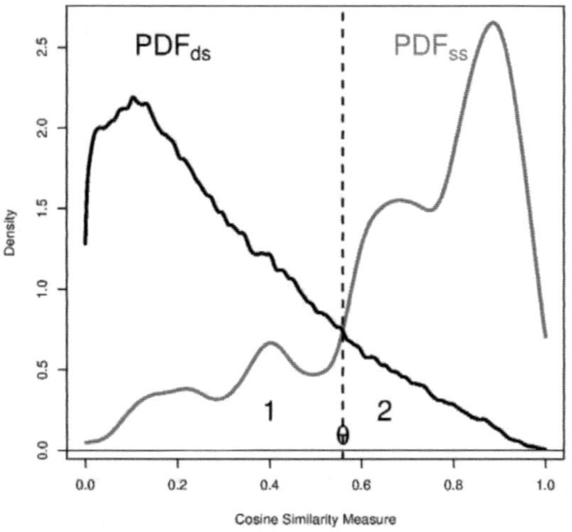

Figure 1: Example of PDF_{ss} (grey curve) and PDF_{ds} (black curve). The vertical dotted line (θ) is the crossing point of PDF_{ss} and PDF_{ds}. Probability density = Y-axis; Cosine similarity measure = X-axis.

4 Test Results and Discussion

In Figure 2, the same speaker (SS) and different speaker (DS) comparisons classification accuracies and the average accuracy between them are plotted separately for the case particles and fillers as a function of the number of vector dimensions.

For the fillers, according to Figure 2, the performance of the SS and DS comparisons are comparable until 20 dimensions, after which the DS comparisons perform better than the SS comparisons. For the case particles, the DS comparisons consistently outperform the SS comparisons. This underperformance of the SS comparisons may be due to the fact that the sample number for estimating the PDF_{ss} (208) is far fewer than that for estimating the PDF_{ds} (86112).

Figure 2 indicates that the average speaker classification accuracy reaches as high as 69.8%

for the case particles with 35 dimensions and 82.7% for the fillers with 25 dimensions, insofar as the performance of speaker classification is consistently better for fillers than case particles. This indicates that fillers carry more speaker-specific information than case particles.

Communication has been traditionally viewed as an intentional act of transferring information. However, whatever the mode of communication (spoken or written), along with the linguistic information about the symbolic content of the intended message, paralinguistic or extralinguistic information about the speaker/writer, such as age, sex, social background, psychological state, health, etc. (Nolan 1983) is also conveyed.

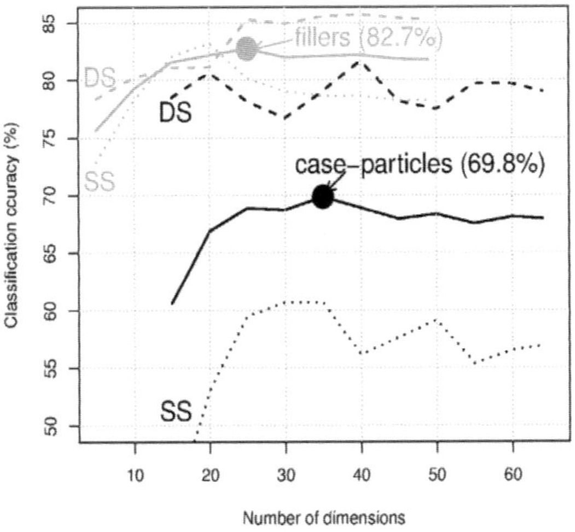

Figure 2: The SS (dotted lines) and DS (dashed lines) comparison accuracies, and their average accuracies are plotted separately for case particles (black) and fillers (grey). The circles indicate the best average accuracy for each type.

Fillers transfer more than the linguistic information encoded in messages, and thus we propose that they are more closely related to paralinguistic and extralinguistic information. This can also be understood from the fact that fillers do not conventionally appear in written texts. It has also been argued based on empirical data that fillers manifest the cognitive process that the speaker is undergoing (Sadanobu and Takubo 1995) and also reflect a speaker's difficulty in conceptual planning and linguistic encoding (Watanabe et al. 2008). The cognitive process is a well-known source of individual differences (Cooper 2002). On the other hand, case particles are key players for linguistic information, such as the syntactic relationship between a noun phrase of a sentence and the predicate of the sentence, the logical relationship between two clauses, etc., which are more directly important for accurately transferring the content information encoded in messages than fillers. Since case particles serve as the dominant carrier of the information directly connected to the propositions of the messages, it is likely that case particles do not have much more capacity to further carry idiosyncratic information of individual speakers. One of the reviewers argues that fillers carry more individualising information mainly because they are relatively free from grammar, which more rigidly controls the use of case particles.

Speaker classification accuracy drastically improves from 15 dimensions (60.6%) to 25 dimensions (69.8%) for case particles. The same increase in accuracy can be observed with fewer dimensions (from 5 dimensions: 75.6% to 15 dimensions: 81.5%) for fillers. This observation that more dimensions need to be included for the case particles in order to reach the same optimal performance level as the fillers is likely due to the fact that the first 15-20 most frequently used case particles are so ubiquitous in the utterances. Hence, the added function of bearing the individualising information of a speaker is too great for case particles. Also note that the curve of the case particles in Figure 2 starts with 15 dimensions because the PDF_{ss} and the PDF_{ds} with less than 15 dimensions become non-monotonic having multiple crossing points between them, and thus sensible results could not be obtained with less than 15 dimensions.

5 Conclusions

It has been demonstrated that Japanese case particles and fillers carry speaker idiosyncratic information to the extent that the average speaker classification accuracy is ca. 69.8% and 82.7%, respectively. We discussed the argument that fillers are more endowed with the idiosyncratic information of speakers than case particles because of the different levels of information with which they operate. Namely, case particles mainly handle a linguistically lower level of structural information, which is directly relevant to the content of messages, whereas fillers assume the task of conveying paralinguistic and extralinguistic information, which have a stronger relevance to a speaker's cognitive processes and are highly diverse at the individual speaker level.

Acknowledgments

The author thanks for the valuable comments and suggestions from the three anonymous reviewers.

References

Baayen, H., Van Halteren, H., and Tweedie, F. (1996) Outside the cave of shadows: Using syntactic annotation to enhance authorship attribution. *Literary and Linguistic Computing 11*(3): 121-132.

Binongo, J. N. G. (2003) Who wrote the 15th book of Oz? An application of multivariate analysis to authorship attribution. *Chance 16*(2): 9-17.

Burrows, J. F. (1987) Word-patterns and story-shapes: The statistical analysis of narrative style. *Literary and Linguistic Computing 2*(2): 61-70.

Cooper, C. (2002) *Individual Differences* (2nd ed.). London: Arnold; New York: Oxford University Press.

Doddington, G. (2001) Speaker recognition based on idiolectal differences between speakers. *Proceedings of 2001 Eurospeech*: 2521-2524.

Halliday, M. A. K., Macintosh, A., and Strevens, P. D. (1964) *The Linguistic Sciences and Language Teaching*. London: Longmans.

Holmes, D. I. (1992) A stylometric analysis of Mormon scripture and related texts. *Journal of the Royal Statistical Society Series a-Statistics in Society 155*: 91-120.

Holmes, D. I., Robertson, M., and Paez, R. (2001) Stephen crane and the New-York Tribune: A case study in traditional and non-traditional authorship attribution. *Computers and the Humanities 35*(3): 315-331.

Ishihara, S., and Kinoshita, Y. (2010) Filler words as a speaker classification feature. *Proceedings of the 13th Australasian International Conference on Speech Science and Technology*: 34-37.

Juola, P., and Baayen, R. H. (2005) A controlled-corpus experiment in authorship identification by cross-entropy. *Literary and Linguistic Computing 20*(Suppl): 59.

Maekawa, K., Koiso, H., Furui, S., and Isahara, H. (2000) Spontaneous speech corpus of Japanese. *Proceedings of the 2nd International Conference of Language Resources and Evaluation*: 947-952.

Manning, C. D., and Schütze, H. (2000) *Foundations of Statistical Natural Language Processing* (2nd ed.). Cambridge, Mass.: MIT Press.

Martin, S. E. (2004) *A reference grammar of Japanese*. Honolulu: University of Hawai'i Press.

Nolan, F. (1983) *The Phonetic Bases of Speaker Recognition.* Cambridge: Cambridge University Press.

Sadanobu, T., and Takubo, Y. (1995) The monitoring devices of mental operations in discourse: A case of 'eeto' and 'ano (o)'. *Gengo kenkyu [Language Studies]*(108): 74-93.

Watanabe, M., Hirose, K., Den, Y., and Minematsu, N. (2008) Filled pauses as cues to the complexity of upcoming phrases for native and non-native listeners. *Speech Communication 50*(2): 81-94.

Weber, F., Manganaro, L., Peskin, B., and Shriberg, E. (2002) Using prosodic and lexical information for speaker identification. *Proceedings of the 2002 IEEE International Conference on Acoustics, Speech, and Signal Processing (ICASSP) 1*: 141-144.

Automatic Climate Classification of Environmental Science Literature

Jared Willett,[♠♡] **Timothy Baldwin,**[♠♡] **David Martinez**[♡] and **J. Angus Webb**[◇]
♠ Department of Computing and Information Systems
♡ NICTA Victoria Research Laboratory
◇ Department of Resource Management and Geography
The University of Melbourne, VIC 3010, Australia
jwillett@student.unimelb.edu.au, tb@ldwin.net,
davidm@csse.unimelb.edu.au, angus.webb@unimelb.edu.au

Abstract

Climate type is one of the potentially most relevant pieces of metadata for identifying studies in evidence-based environmental management. In this paper, we propose a method for automatically predicting the climate type in environmental science literature using NLP techniques, relative to a pre-existing set of climate type categories. Our main approaches combine toponym detection and resolution using two different resources with support vector machines. The results show great promise, but also further challenges, for using NLP to extract information from the vast and rapidly growing collection of environmental sciences literature.

1 Introduction

In this paper, we investigate the task of automatic prediction of climate type (e.g. temperate or arid) in environmental science abstracts. The climate type of an environmental science study is crucial information, which gives context to the research and insight into its wider implications and applicability. Availability of climate information as metadata has clear value to researchers performing a systematic review of the literature or comprehensive analysis of the evidence. However, the manual annotation of climate type over a large volume of literature is a time-consuming task. In this paper, we seek to automate the climate annotation process with natural language processing (NLP) techniques. The task of climate type classification is complex as although the label set is relatively small, the geographic granularity is fine and toponym ambiguity becomes a significant problem — toponyms commonly mentioned in the environmental sciences (e.g. *Murray River*) are often large and cover multiple climates, which presents difficulties for a point-based representation of toponyms. Initially, experiments are run to examine the effectiveness of the direct application of the classifiers developed by Willett et al. (2012) for study region classification. We then investigate methods for adapting these techniques to the climate task through the modification of the toponym resolution component of our classifiers. These approaches include utilizing a Köppen-Geiger climate classification world map to resolve toponyms to climate instead of region, in addition to experiments with targeting types of toponyms reliable for identifying climate.

2 Related Work

The methodology used to extract and disambiguate toponyms is based on a standard approach to geographic information retrieval, which was presented, e.g., by Stokes et al. (2008) in their study on the performance of individual components of a geographic IR system. In particular, the named entity recognition and classification (NERC) and toponym resolution (TR) components are the basis for the main classifiers in this study.

The unique opportunities and challenges specific to retrieving geospatial information have been well documented, particularly in the context of geospatial information retrieval where queries and documents have a geospatial dimension (Santos and Chaves, 2006). Aside from finding locations in the text, the disambiguation of what exact location a term in a text is referring to presents a unique challenge in itself, and a variety of approaches have been suggested and demonstrated for this task (Overell and Rüger, 2006).

Toponym resolution is the process of taking each identified named entity from the NERC, and attempting to determine the specific location to which it is referring. This involves strategies such as shared relationships between potential identifications of locations, prominence in Wikipedia, and population statistics.

As a specific instance of toponym resolution over environmental sciences data, Willett et al. (2012) proposed a method for predicting the "study region" of a published abstract, based on text categorisation techniques using features including frequency distributions of resolved toponyms and a bag of word unigrams. Their best method was able to determine the study region with an accuracy of 0.892, combining toponym resolution from DBpedia and GeoNames with the bag-of-toponyms features. We adapt this method to climate type classification, and present details of the method in Section 5.

This work is inspired in part by work on evidence based medicine (EBM). As Sackett et al. (1996) define it: "Evidence based medicine is the conscientious, explicit, and judicious use of current best evidence in making decisions about the care of individual patients." The reasons for moving towards an evidence-based model of environmental management have obvious parallels to the motivation for the practice of EBM. Although the structure of evidence will differ between the domains, many of the techniques applied in research for EBM are likely to have application for our current task. Successful applications of NLP to EBM include sentence categorization for information on randomized controlled trials (Chung, 2009; Kim et al., 2011), the labelling of sentences with "PICO" (Patient/Problem, Intervention, Comparison and Outcome) labels to aid clinical information retrieval (Boudin et al., 2010), and the automatic assignment of Medical Subject Headings (MeSH) terms to PubMed abstracts (Gaudinat and Boyer, 2002).

3 Resources

In this section, we provide details of key resources used in this paper, namely:

- Eco Evidence, a manually-curated database of metadata for environmental science literature, which provides the basis of the data used in our experiments
- DBpedia and GeoNames, as resources for toponym resolution
- the Köppen-Geiger Climate Map of Peel et al. (2007)

3.1 Eco Evidence

Eco Evidence (Webb et al., 2011) is a tool for literature review and evidence synthesis, consisting of two parts. The first is the underlying Eco Evidence Database (EED) (Webb et al., 2012a), in which the evidence items are stored. The citations for environmental studies are catalogued in the database as separate entities, and evidence items may be stored by means of linking them to the citation for the study from which the information came. Additional details about the study's location, scale and ecosystem can also be stored with each citation to aid the process of filtering relevant evidence. An example of a record in the EED is given in Figure 1. The database is in active use in a number of research projects currently, and evidence therein has also formed the basis of several published systematic reviews (Webb et al., 2012b).

The Eco Evidence Analyser (EEA) retrieves the potentially relevant evidence from the EED for a hypothesised cause and effect, then weights and analyses the selected evidence to determine whether there is adequate evidence to support or reject the hypothesis. For the Eco Evidence Analyser to be effective, the underlying EED must contain as much evidence as possible. However, the database has to date been populated through manual annotation of citations with their evidence items, which is a time-consuming process (Webb et al., 2012b). Our work is motivated by the possibility of streamlining the population of the EED, by automatically extracting climate information, but potentially in the future extending NLP-based extraction to other evidence items.

3.2 Toponym Resolution

Toponym resolution is a key component of our experiments, and we worked with two different resources in disambiguating toponyms: DBpedia and GeoNames.

DBpedia (`http://www.dbpedia.org`) is a database of structured content extracted from Wikipedia. We utilize DBpedia as a source of information for resolving ambiguous toponyms by finding the DBpedia pages for likely candidates based on the toponym name, and extracting geographic coordinates to identify their location. For terms with multiple meanings, DBpedia will contain a disambiguation page. We use the disambiguation page in one of two ways:

1. the top-result TR approach: the top-ranked

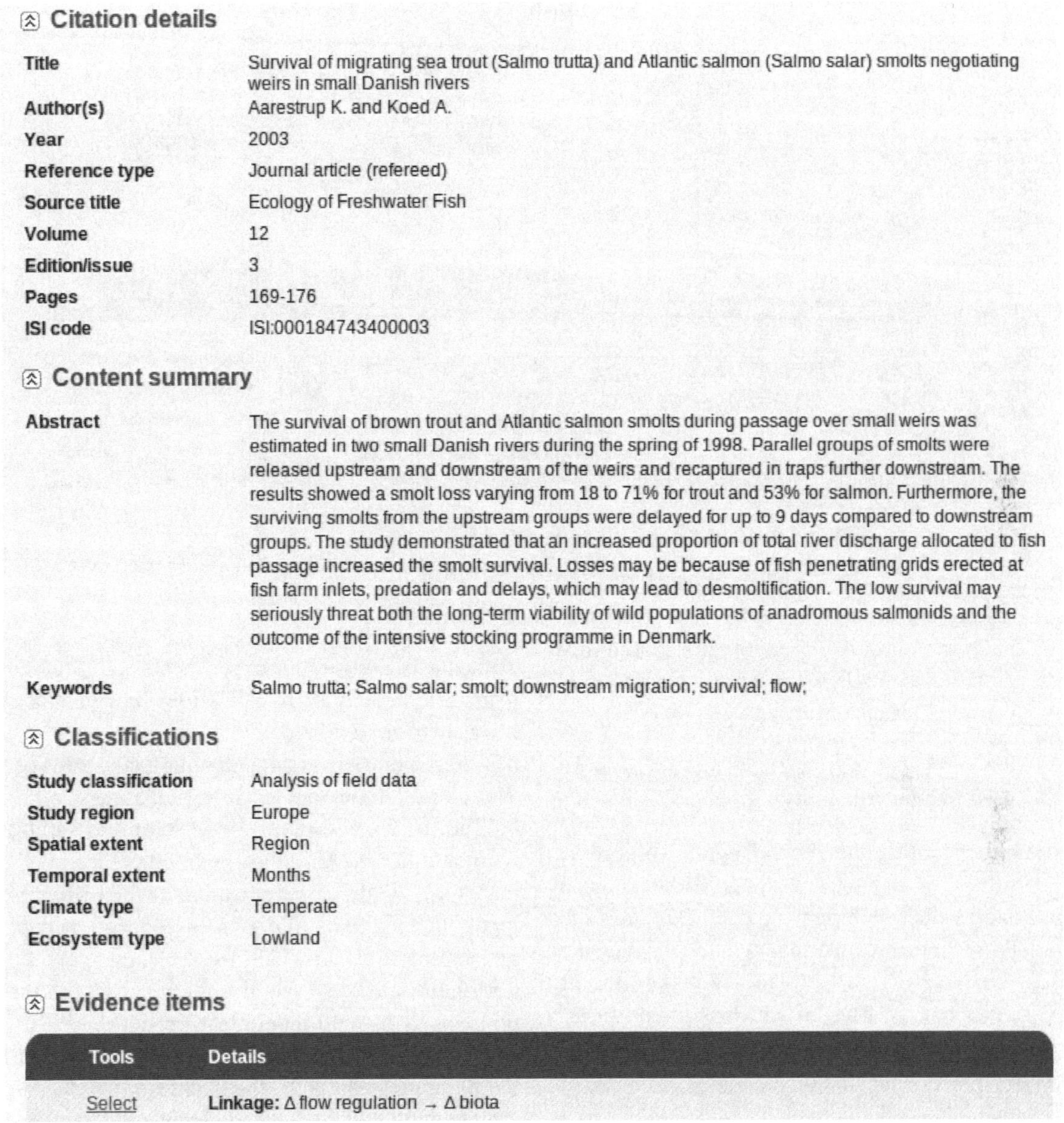

Citation details

Title	Survival of migrating sea trout (Salmo trutta) and Atlantic salmon (Salmo salar) smolts negotiating weirs in small Danish rivers
Author(s)	Aarestrup K. and Koed A.
Year	2003
Reference type	Journal article (refereed)
Source title	Ecology of Freshwater Fish
Volume	12
Edition/issue	3
Pages	169-176
ISI code	ISI:000184743400003

Content summary

Abstract	The survival of brown trout and Atlantic salmon smolts during passage over small weirs was estimated in two small Danish rivers during the spring of 1998. Parallel groups of smolts were released upstream and downstream of the weirs and recaptured in traps further downstream. The results showed a smolt loss varying from 18 to 71% for trout and 53% for salmon. Furthermore, the surviving smolts from the upstream groups were delayed for up to 9 days compared to downstream groups. The study demonstrated that an increased proportion of total river discharge allocated to fish passage increased the smolt survival. Losses may be because of fish penetrating grids erected at fish farm inlets, predation and delays, which may lead to desmoltification. The low survival may seriously threat both the long-term viability of wild populations of anadromous salmonids and the outcome of the intensive stocking programme in Denmark.
Keywords	Salmo trutta; Salmo salar; smolt; downstream migration; survival; flow;

Classifications

Study classification	Analysis of field data
Study region	Europe
Spatial extent	Region
Temporal extent	Months
Climate type	Temperate
Ecosystem type	Lowland

Evidence items

Tools	Details
Select	**Linkage:** Δ flow regulation → Δ biota

Figure 1: Screen capture of an example citation in the Eco Evidence Database, with associated classifications and an evidence item.

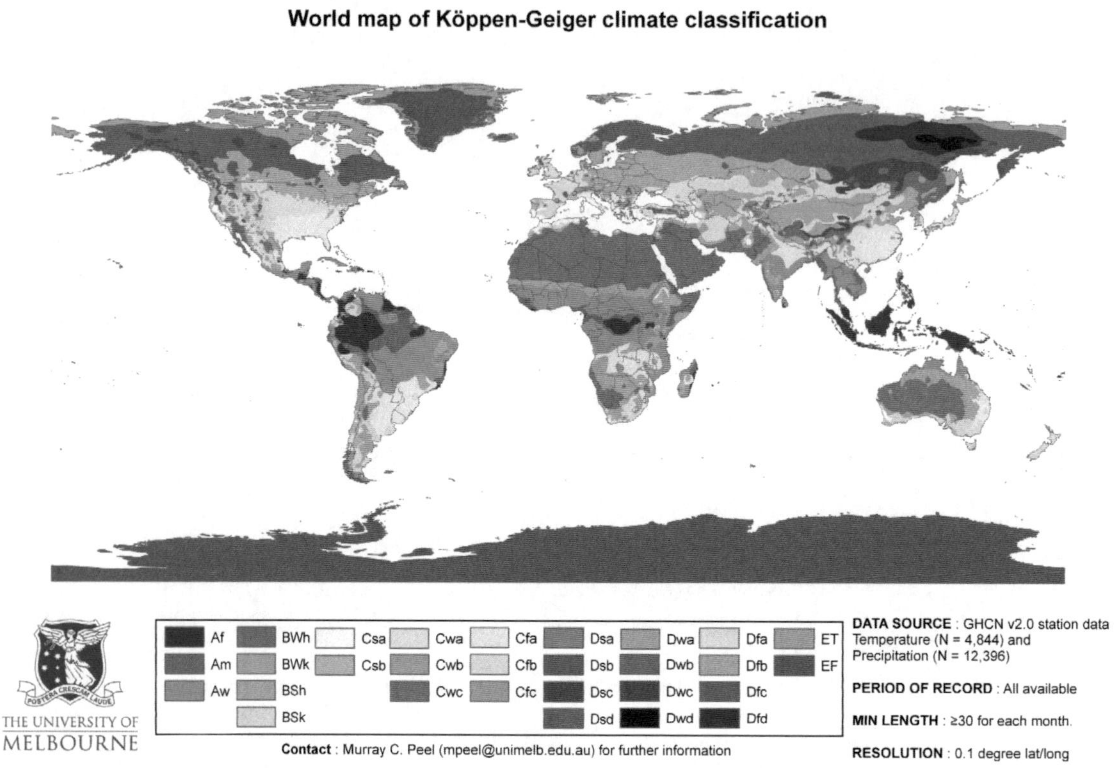

Figure 2: World map of Köppen-Geiger climate classification.

result is returned; in the event that coordinates are unavailable for the first possibility on the disambiguation page, no resolution is recorded for the term.

2. the top-5 approach: up to the top-5 results are used to represent a given toponym

Another tool we use for toponym resolution is GeoNames (`http://www.geonames.org`), a gazetteer which is based on data from a wide variety of sources. A toponym query via the GeoNames search API provides a ranked list of geospatial results, each of which is linked to information such as geo-coordinates, and the population of towns/cities.

3.3 Köppen-Geiger Climate Map

We map geographic coordinates from DBpedia to a world map of Köppen-Geiger climate classification (Peel et al., 2007). The Köppen-Geiger climate classification system divides climates into five main groups, as detailed in Figure 2 (with each climate type represented by subclasses of the prefix indicated in parentheses): Tropical ("A*"), Arid ("B*"), Temperate ("C*"), Cold ("D*") and Polar ("E*").

4 Dataset

The dataset used in our experiments was sourced from the collection of 3977 titles and abstracts from the Eco Evidence database, each of which has been manually annotated with a climate type. The climate types are made up of 5 basic types — Temperate, Tropical, Dry, Polar and Alpine — in addition to Multiple (i.e. multiple basic climate types, without specification of which specific types) and Other. Eco Evidence does not capture information on which basic classes make up a Multiple label, so we are not able to treat the problem as a multi-label classification task. Instead, Multiple is represented in the same way as the basic classes. Note the slight mismatch with the climate types used in the Köppen-Geiger climate classification.

The Eco Evidence dataset is quite unbalanced, as detailed in Table 1: Temperate is the majority class by a very large margin, and Polar and Other are very small minority classes.

5 Methodology

We build classifiers using the continent-level study region classification method of Willett et al.

Climate	EU	AU	AF	AN	AS	NA	SA	OC	MU	OT	TOTAL
Temperate	**768**	**390**	46	0	**98**	**1055**	9	**98**	13	1	**2478**
Tropical	1	102	45	0	65	51	**98**	10	7	1	380
Dry	9	89	**67**	0	21	162	7	0	1	0	356
Polar	2	0	0	**1**	0	5	1	1	2	0	12
Alpine	139	1	0	0	39	278	3	0	1	**2**	463
Multiple	22	24	9	0	13	102	1	1	**113**	1	286
Other	0	1	0	0	0	1	0	0	0	0	2
TOTAL	941	607	167	1	236	1654	119	110	137	5	3977

Table 1: Distribution for the gold standard climate classifications across the gold standard study region classifications (EU = Europe, AU = Australia, AF = Africa, AN = Antarctica, AS = Asia, NA = North America, SA = South America, OC = Oceania [other than Australia], MU = Multiple, OT = Other; the boldfaced number indicates the majority-class for a given continent)

(2012). First, the Stanford Named Entity Recogniser (Finkel et al., 2005) is used to identify location-type NEs in each abstract. Each NE is then mapped to a set of toponyms, based on DBpedia or GeoNames, and the counts of toponyms are aggregated into bag-of-toponyms (BoT) features. Finally, a linear-kernel support vector machine (SVM) is used to train a supervised classifier.

We experiment with both: (1) study region classification (at the continent level), and a majority-class classification for that continent; and (2) replacement of continent-level classes from the original paper with climate-based classes. In the latter case, the toponyms are resolved to climates using the Köppen-Geiger climate classification system. One issue that arises with the use of the climate map is that the classifications of the climate map do not all directly correspond to labels used in the dataset. Temperate, Tropical and Polar have direct matches, but the climate map classes Cold and Arid do not. These two labels were mapped to the Alpine and Dry labels respectively for the benchmark system. Note that this is only relevant for the majority-class classification; in the case of the toponym resolution, the supervised classifier is able to learn its own mapping between the Köppen-Geiger climate classification system and the 5+2-class climate system used by Eco Evidence.

We also include structured features. That is, separate frequency distributions of the number of tags resolving to each climate type are used for each zone of the abstract, based on partitioning the abstract into 4 equal-sized zones (based on word count). Each of these frequency distributions are treated as separate vectors of unique features. The title of the paper is treated as an additional fifth zone and feature vector.

We also present a majority class baseline, that selects the majority climate type from the training data (Temperate). In addition, we experiment with taking a majority vote across the climate type(s) that each toponym in the abstract resolves to.

Subsequent experiments attempt to target only toponyms more likely to reliably identify climate. This was done by excluding toponyms of the GeoNames feature code "A", which identifies countries, states, regions, and similar entities.[1] These experiments are only completed with the GeoNames multiple result classifiers, as no reliable method of identifying the form of toponym is available in DBpedia. These experiments are performed based on the hypothesis that the point-based representation of coordinates extracted from GeoNames for these coarse-grained toponyms may prove problematic, as larger areas are more likely to contain more than one climate type. Precision may therefore be enhanced by filtering these toponyms out.

For all classifiers, we evaluate our model with classification accuracy, measured using 10-fold stratified cross-validation over the full dataset. As our learner, we use LIBSVM with a linear kernel (Chang and Lin, 2011).

6 Results

We first present results based on the methodology of Willett et al. (2012) for classifying study region, simply mapping toponyms onto continental study

[1]See `http://www.geonames.org/export/codes.html` for a comprehensive list.

Classifier	Accuracy
Zero-R	0.623
Bag-of-Toponyms (BoT)	0.681
Bag-of-Words (BoW)	0.654
BoT + BoW	0.659
DBpedia + GeoNames top result ("dbp+Geo:TR")	0.623
dbp+Geo:TR + BoT	0.681
dbp+Geo:TR + BoW	0.681
dbp+Geo:TR + BoT + BoW	**0.687**

Table 2: Accuracy for classifiers based on the method of Willett et al. (2012) when trained and tested on climate type labels.

Classifier	dbp:TR	Geo:TR	dbp+Geo:TR	dbp:MR	Geo:MR	dbp+Geo:MR	Geo(F)
MV	0.550	0.518	0.555	0.543	0.536	0.555	0.554
SVM	0.662	0.656	0.667	0.652	0.664	0.674	0.650
+ S	0.658	0.661	0.667	0.650	0.657	0.663	0.645
+ T	**0.692**	0.689	**0.695**	**0.687**	0.692	0.692	0.690
+ ST	0.691	**0.691**	0.694	**0.687**	0.689	0.685	0.689
+ W	0.674	0.677	0.681	0.673	0.678	0.682	0.674
+ SW	0.668	0.674	0.682	0.671	0.681	0.682	0.675
+ TW	0.680	0.682	0.686	0.679	0.683	0.685	0.680
+ STW	0.673	0.677	0.683	0.673	0.686	0.686	0.676

Table 3: Accuracy for DBpedia/GeoNames classifiers resolving toponyms to climate type using the climate map ("TR" = only the top resolution being collected for a given topoynm; "MR" = multiple resolutions; "S" = zone-based structural features; "T" = bag-of-toponyms; "W" = bag-of-words; Geo(F) = Geo:MR without toponyms of GeoNames feature class 'A')

regions, and replacing the class set with climate types. The results are presented in Table 2. The best results are achieved by using the DBpedia and GeoNames top results ("TR") together with both bag-of-toponyms and bag-of-words features, although this performs only marginally better than the bag-of-toponyms by itself. The results in this table suggest the continent resolution features add no relevant information for climate classification over bag-of-words/toponyms features. However, location-based features do appear to have added relevance, as the bag-of-toponyms outperforms the bag-of-words.

We next experiment with resolving toponyms to climate types, as detailed in Table 3. As we can see, our classifiers struggle to outperform our baseline classifiers. The majority vote classifiers ("MV") — where the majority climate type for the different toponyms is returned — performs very poorly on this dataset, achieving an accuracy below the Zero-R classifier which simply labels every instance with the majority class. The SVM-based supervised approach ("SVM") is more successful, with the top accuracy of 0.695 achieved by the DBpedia ("dbp") and GeoNames ("Geo") top-result ("TR") classifier in combination with a bag-of-toponyms ("T"). Bag-of-toponyms is clearly the most effective set of the standalone features, with classifiers of any toponym resolution method consistently achieving the greatest accuracy when used in combination with bag-of-toponyms features. However, even the highest-performing classifiers achieve only a minor improvement over the best baseline scores, and the overall accuracy is well below that achieved in the study region task.

The difference between DBpedia and GeoNames is negligible on all supervised classifiers. Features which provide structural data ("S") have no substantial effect on the performance of the classifiers, consistent with the findings of Willett et al. (2012). The granularity filter, although providing a slight boost to the majority vote classifier, is similarly ineffective: a total of 2991 possible resolutions were filtered out across 1280 unique

Label	Tropical	Arid	Temperate	Cold	Polar
Tropical	**0.445**	0.143	0.384	0.027	0.000
Dry	0.032	**0.446**	0.353	0.166	0.003
Temperate	0.009	0.186	**0.541**	0.260	0.004
Alpine	0.002	0.141	0.184	**0.658**	0.015
Polar	0.000	0.000	0.278	0.611	**0.111**
Multiple	0.023	0.202	0.427	0.344	0.004
Other	0.000	0.333	0.667	0.000	0.000

Table 4: Toponym mapping of resolved climate from the Köppen-Geiger climate map to the corresponding abstract's gold standard climate label.

toponyms, but due to the sparsity of toponyms in the text, the loss of information from filtering out these resolutions outweighs any gain in precision from avoiding ambiguity in climate resolution.

In order to investigate how much of the problem could be attributed to incorrect disambiguation, a classifier with "oracle" toponym disambiguation is also tested. This oracle determined the proportion of instances in the dataset that had at least one climate resolution of a toponym that matches the gold standard label out of all the possible disambiguations from the top 5 results of both DBpedia and GeoNames. The number of matches was only 2552 out of 3977 (64.2%) abstracts. This low percentage suggests that the source of error cannot be primarily explained by toponym disambiguation. Another possible source of error for correctly disambiguated toponyms is that the toponym is resolved to the incorrect climate.

Based on the chosen set of label mappings, the distribution of resolved toponyms using the top result in DBpedia across the set of abstracts for each gold standard label was collected (Table 4). For each map label, the highest proportion of toponyms resolves to the expected dataset label. However, significant proportions are mismatched in all cases. One cause of the poor accuracy in climate resolution is that identifying climate generally requires a greater degree of geographic accuracy than resolving toponyms to a continent. Regions of continental scale generally contain more than one climatic zone (as seen in Figure 2). Therefore, coarse-grained toponyms representing countries or continents that provided valuable information in classification of study region are no longer of use. The granularity filter classifiers were developed with the intention of filtering these out of the dataset. However, there was too much loss of information from the already small number of available toponyms.

7 Conclusion

In this paper, we have explored NLP approaches to classifying climate type in environmental science abstracts based on resolving toponyms detected within the abstract to their climate type. This was done by first disambiguating the toponym with DBpedia and/or GeoNames to a set of geographic coordinates, then referencing the coordinates on a world map of climate classification. Supervised approaches with support vector machines also included features based on bag-of-words, bag-of-toponyms, and structural information. The classifiers developed in these experiments had limited success in outperforming baseline approaches. Bag-of-toponyms were demonstrated to be the most useful feature set, and the highest-performing classifier was DBpedia and GeoNames top-result toponym resolution in combination with bag-of-toponyms, achieving 0.695 classification accuracy.

Acknowledgments

NICTA is funded by the Australian Government as represented by the Department of Broadband, Communications and the Digital Economy and the Australian Research Council through the ICT Centre of Excellence program.

References

F. Boudin, J.Y. Nie, and M. Dawes. 2010. Clinical information retrieval using document and PICO structure. In *Human Language Technologies: The 2010 Annual Conference of the North American Chapter of the Association for Computational Linguistics*, pages 822–830, Los Angeles, USA.

C.-C. Chang and C.-J. Lin. 2011. LIBSVM: A library for support vector machines. *ACM Transactions on Intelligent Systems and Technology*, 2:27:1–27:27. Software available at `http://www.csie.ntu.edu.tw/~cjlin/libsvm`.

G. Chung. 2009. Sentence retrieval for abstracts of randomized controlled trials. *BMC Medical Informatics and Decision Making*, 9(1):10.

J.R. Finkel, T. Grenager, and C. Manning. 2005. Incorporating non-local information into information extraction systems by Gibbs sampling. In *Proceedings of the 43rd Annual Meeting on Association for Computational Linguistics*, pages 363–370, Ann Arbor, USA.

A. Gaudinat and C. Boyer. 2002. Automatic extraction of MeSH terms from Medline abstracts. In *Workshop on Natural Language Processing in Biomedical Applications*, pages 53–57, Nicosia, Cyprus.

S. Kim, D. Martinez, L. Cavedon, and L. Yencken. 2011. Automatic classification of sentences to support evidence based medicine. *BMC Bioinformatics*, 12(Suppl 2):S5.

S.E. Overell and S. Rüger. 2006. Identifying and grounding descriptions of places. In *3rd Workshop on Geographic Information Retrieval*, Seattle, USA.

M.C. Peel, B.L. Finlayson, and T.A. McMahon. 2007. Updated world map of the Köppen-Geiger climate classification. *Hydrology and Earth System Sciences*, 11:1633–1644.

D.L. Sackett, W. Rosenberg, JA Gray, R.B. Haynes, and W.S. Richardson. 1996. Evidence based medicine: what it is and what it isn't. *British Medical Journal*, 312(7023):71–72.

D. Santos and M.S. Chaves. 2006. The place of place in geographical IR. In *3rd Workshop on Geographic Information Retrieval*, Seattle, USA.

N. Stokes, Y. Li, A. Moffat, and J. Rong. 2008. An empirical study of the effects of NLP components on geographic IR performance. *International Journal of Geographical Information Science*, 22(3):247–264.

J.A. Webb, S.R. Wealands, P. Lea, S.J. Nichols, S.C. de Little, M.J. Stewardson, R.H. Norris, F. Chan, D. Marinova, and R.S. Anderssen. 2011. Eco Evidence: using the scientific literature to inform evidence-based decision making in environmental management. In *MODSIM2011 International Congress on Modelling and Simulation*, pages 2472–2478, Perth, Australia.

J.A. Webb, S.C. de Little, K.A. Miller, and M.J. Stewardson. 2012a. Eco Evidence Database: a distributed modelling resource for systematic literature analysis in environmental science and management. In *2012 International Congress on Environmental Modelling and Software*, pages 1135–1142, Leipzig, Germany.

J.A. Webb, E.M. Wallis, and M.J. Stewardson. 2012b. A systematic review of published evidence linking wetland plants to water regime components. *Aquatic Botany*, 103:1–14.

J. Willett, T. Baldwin, D. Martinez, and A. Webb. 2012. Classification of study region in environmental science abstracts. In *Proceedings of the Australasian Language Technology Association Workshop 2012*, pages 118–122, Dunedin, New Zealand.

ALTA Shared Task papers

Overview of the 2013 ALTA Shared Task

Diego Molla
Department of Computing
Macquarie University
Sydney, NSW 2109
diego.molla-aliod@mq.edu.au

Abstract

The 2013 ALTA shared task was the fourth in the ALTA series of shared tasks, where all participants attempt to solve the same problem using the same data. This year's shared task was based on the problem of restoring casing and punctuation. As with last year, we used Kaggle in Class as the framework to submit the results and maintaining a leaderboard. There was a strong participation this year, with 50 teams participating, of which 21 teams submitted results that improved on the published baseline. In this overview we describe the task, the process of building the training set, and the evaluation criteria, and present the results of the submitted systems. We also comment on our experience with using Kaggle in Class.

1 Introduction

There are many situations when a piece of English text does not have information about capitalisation or punctuation. These situations may arise, for example, when the text is the result of automatic transcription from speech, or when the text has been typed in a hurry, such as when taking quick notes or in quick responses in Web forums, or when using media such as text messages. If such a text is to be processed automatically, one may want to restore the missing capitalisation and punctuation, so that the text can be processed using conventional text processing tools and resources. It has been shown that introducing a preliminary step that automatically restores case information improves the results of machine translation (Lita et al., 2003) and information extraction from speech transcripts (Niu et al., 2004).

The task of case and punctuation restoration takes text such as the following as input:

> ... stored at the ucla television archives the archived episodes were telecast march 8 16 and 24 1971 april 1 and ...

The expected output is:

> ... stored at the UCLA Television Archives. The archived episodes were telecast: March 8, 16, and 24, 1971, April 1 and ...

An interesting feature of case and punctuation restoration is that training data can be obtained cheaply. One only needs to take a piece of text and remove case and punctuation. By doing this we can obtain the input data (the text with the case and punctuation information removed) and the target data (the original text). It has been observed that using this approach to generate training data suffices to obtain reasonable results (Niu et al., 2004), and this observation agrees with the results obtained in this shared task, as we will show in this paper.

2 The 2013 ALTA Shared Task

Case and punctuation restoration can be formulated as a text classification task. Baldwin and Joseph (2009) used a multi-label classification approach where a word can have multiple labels, each label indicating the information to be restored in the word. For example, the set of labels `CAP1+FULLSTOP+COMMA` indicates that the word has the first character as uppercase and is followed by a full stop and a comma. Thus, if the word was *corp*, the labels indicate that the word should be restored to *Corp.,*. There is a label `ALLCAPS` to indicate that all letters in the word need to be uppercased, and the specific label `NOCHANGE` indicates that the word does not need any special restoration.

```
ID WORD
255 stored
256 at
257 the
258 ucla
259 television
260 archives
261 the
262 archived
263 episodes
264 were
265 telecast
266 march
267 8
268 16
269 and
270 24
271 1971
271 april
273 1
274 and
```

Figure 1: Example of input text

The ALTA shared tasks primarily target university students with programming experience, but without necessarily much background on text processing techniques. For this reason, the 2013 ALTA shared task is a simplification of the more general task of case and punctuation restoration. The participants are asked to build automatic systems that predict where a word should have any of its characters in uppercase, and whether the word is followed by any punctuation mark. They are not required to predict which specific characters are in uppercase, or which specific punctuation marks are attached to the word. Furthermore, the only punctuation characters to consider for the task are:

,.;:?!

The shared task was presented as a task of multi-label classification with two possible labels: `Case` and `Punct`. A word could be labelled with any of the labels, both, or none. The participants were given text that had been tokenised, all case removed, and all punctuation (,.;:?!) removed. Figures 1 and 2 show an example of input text and the target, using the specific format required for the task. According to the example in the figures, word with ID 258 (*ucla*) has at least one character in uppercase, and word with ID 260 (*archives*) has

```
Id,documents
Case,258 259 260 261 266 272
Punct,260 265 267 268 270 271
```

Figure 2: Example of target output

uppercase characters and punctuation marks.

3 The Training and Test Sets

We used the data by Baldwin and Joseph (2009) to produce a training set and two test sets, plus text from Wikipedia to produce additional training data.

The data by Baldwin and Joseph (2009) are from the AP Newswire (APW) and New York Times (NYT) sections of the English Gigaword Corpus. Of the two test sets, one was used as a "public" test set that participants could use to check their progress in the development of their systems. The participants did not have access to the target output but they could submit the output of their systems and they would receive instant feedback with the results and how they compare against other participants in the leaderboard. The second test set was a "private" test set that was used to determine the final scores. By having separate "public" and "private" test sets we aimed to reduce the risk of some systems overfitting to the actual test set, since each participant could submit up to two runs every day. As training data we used the third partition from Baldwin and Joseph (2009) plus an extract from Wikipedia.

To download the Wikipedia text, shuffle the paragraphs, and split the contents into smaller files we used a method and scripts based on a blog post[1]. We then used the Python NLTK toolkit (Bird et al., 2009) to tokenise the words. We lowercased the tokens and removed those that matched our list of punctuation marks.

The Wikipedia training data consisted of 18 files with a total of 306,445 words. The data from Baldwin and Joseph (2009) consisted of a "train" file with 66,371 words, the "public" test file with 64,072 words, and the "private" test file with 65,903 words.

[1]http://blog.afterthedeadline.com/2009/12/04/generating-a-plain-text-corpus-from-wikipedia/

4 Kaggle in Class

Kaggle[2] is a Web-based framework for the creation of data-driven competitions. Kaggle provides the means for competition designers to upload the training data to distribute among participants, and private test data that is used when participants submit a run. The winner is automatically determined as the team who produces the highest score on the private data.

Kaggle targets data analytics companies who can use this framework to hire data modelling specialists. At a cost, Kaggle offers their outreach solutions to find participants to the competitions. Kaggle in Class[3] is a free variant that allows class instructors and organisations hold shared tasks without incurring in management fees. The main differences between Kaggle and Kaggle in class are that Kaggle in Class has limited support services, it has less flexibility in its setup, and does not use Kaggle's outreach services.

A very attractive feature of Kaggle in Class is its ability to maintain a leaderboard that allows participants to keep track of how they stand against other participants. Participants can submit results up to two times a day using the test set. The test set has a "public" partition that is used to display the participants' results in a public leaderboard, and a "private" partition that is used for the final rating. Kaggle in Class also includes a competition-specific Web forum for communication among participants and between organisers and participants.

Kaggle in Class offers an array of evaluation metrics. For this shared task we used the macro-averaged F1 score, which allowed the evaluation of the output of multi-label classification tasks by averaging the class-specific F1 score. For example, if the target output is as shown in Table 2, and a system returns the following output:

```
Id,documents
Case,258 259 260 262 270
Punct,259 260 265 270
```

Then the computed F-scores are:

Case: P = 3/5; R = 3/6; F1 = 0.54

Punct: P = 3/4; R = 3/6; F1 = 0.6

Final score: (0.54+0.6)/2 = **0.57**

[2] http://www.kaggle.com

[3] http://inclass.kaggle.com

Training data	F1 (private)	F1 (public)
Train data	0.2895	0.4355
Wikipedia 0-5	0.2761	0.4077
Wikipedia 0-10	0.2791	0.4173
Wikipedia 0-17	0.2789	0.4226
Train + Wikipedia	0.2876	0.4493

Table 1: Impact of training data on the baseline

5 The Baseline

We built a simple baseline and made the code available to the participants. The baseline was written in Python and it used NLTK's Hidden Markov Model (HMM) trained on a single-labelling variant of the task. The single-labelling variant had 4 classes, one for each combination of the `Case` and `Punct` labels. Table 1 shows the result of the system when trained on the "train" data, and when trained on increasing portions of the Wikipedia train data. We observed that the "train" data was better than the Wikipedia train data, but adding more Wikipedia data might have improved the results. These findings are in line with the findings of the winner of the shared task (Lui and Wang, 2013, in these proceedings), who observed better results as they added more training data. We also observed a considerable difference between the results of the "public" and the "private" test. This may indicate that these two partitions do not represent each other, although as we will observe in Section 6, the results of the top participants are consistent across the two test partitions.

6 Results

The specific format required for submitting the results to Kaggle in Class using the macro-averaged F1 score did not allow to specify "public" and "private" partitions on the test file. For this reason we created two Kaggle in Class competitions: a "public" competition where participants could submit and observe the results in the leaderboard, and a "private" competition for the final results. However, it turned out that many participants who submitted to the public competition did not submit to the private competition. Table 2 shows the results of all teams in the public competition, including the baseline (in **boldface**), and a test system that used the same training data as the baseline plus the private set. Table 3 shows the results of the private submissions. All team names have been anonymised, and we have kept the same names in both tables.

We can observe a number of participants with the same score as the baseline. Since the code of the baseline was made available, it is likely that these participants simply ran the baseline. The two top participants in the public competition submitted to the private competition and obtained similar results. We could not locate one of the two remaining participants of the private competition in the public competition, but we observed a very different score for one participant ("Team A") across the two competitions. Unfortunately too few participants submitted to the private competition to confirm whether the "private" test data tends to lower the scores of poor submissions. Given that our baseline also had a reduced score with the private test data, it appears that this is the case.

7 Conclusions

This year's shared task had a much larger participation than in past tasks. The main reason for this was the use of the task as part of an assignment of a Masters unit at University of Melbourne.

A large percentage of participants outdid our baseline task, and the top participants did much better than our baseline. The best results outperformed the results reported by Baldwin and Joseph (2009), who achieved an F-score of 0.619. Even though our shared task was a simplification, it shows the good skills of the top participants, who were PhD and Masters students. The top team used Conditional Random Fields and is described elsewhere in these proceedings (Lui and Wang, 2013).

We observed that a key component to improve the results was the use of additional training data. Since training data is easy to obtain for this task, the only issue would be the increasing computational costs involved in adding additional data.

The use of Kaggle in Class was very convenient due to its easy interface for the creation of the task, its ability to maintain a leaderboard, and its automatic partition into public and private test data. Unfortunately, the actual evaluation score that we used, macro-averaged F1, did not allow the automatic partition into public and private test sets. Our solution was to create an additional "private" competition, but very few participants submitted to the new competition, possibly because they could observe that they were not at the top of

Rank	Team	Score
1	Winner	0.73763
2	Second	0.68360
3	(anonymous)	0.63232
4	(anonymous)	0.63109
5	(anonymous)	0.60251
6	(anonymous)	0.60147
7	(anonymous)	0.59517
8	(anonymous)	0.58332
9	(anonymous)	0.56832
10	(anonymous)	0.56747
11	(anonymous)	0.55793
12	(anonymous)	0.55606
13	(anonymous)	0.55087
14	(anonymous)	0.52261
15	(anonymous)	0.51954
16	(anonymous)	0.51167
17	(anonymous)	0.49311
18	(anonymous)	0.47622
19	*(test system)*	0.46667
20	(anonymous)	0.46490
21	(anonymous)	0.45986
22	(anonymous)	0.45291
	Baseline	**0.44930**
23	(8 systems)	0.44930
32	(anonymous)	0.44914
33	(anonymous)	0.42710
34	(anonymous)	0.42257
35	(anonymous)	0.41692
36	(anonymous)	0.40239
37	(anonymous)	0.38812
38	(anonymous)	0.38113
39	(anonymous)	0.32594
40	(anonymous)	0.32320
41	(anonymous)	0.30988
42	(anonymous)	0.29891
43	(anonymous)	0.29304
44	(anonymous)	0.27642
45	(anonymous)	0.23504
46	Team A	0.23108
47	(anonymous)	0.21930
48	(anonymous)	0.21771
49	(anonymous)	0.21291
50	(anonymous)	0.20226
51	(anonymous)	0.13397
52	(anonymous)	0.00000

Table 2: Results of the public submissions

Rank	Team	Score
1	**Winner**	**0.73660**
2	Second	0.64934
3	(anonymous)	0.30037
4	Team A	0.07656

Table 3: Final results of the private submissions

the leaderboard.

References

Timothy Baldwin and Manuel Paul Anil Kumar Joseph. 2009. Restoring Punctuation and Casing in English Text. In *AI '09 Proceedings of the 22nd Australasian Joint Conference on Advances in Artificial Intelligence*, pages 547–556.

Steven Bird, Ewan Klein, and Edward Loper. 2009. *Natural Language Processing with Python*. O'Reilly Media.

Lucian Vlad Lita, Abe Ittycheriah, Salim Roukos, and Nanda Kambhatla. 2003. tRuEcasIng. In *Proc. ACL 2003*, pages 152–159.

Marco Lui and Li Wang. 2013. Recovering casing and punctuation using conditional random fields. In *Proceedings of the 2013 Australasian Language Technology Workshop*, Brisbane, Australia.

Cheng Niu, Wei Li, Jihong Ding, and Rohiri K. Srihari. 2004. Orthographic Case Restoration Using Supervised Learning without Manual Annotation. *International Journal on Artificial Intelligence Tools*, 13(1):141–156, March.

Recovering Casing and Punctuation using Conditional Random Fields

Marco Lui, Li Wang
NICTA VRL
Department of Computing and Information Systems
University of Melbourne
mhlui@unimelb.edu.au, li@liwang.info

Abstract

This paper describes the winning entry to the ALTA Shared Task 2013. The theme of the shared task was recovery of casing and punctuation information from degraded English text. We tackle the task as a sequential labeling problem, jointly learning the casing and punctuation labels. We implement our sequential classifier using conditional random fields, trained using linguistic features extracted with off-the-shelf tools with simple adaptations to the specific task. We show the improvement due to adding each feature we consider, as well as the improvment due to utilizing additional training data beyond that supplied by the shared task organizers.

1 Introduction

The ALTA Shared Task 2013[1] required participants to recover casing and punctuation information from degraded English text. The task focused specifically on English text where casing and punctuation were entirely absent (i.e. all characters had been reduced to lowercase, and all non-alphanumeric symbols had been omitted). Participants were required to submit word-level predictions, identifying on a word-by-word basis whether (1) the word in its original form has any characters in uppercase, and (2) whether the word is followed by one of a closed set of punctuation marks.

Our approach to the task treats the task as a sequential labeling problem, a common technique in modern natural language processing (NLP). We implement a word-level sequential classifier using conditional random fields (CRFs), a sequential labeling technique that has been successfully applied to a variety of NLP problems. We make use of a number of linguistic features extracted using off-the-shelf NLP tools, with some simple adaptations to the specific problem at hand. We also make use of additional training data beyond that supplied by the shared task organizers, and show that this has a large impact on the final result. Overall, our approach was the most effective in the shared task by a reasonable margin, outperforming 50 other participants (22 of which outperformed the organizer-supplied baseline).

[1] http://www.alta.asn.au/events/sharedtask2013

2 Task Description

Participants were required to implement an automated system that could accept as input a stream of words without any casing or punctuation. On the basis of this stream, participants were asked to infer which words in the stream should (1) have some form of casing, and (2) be followed by punctuation. The setting was meant to simulate scenarios whereby such information is missing, such as from audio transcriptions, or from user-generated content in social media.

For purposes of the shared task, the text supplied to participants was an automatically-converted version of original English documents with "standard" casing and punctuation. These documents constitute the "original" goldstandard, and were not supplied to participants. Participants only received the transformed (i.e. lowercased and punctuation removed) version. Additionally, for training documents, participants were provided with a "simplified" goldstandard consisting of word-level annotation of which words in the original text (1) contained any uppercase characters and/or (2) were followed by a punctuation mark. Participants were only required to provide predictions corresponding to the "simplified" goldstandard, not to restore the text to the "original" goldstandard.

The shared task was hosted on Kaggle[2], a web platform for crowdsourced competitive data analytics. Kaggle provides the infrastructure for running a shared task, including user management, results tabulation and discussion forums. For evaluation, the macro-averaged F-score across the two types of word-level labels (casing and punctuation) was used. Participants were able to submit two attempts daily and received immediate feedback on the score obtained, which was also posted on a publicly-visible ranking known as the leaderboard. The initial data released to participants consisted of a "basic" training set of ≈66k words and a test set of ≈64k words, with a further ≈300k words from English Wikipedia. The source of the "basic" training data and the test data was not officially revealed, but manual inspection showed that it was newswire data.

3 Methodology

Our main focus was to treat the task as a sequential labeling problem, which in recent NLP research has frequently been tackled using conditional random fields (Lafferty et al., 2001), a class of probabilistic graphical model that integrates information from multiple features, and has enjoyed success in tasks such as shallow parsing (Sha and Pereira, 2003). We apply CRFs to learn a sequential labeler for the shared task on the basis of 4 automatically-extracted features: the surface form of the word (WORD), the part-of-speech of the word in context (POS), IOB tags for verb and noun phrases (CHUNK) and named entity recognition with NE type such as person (NER).

POS, CHUNK and NER were extracted using SENNA v3.0 (Collobert et al., 2011), an off-the-shelf shallow parsing system based on a neural network architecture. We chose SENNA for this task due to its near state-of-the-art accuracy on tagging tasks and relatively fast runtime. One challenge in using SENNA is that it expects input to be segmented at the sentence level. However, this information is obviously missing from the stream-of-words provided for the shared task. Restoring sentence boundaries is a non-trivial task, and automatic methods (e.g. Kiss and Strunk, 2006) typically make use of casing and punctuation information (e.g. a period followed by a capitalized word is highly indicative of a sentence boundary). In order to obtain POS, CHUNK and NER tags from SENNA, we segmented the text using a fixed-size sliding window approach. From the original stream of words, we extracted pseudo-sentences consisting of sequences of 18 consecutive words. The start of each sequence was offset from the previous sequence by 6 words, resulting in each word in the original appearing in three pseudo-sentences (except the words right at the start and end of the stream). SENNA was used to tag each pseudo-sentence, and the final tag assigned to each word was the majority label amongst the three. The rationale behind this overlapping window approach was to allow each word to appear near the beginning, middle, and end of a pseudo-sentence, in case sentence position had an effect on SENNA's predictions. In practice, for over 92% of words all predictions were the same. We did not carry out an evaluation of the accuracy of SENNA's predictions due to a lack of gold-standard data, but anecdotally we observed that the POS and CHUNK output generally seemed sensible. We also observed that for NER, the output appeared to achieve high precision but rather low recall; this is likely due to SENNA normally utilizing casing and punctuation in carrying out NER.

3.1 Sequence Labeler Implementation

To implement our sequence labeler, we made use of CRFSUITE version 0.12 (Okazaki, 2007). CRFSUITE provides a set of fast command-line tools with a simple data format for training and tagging. For our training, we used L2-regularized stochastic gradient descent, which we found to converge faster than the default limited-memory BFGS while attaining comparable extrema. We also made use of the supplied tools to facilitate sequential attribute generation. We based our feature template on the example template included with CRFSUITE for a chunking task. For WORD, single words are considered for a (-2,2) context (i.e. two words before and two words after, as well as word bigrams including the current word. For POS, CHUNK and NER, we used a (-2,2) context for single tags, bigrams and trigrams. This means that for word bigrams, we also utilized features that captured (1) two words before, and (2) two words after, in both cases excluding the target word itself.

We treated the task as a joint learning problem over the casing and punctuation labels, reasoning that the two tasks are highly mutually informative,

[2] http://www.kaggle.com

Feature	Case	Punc	Avg
WORD	0.469	0.453	0.461
+POS	0.607	0.577	0.592
+CHUNK	0.627	0.592	0.610
+NER	0.636	0.597	0.617

Table 1: F-score attained by adding each feature incrementally, using only the organizer-supplied `train` data, broken down over the two component tasks. The average of the two components is the metric by which the shared task was judged.

as certain punctuation strongly influences the casing in the immediate context, e.g. a period often ends a sentence and thus a word followed by a period is expected to be followed by a capitalized word. We trained the labeler to output four distinct labels: (FF) the word should not be capitalized and should not be followed by punctuation, (FT) the word should not be capitalized and should be followed by punctuation, (TF) the word should be capitalized and should not be followed by punctuation, and (TT) the word should be capitalized and should be followed by punctuation.

We applied the same pseudo-sentence segmentation to the text that was carried out to pre-process the word stream for use with SENNA, and again the majority label amongst the three predictions was used as the final output.

Table 1 summarizes the effect of adding each feature to the system, using only the "basic" training data. The result attained using only word features is marginally better than the organizer-supplied hidden Markov model baseline (0.461 vs 0.449). The biggest gain is seen by adding POS, and further improvements are achieved by using CHUNK and NER.

4 Additional Data Used

The feature set and labeler setup we outline above, combined with the "basic" training data provided by the shared task organizers resulted in a system that attained F-score of 0.617, comfortably exceeding the organizer-posted baseline of 0.449 utilizing a hidden Markov model on the same training data. Adding the organizer-provided Wikipedia data further improved this result to 0.664.

Banko and Brill (2001) observed that for confusion set disambiguation, the performance of learners can benefit significantly from increasing the training set size substantially. Confusion set disambiguation is representative of many NLP tasks, in that it relies on statistical models of word sequences. Due to the large vocabulary, only a very small proportion of valid sequences is observed in any given dataset, and hence adding more data allows us to better estimate the parameters of the model. Our task suffers the same problem, and we thus expect that increasing the quantity of training data will increase performance, a hypothesis is supported by the results obtained by adding the Wikipedia data to the "basic" training data.

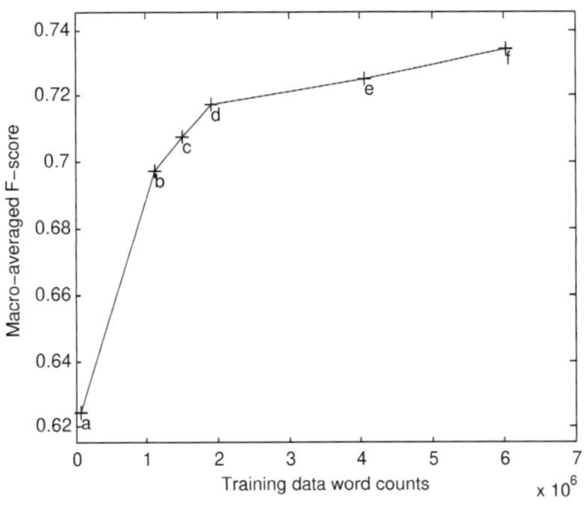

Figure 1: Effect of adding training data. Left to right, each point represents the cumulative addition of training data. (i.e. `a` uses only `train`, and `f` uses all the data in Table 2.) Datasets are added in the order listed in Table 2.

Table 2 summarizes the training data we used in our best-scoring system. As previously discussed, manual inspection of the training data suggested that it was derived from a newswire source. We thus sought additional training data from newswire sources. We made use of all the treebanked Wall Street Journal (WSJ) data from the Penn Treebank (Marcus et al., 1993), as well as a sample of data from RCV1 (Lewis et al., 2004). We opted not to use the organizer-supplied sample of English Wikipedia in our further experiments, instead utilizing our own sample which gave us access to a larger number of documents. For purposes of discussion, we divide the Wikipedia and Reuters data into two partitions each.

Table 2 also shows the score attained using each dataset individually as training data. Here we see the effect of affinity between datasets; the organizer-supplied `train` is assumed to be the most similar to the test data, and hence attains a

Label	Source	Size (words)	F-score
train	Competition Organizer	66371	0.617
wsj	Wall Street Journal	1082959	0.617
enwiki1	English Wikipedia	372547	0.553
enwiki2		383368	0.564
reut1	Reuters RCV1	2244959	0.604
reut2		2052119	0.606

Table 2: Datasets used in our best-scoring system. F-score is the macro-averaged F-score for the task attained by using each dataset individually as training data, using the full feature set.

high score despite having a relatively low word count. An interesting comparison can be made with the wsj result, where much more data is required to attain the same score. Figure 1 illustrates the effect of training models on successively greater amounts of training data. The order in which data was added for Figure 1 was largely arbitrary, though several trends can be observed: adding each successive dataset reduces the improvement obtained per word added, and for each of Wikipedia and RCV1, adding the same amount of data results in a near-linear increase in performance.

5 Negative Results

CRFSUITE is not able to train a model incrementally, and so adding additional training data required retraining the entire model from scratch. We attempted to circumvent this problem by implementing a voting system over models from different partitions of the training data, but found that the performance was not competitive with the monolithic model.

We also tested crfsgd,[3] but found that CRFSUITE was faster and attained slightly better F-score for comparable setups. We believe that the default parametrization of the CRF model differs slightly between tools, but did not investigate.

Much of the additional training data we used was pre-tokenized in Penn Treebank format, which utilizes special sequences to represent different types of brackets. As the organizer-supplied data did not follow this convention, we tested "de-escaping" the Penn Treebank brackets (e.g. converting -LCB- back to {). Surprisingly, we found that this actually reduced our F-score, though the reasons for this remain unclear.

We introduced gazetteer features on the basis of observing that despite low recall, the NER features produced by SENNA had an overall positive impact on our task score. Our gazetteer features are based on word lists of common named entities. For place names, we used data from GeoNames,[4] and for first names we used a wordlist included with Apple's OS X. We used each wordlist to produce a single Boolean feature indicating whether the word was present in the given wordlist. This approach showed some promise in internal cross-validation, but was abandoned as we found that it did not improve our score on the leaderboard.

6 Further Work

The CRF feature template (i.e. the set of rules for generating sequential features) that we used was derived with minimal modification from a template for a chunking task. Tuning the template to this task may yield further improvements. Furthermore, CRFs are able to provide a probability distribution over labels, and this information may be useful in weighting a voting approach to model combination. Finally, the amount of data we used was primarily limited by computation resources available, so it is likely that increasing data quantity will further improve performance.

7 Conclusion

In this paper we detailed the winning entry to the ALTA 2013 Shared Task. We treat the task as a sequence labeling problem, jointly learning the casing and punctuation labels. We implemented a classifier using conditional random fields, trained using linguistic features extracted using off-the-shelf tools, using a simple windowing approach to generate pseudo-sentences. We find that the linguistic features out-perform simple word features, and that further improvements can be made by further adding training data. We briefly discussed

[3] http://leon.bottou.org/projects/sgd

[4] http://www.geonames.org

negative results in our development process, and outlined some avenues for further work.

Acknowledgments

NICTA is funded by the Australian Government as represented by the Department of Broadband, Communications and the Digital Economy and the Australian Research Council through the ICT Centre of Excellence program.

References

Michele Banko and Eric Brill. 2001. Scaling to very very large corpora for natural language disambiguation. In *Proceedings of the 39th Annual Meeting of the ACL and 10th Conference of the EACL (ACL-EACL 2001)*, pages 26–33. Association for Computational Linguistics, Toulouse, France.

Ronan Collobert, Jason Weston, Léon Bottou, Michael Karlen, Koray Kavukcuoglu, and Pavel Kuksa. 2011. Natural language processing (almost) from scratch. *The Journal of Machine Learning Research*, 12:2493–2537.

Tibor Kiss and Jan Strunk. 2006. Unsupervised multilingual sentence boundary detection. *Computational Linguistics*, 32(4):485–525.

John Lafferty, Andrew McCallum, and Fernando Pereira. 2001. Conditional random fields: Probabilistic models for segmenting and labeling sequence data. In *Proceedings of the 18th International Conference on Machine Learning*, pages 282–289. Williamstown, USA.

David D Lewis, Yiming Yang, Tony G Rose, and Fan Li. 2004. Rcv1: A new benchmark collection for text categorization research. *The Journal of Machine Learning Research*, 5:361–397.

Mitchell P. Marcus, Beatrice Santorini, and Mary Ann Marcinkiewicz. 1993. Building a large annotated corpus of English: the Penn treebank. *Computational Linguistics*, 19(2):313–330.

Naoaki Okazaki. 2007. Crfsuite: a fast implementation of conditional random fields (crfs). URL `http://www.chokkan.org/software/crfsuite/`.

Fei Sha and Fernando Pereira. 2003. Shallow parsing with conditional random fields. In *Proceedings of the 3rd International Conference on Human Language Technology Research and 4th Annual Meeting of the NAACL (HLT-NAACL 2003)*, pages 213–220. Edmonton, Canada.

e-Learning with *Kaggle in Class*: Adapting the ALTA Shared Task 2013 to a Class Project

Karin Verspoor[1,2] **and Jeremy Nicholson**[2]
[1]National ICT Australia
[2]Department of Computing and Information Systems
The University of Melbourne
Melbourne VIC 3010 Australia
karin.verspoor@nicta.com.au, nj@unimelb.edu.au

Abstract

The 2013 ALTA Shared Task was utilised as a class project for a subject taught at The University of Melbourne in the second semester of 2013. This paper reviews the experience of using an on-line, *Kaggle in Class*-based shared task for class work. Adoption of the shared task enables a *blended learning* paradigm that engages students in problem-based learning in a shared and open context.

1 Introduction

As in recent years, the Australasian Language Technology Association sponsored a shared task in 2013 to stimulate interest in language technology tasks among university students (Molla, 2013). This year's task was primarily organised by Diego Molla of Macquarie University and addressed the restoration of normal case (capitalisation) and punctuation to a noisy text input not conforming to conventional use of case and punctuation. As described in (Molla, 2013) the task is framed as a simplification of the general task explored by (Baldwin and Joseph, 2009).

Because the task is specifically aimed at university students with programming skills, and as it can be approached as a classification task, it is appropriate to consider as a project for a university subject that addresses machine learning algorithms. Furthermore, it provides an opportunity to make use of *blended learning* (Garrison and Kanuka, 2004) in the classroom; that is, integrating face-to-face learning with on-line asynchronous learning opportunities. Enrichment of the traditional classroom learning experience with on-line activities has been suggested to have positive benefits for student learning, in addition to student satisfaction and retention.

The task was therefore selected as a project for approximately 115 students registered for The University of Melbourne's *Knowledge Technologies* subject, a subject in the Department of Computing and Information Systems for which the stated objective is to "learn algorithms and data structures for extracting, retrieving and storing explicit knowledge from various data sources, and methods for data mining and machine learning with complex data." The students were given the option to register for the shared task formally through the *Kaggle In Class* system.

2 Organisation

To adapt the shared task to the classroom context, the project was split into several stages.

2.1 Data pre-processing and task familiarisation

The students were introduced to the task through the ALTA shared task data, without an explicit reference to the shared task itself. They were given the context of the task in a project specification, provided with the training data and asked to write scripts to manipulate the data in various ways. In one subtask, they were asked to map the provided ALTA Shared Task data format to the ARFF (Attribute-Relation File Format) format which is used in several machine learning frameworks. This was intended to get the students comfortable with regular expressions for simple data transformations, and to enable them to produce files appropriate for use in the next stage of the project.

A second subtask required the students to write a program for producing training data for the task from natural language data. That is, to write a program that given normally cased and punctuated text, would produce the appropriate lower-cased and unpunctuated, but appropriately tokenised and labelled structured output for the task. The hope with this subtask was that students would realise that they could in principle produce very large quantities of their own training data for their eventual shared task solutions, by downloading text sources and stripping case and appropriate punctuation.

In a third subtask, post-graduate students (primarily Master by coursework students) were additionally asked to explore some preliminary rule-based methods for solving the classification tasks. This step was optional for undergraduate students, however they were encouraged to attempt an initial solution. The purpose of this subtask was to encourage the students to begin thinking about the features that might be relevant to addressing the problem, and to give them some sense of the difficulty of a rule-based approach to the task.

2.2 Machine learning-based problem exploration

The students were introduced to various machine learning algorithms in class, as well as approaches to feature engineering and system evaluation. They were pointed specifically towards the WEKA machine learning toolkit, which provides good implementations of many algorithms (Hall et al., 2009), although they were allowed to use any machine learning implementation they were familiar with. The students were instructed to construct and experiment with different features that would be helpful for solving the two classification tasks (i.e. features that may be useful indicators of the appropriate punctuation and capitalisation of a word), and to explore different classification algorithms on the shared task data. The distributed ALTA Shared Task data was divided into pre-defined training and development subsets, with the test set provided as held-out (blind), unlabelled data.

2.3 Kaggle In Class

Along with the project specification for the second, machine learning-based problem exploration stage, the students were introduced to the ALTA Shared Task platform in the *Kaggle in Class* site and provided with invitation links associated to their student IDs. Submission of the results to the Kaggle In Class site for the shared task was entirely optional, although the students were encouraged to participate. Submitting to Kaggle required the students to work out how to map their system results (from WEKA, or whatever toolkit they selected), back into the ALTA Shared Task format.

Participation in the official shared task gave students access to a baseline solution, and allowed them to receive an immediate evaluation of their system results on the held-out test data. It provided an opportunity for immediate feedback on the effectiveness of their solutions; through the Leaderboard the students could see concretely how well their solutions were performing relative to other students.

2.4 Report writing

The students were asked to write a report describing their approach, summarising their exploration of the features and algorithms on the task, and providing observations and critical analysis of their results. The objective of the report was to demonstrate their understanding of the task, methods, and results and to highlight creativity in their solution. Marks were primarily based on the student's critical analysis of their results, rather than the overall score of their solution.

2.5 Peer review

Using an on-line peer review system, TurnItIn's PeerMark, that is integrated into The University of Melbourne's on-line Learning Management System, each student provided feedback on two other students' reports. This enabled Contributing Student Pedagogy (CSP) (Hamer et al., 2008), a participatory learning strategy in which students are encouraged to contribute to the learning of others and to value the contributions of others.

The students were specifically asked to address three points:

1. A summary of the author's work; the approach to the task and the analysis in the report.

2. What they felt that the author had done well, and for what reasons. For example, novel use of features, interesting methodology, or insightful discussion.

3. What they felt were the weak points of the submission, including suggestions of avenues for further research.

The quality of the student peer review reports was quite high; students largely provided thoughtful feedback and critical assessment of their peers' work.

3 Results

The students generally appeared to find the task quite challenging. For most students it was their first exposure to hands-on application of machine learning algorithms to solve a problem, as well as their first exposure to text classification. Lectures covered algorithms and evaluation strategies in detail, and several pointers were provided about good features to experiment with, such as token "shape" and character or token n-grams. However, many student solutions applied WEKA in a narrow range of configurations and with a limited set of features. Some students—typically those with prior exposure to natural language processing through another subject in the department—made use of linguistic features such as part of speech tags, and some used gazetteers of English names or common words specifically to help with the capitalisation task. A few students used machine learning frameworks other than WEKA.

A number of students did submit their results to the main Kaggle ALTA Shared Task site, and some even included those results in their project reports. It was observed that several of the students' submissions to the Kaggle site displayed identical performance. Further investigation revealed that their scores matched exactly the performance of the baseline model provided along with the ALTA Shared Task data upon registration to Kaggle In Class. This suggests that these students likely made test submissions using the baseline model, rather than submitting results based on their own systems or solutions.

4 Discussion

4.1 Interaction with Kaggle

Since the ALTA Shared Task was run using the Kaggle in Class framework (`https://inclass.kaggle.com/c/alta-2013-challenge`), students were encouraged to submit results directly to the on-line system. This required generating individual invitation links to join the shared task site for each student. While this was easily generated through the Kaggle system by the organiser of the task, it was also important to associate Kaggle logins with individual student IDs, so that Kaggle submissions from our student cohort could be identified. For a class with over one hundred students, this created a logistical hassle for managing login-student ID associations, and the distribution of the invitation links to the individual students.

4.2 Timing considerations

An important factor in the decision to utilise the ALTA Shared Task as a class project was whether the timing would fit in with the overall timeline for the subject. The dates generally aligned well; the shared task was announced in mid-July, while the semester began at the end of July.

The final submission date for the official ALTA Shared Task was set at 04 October. That date fell during the non-teaching week of the semester (semester break) and did not allow adequate time for a second project during the second half of the semester. Therefore it was decided to set the deadline for the class project ahead of the final ALTA Shared Task deadline, on 20 September. In the end, as the students found the assignment challenging, the deadline was extended to 27 September (compressing the second project somewhat) to give them more time to make adequate progress.

Since the deadline for the class project was ahead of the shared task deadline, the students were told that they could continue to attempt to improve their results after submission of the project report if they were enjoying participating in the shared task. Reviewing the time stamps on the Kaggle Leaderboard, most students did not continue working on the project after the submission deadline. Three students did at least take the time to submit results on the "final" ALTA Shared Task data (on a sister Kaggle site, `https://inclass.kaggle.com/c/alta-2013-challenge-final`) on 06 October; two did not do particularly well (obtaining scores of 0.3 and 0.08, respectively), while one student obtained 0.65, second to the winning system score of 0.74. This second-place result was consistent with the leader board results for the original shared task; i.e. that student also placed second to the winning system on the original data. Interestingly, one of the students who submitted results on the final data hadn't participated in the original shared task leader board at all.

4.3 Set-up of the Shared task

Due to the separation of the ALTA Shared Task into a development competition and a "final" competition, with the final data not being released until well after the class project deadline, it proved difficult for the students enrolled in the subject to submit results to the final test. As indicated above, only three students did so while there were about 50 students who made at least one submission to the original Kaggle ALTA Shared Task site.

4.4 The Leaderboard

The students who participated in the on-line competition were not systematically compared to the students who did not participate on-line; significant variations in how students set up their training and testing scenarios for their final reports would have made this very difficult. In contrast, the availability of the on-line framework and the Leaderboard provided a consistent testing scenario for comparing student performance on the task: the relative performance of different systems over the same held-out data were immediately available upon submission. While we did not systematically cross-reference Kaggle results with student reports, our general impression was that students who showed creativity in their feature engineering did appear to achieve higher results on the leader board for the shared task. Participating in the on-line task seemed to spur experimentation. While we cannot know how many configurations the students who did not participate on-line explored, most students participating on-line submitted multiple runs. This suggests that they were experimenting with various configurations to obtain better results. One student made 14 entries, and indeed the winning system submitted 13 sets of results.

4.5 Emphasis

The focus of the shared task is competitive; entrants aim to achieve the best possible results on the task. In contrast, the aim of the class project was to provide the students with an opportunity to apply newly acquired knowledge of machine learning and feature engineering, and to demonstrate understanding of that application through critical exploration of the problem and different approaches to solving it. A student who scored high on the leader board was not guaranteed to have a good mark for the project; as indicated above, the mark was based on the report. Conversely, a student could achieve a good mark for the project without creating a high-performing solution to the task, for instance by exploring and explaining the performance of a broad range of features that may not have proven particularly effective for solving the task. However, given the above observation that participation in the on-line shared task seemed to result in substantial experimentation, and the context of comparative, immediate feedback, it seems likely that students who actively participated on-line would have been thinking relatively more creatively about their approach. In turn, the objectives of the project would have been met, and their marks would likely have reflected this creativity.

5 Conclusions

Nearly one-half of the students in a subject taught at The University of Melbourne who were given the (completely voluntary) opportunity to participate in the *Kaggle in class* on-line component for the ALTA Shared Task elected to sign up and participate in the open competition. While the emphasis of the students' assignment was on problem exploration rather than system performance, it appeared, based on an informal and unsystematic review of the assignments, that students who performed well on the on-line task also had made a significant effort to explore creative strategies for solving the task.

Use of the ALTA Shared Task as a class project was generally successful despite some differences in objectives. Participation in the on-line experience afforded by the ALTA Shared Task seemed to enhance overall student learning.

Acknowledgements

Dr. Verspoor's teaching and research time is supported by National ICT Australia (NICTA). NICTA is funded by the Australian Government through the Department of Communications and the Australian Research Council through the ICT Centre of Excellence Program. Mr. Nicholson is supported by The University of Melbourne Department of Computing and Information Systems as Head Tutor of the Knowledge Technologies subject, among several other subjects.

References

Timothy Baldwin and Manuel Paul Anil Kumar Joseph. 2009. Restoring punctuation and casing in english text. In *AI 09 Proceedings of the 22nd Australasian Joint Conference on Advances in Artificial Intelligence*, pages 547–556.

D. Randy Garrison and Heather Kanuka. 2004. Blended learning: Uncovering its transformative potential in higher education. *The Internet and Higher Education*, 7(2):95–105.

Mark Hall, Eibe Frank, Geoffrey Holmes, Bernhard Pfahringer, Peter Reutemann, and Ian H. Witten. 2009. The WEKA data mining software: An update. *SIGKDD Explorations*, 11(1):10–18.

John Hamer, Quintin Cutts, Jana Jackova, Andrew Luxton-Reilly, Robert McCartney, Helen Purchase, Charles Riedesel, Mara Saeli, Kate Sanders, and Judithe Sheard. 2008. Contributing student pedagogy. *ACM SIGCSE Bulletin*, 40(4):194–212.

Diego Molla. 2013. Overview of the 2013 alta shared task. In *Proceedings of the Australasian Language Technology Association Workshop 2013*, pages 132–136, Brisbane, Australia, December.